Salsa Consciente

LATINOS IN THE UNITED STATES SERIES

Salsa Consciente: Politics, Poetics, and Latinidad in the Meta-Barrio

Andrés Espinoza Agurto

Michigan State University Press • *East Lansing*

⊛ The paper used in this publication meets the minimum requirements
of ANSI/NISO Z39.48-1992 (R 1997) (Permanence of Paper).

Michigan State University Press
East Lansing, Michigan 48823-5245

Funding provided by the AMS 75 PAYS Fund of the American Musicological Society,
supported in part by the National Endowment for the Humanities and the Andrew W.
Mellon Foundation.

Library of Congress Cataloging-in-Publication Data
Names: Espinoza Agurto, Andrés, author.
Title: Salsa consciente : politics, poetics, and latinidad in the
meta-barrio / Andrés Espinoza Agurto.
Description: [First.] | East Lansing : Michigan State University Press,
2021. | Series: Latinos in the United States series | Includes
bibliographical references and index.
Identifiers: LCCN 2021016773 | ISBN 9781611864014 (paperback) | ISBN
9781609176761 | ISBN 9781628954432 | ISBN 9781628964370
Subjects: LCSH: Salsa (Music)–History and criticism. | Salsa
(Music)–Political aspects–Latin America. | Salsa (Music)–Social
aspects–Latin America. | Salsa (Music)–Political aspects–United
States. | Salsa (Music)–Social aspects–United States.
Classification: LCC ML3535.5 .E89 2021 | DDC 781.64–dc23
LC record available at https://lccn.loc.gov/2021016773

Composition by Peter Holm
Cover design by Charlie Sharp, Sharp Des!gn, East Lansing, MI

Michigan State University Press is a member of the Green Press Initiative and is
committed to developing and encouraging ecologically responsible publishing practices.
For more information about the Green Press Initiative and the use of recycled paper in
book publishing, please visit www.greenpressinitiative.org.

Visit Michigan State University Press at *www.msupress.org*

A Latinoamérica

Un barrio que va desde Nueva York hasta la Patagonia (A neighborhood that goes from New York to Patagonia).

—Rubén Blades

Salsa is an idea, a concept, the result of a way of approaching music from the Latin American cultural perspective.

—Willie Colón

Contents

Foreword

Rubén O. Martinez

Historically, the relationship between art and politics has been a matter of controversy in society. There are those who want art to be apolitical, exhibiting the best in aesthetics, while others see art as political and want to use it politically as part of expressive culture. Who is most likely to use art politically? I believe it is oppressed peoples and those actively promoting social justice in society, although nationalist and other movements also use art and music to promote solidarity. As with all social relations, the relationship between art and politics is historical and contextual. In this book, Andrés Espinoza Agurto traces the roots of *Salsa consciente*. That is, salsa as a musical genre that exposes the racial and colonial aspects of the lives of Latinos and Latin Americans, and promotes Latinidad, a collective identity that transcends national boundaries.

Salsa consciente gives voice to the racial and class issues that Latinos and most Latin Americans experience in everyday life and have for several centuries. However, they tend to understand the hardships they experience as personal problems rather than public issues, a broad concern raised by

C. Wright Mills several decades ago. As such, the separation of the private and public spheres is an important feature of the context in which the political aspects of art are to be understood.

Attending the rise of the nation-state and notions of sovereignty were countervailing efforts to define a private sphere in which individuals were free from the encroaching power of the state. Rooted in medieval conceptions of property, public law had been fused with property, with officeholders able to claim property interests in the office. In the United States and in England, the public realm was not made distinct until the nineteenth century, when legal thought made a clear separation between public (regulatory) law and constitutional, criminal, tort (property), and commercial laws. In these capitalist societies the ideologies of the ruling class have prevailed in the consciousness of working classes despite ideological ruptures here and there across the decades.

In this context, market influences became central to the public/private sphere separation, and legal discourse increasingly performed ideological functions in which people come to believe that the social order is rational, just, and, therefore, legitimate. For example, political ideology following the French Revolution of 1848, when the monarchy was overthrown and the promise of democracy seemed to have taken hold, class struggles between French capitalists and the working masses, over time, were hidden behind the separation of public and private spheres. Although never an absolute separation, the marketplace offered universal status for consumers, while the private sphere offered security and autonomy. Market transactions were made to appear like private transactions, and consumers, now in a mass society, were seen as equal. Private transactions were shielded from public power. This included employment relations, with employees having entered into a private transaction with their employers.

Implementation of the National Labor Relations Act began to expand the idea of the public sphere in that it expressed a public interest in workers having the right to collective bargaining even if that bargaining occurred in the private sphere. Years later, public concerns regarding racism, sexism, and other forms of discrimination intervened in employment relations, further blurring the lines between the public and private spheres. Coupled with the ideology of individualism, which is taken to an extreme by neo-liberalism, the quality of life and the chances for upward mobility tend to be interpreted as individual problems. Framing those experiences as general and unjust, Salsa consciente translates personal problems into public issues. Like the ideological struggle that occurs in the economy, Salsa consciente is an expression of expressive culture in the context of racial and colonial ideological struggles.

Where there is group oppression, there is an expressive culture of resistance, whether it be through political rhetoric, song, poetry, literature, visual, or other forms of art. It does not matter if it is a rural or urban culture. Group domination can never be absolute, except through extermination. For example, in the American system of slavery, which was an extreme form of total domination, there were multiple forms and instances of rebellion. Resistance movements tend to use music to promote critical consciousness and to build collective solidarity, and slavery gave rise to spiritual songs that affirmed the humanity of the slaves, suggested freedom, and often pointed to the North as the place of freedom. Those spirituals, often using coded language, were the forerunners of the protest songs that were sung in the decades following emancipation. In 1936, Lawrence Gellert published a collection of African American songs in his book *Negro Songs of Protest*.

Other movements sparked protest songs. The labor movement at the turn of the twentieth century had songs on solidarity, unionization, child labor, and labor strikes. The Industrial Workers of the World (IWW), an international labor union founded in Chicago in 1905, promoted revolutionary culture through various art media, and in 1909 published the *Little Red Songbook*, which contained songs intended to "fan the flames of discontent" among workers. Such songs as "There Is Power in the Union," "Solidarity Forever," and "Roll the Union On" promoted collective solidarity and unionization. The book contained songs in Spanish that served the same function. For example, "Hijos del Pueblo," "Porque los Pobres no Tienen," and "A las Barricadas!" sought to engender a critical consciousness and motivate workers to action, while "Joe Hill" exalted the immigrant martyr. The tradition of labor songs by the members of the IWW, known as the Wobblies, was carried on by such singers as Woody Guthrie and Pete Seeger.

In Mexico, the Mexican Revolution engendered numerous songs of protest that chronicled the experiences of the revolutionaries and promoted their movement as a just cause. The songs highlighted the virtues of leaders such as Francisco "Pancho" Villa, as well as the women of the Revolution known as *soldaderas*. "El Corrido de la Cucaracha" was quite popular during the Revolution, especially among Villa's troops. After the Revolution, the Cristero Rebellion, a countermovement based on opposing the secularist components of the country's new constitution and restoring religious freedom, included protest songs that are still sung today both in Mexico and the U.S. Southwest. One of the most popular is "Valentín de la Sierra," although it is often mistaken for a song of the Revolution.

In the 1950s, restive political climates across South America gave rise to the renewal of folkloric music and what would come to be known as *nueva canción* through the works of Atahualpa Yupanqui in Argentina and Violeta Parra in Chile. She influenced Victor Jara, who became a popular protest-song musician who was killed by the Pinochet regime. In Cuba, the revolution gave rise to *nueva trova* or new ballad in the 1960s. In 1965, "Hasta Siempre Comandante" was written following Fidel Castro's public reading of the farewell letter from Che Guevara to him. *Nueva trova* became popular in support of the revolution. In 1967, the First Protest Song Conference was held in Havana, with some fifty musicians from Latin American and European countries gathered to promote a protest-song movement. This was followed by the establishment of a Protest Song Centre (Centro de la Canción Protesta) at the House of the Americas (Casa de las Américas) in Havana by the Cuban government. Notable musicians of *nueva trova* include Pablo Milanes, Silvio Rodriguez, and others. In Mexico, Oscar Chavez and Mercedes Sosa led the *nueva canción* movement.

In the United States, the civil rights movement was a fertile period for both songs of protest and revolution. The movement consisted of many threads and was embedded in a broader societal climate in which youths were beginning to resist the "cog in a wheel" lifestyles that were part of advanced capitalism. In 1963 this was probably best stated by Bob Dylan in his song "The Times They Are A-Changin'," in which he articulated an anti-establishment message and which achieved anthem-like status among young adults. In 1965, El Teatro Campesino was formed as the consciousness-raising arm of the National Farmworkers Association led by César Chávez. The troupe was intentionally formed to promote solidarity on issues being addressed by the union. In 1968, James Brown promoted Black pride with his song "Say It Loud (I'm Black and I'm Proud)." It was during this period that Salsa consciente was coming into being, and that is the historical account that Andrés Espinoza Agurto provides in this volume.

Salsa consciente, like all protest music, speaks both to local and universal issues of social justice and the desire for a better social order. Thus, it has individual and collective dimensions, with individuals developing a critical consciousness that breaks through the ideological hegemony of the dominant group and embracing a collective identity with similar others. What is interesting about Salsa consciente is that it emerges from dance music. Popular dance music is more an escape from the travails of everyday life than it is a critical consciousness-raising genre. But that is exactly what Salsa consciente does: it blends protest lyrics with dance music. Salsa as protest music is greatly understudied. This volume by Andrés Espinoza Agurto makes a pioneering contribution to filling the void.

Preface

Usa la conciencia Latino, no la dejes que se te duerma, no la dejes que muera.
(Latino, use your consciousness/conscience, don't let it fall asleep,
don't let it die).

This was the injunction by Rubén Blades in what became the biggest
selling Salsa[1] album of all time: *Siembra* (Fania 1978).[2] The musical
and poetic discourse encapsulated by this release, which came to be
known as *Salsa consciente*, referenced in its lyrical content alongside specific
sonic markers, political and social issues facing U.S. Latinos as well as the
people of their ancestral homes across Latin America, evoking the overarching cultural-nationalist idea of *Latinidad* (Latin-ness).[3] The new style was
even supported by New York record executives as a way to build sales in
South American markets.

This book explores the significations and developments of the Salsa
consciente movement. Sociologically, the music is treated as an index of
ongoing ethnic identity formation among continental and Caribbean Latin
Americans who migrated to the New York City environment and became
Latinos. I argue that the urban Latino identity expressed in Salsa consciente
was constructed from diasporic, deterritorialized, and at times imagined
cultural memory, as analyzed through processes that Stuart Hall (1991) has

referred to as "old and new identities, old and new ethnicities." As part of this understanding, throughout the book I utilize the metaphorical term *meta-barrio* (meta-neighborhood) to denote semiotically constructed meeting spaces where Latinos and Latin Americans interact and advance Latino ethnic consciousness, and where Salsa consciente functions as the engine of these advances. Previous scholarship on Salsa consciente only accounts for a relatively small part of the foregoing perspective, which I seek to analyze more systematically and in greater detail. In a short article, Perez refers to "socio-political *Salsa*" (1987, 155) while admitting that "the contributions of Willie Colón, Catalino [Tite] Curet Alonso and Rubén Blades . . . deserve more attention than can be given here" (154). Padura Fuentes (2002) brings the important perspective of treating Salsa from a literary point of view, which helps to clarify differences between Salsa and Cuban *son*. Padilla briefly observes that "content analysis of lyrics of popular Salsa music reveals the emergence over the last fifteen years of cultural themes emphasizing the shared lives of Spanish speaking groups in the United States" (1989, 28).

Defining Salsa consciente first requires a definition of Salsa itself. It is widely accepted that Salsa's musical aesthetics originated mainly from Cuban *son, guaracha,* and *son montuno* (see Waxer 2002b, Steward 2000, Duany 1984, García 2006) and were then reimagined and hybridized in New York, following the break of legal trade and legal migration between Cuba and the United States in 1962. This process was operated mainly by *Nuyoricans* (New York Puerto Ricans) as well as other people who we can call *Nuyolatinos*.[4] Although the Nuyorican Salsa sound became a symbol of Latinidad, any specific equation of Salsa with Puerto Ricanness is challenged by artists such as Rubén Blades and Catalino "Tite" Curet Alonso, who claimed the music for a wider social scene not bound to one particular geographical location. This broader conceptualization of Salsa as Nuyolatino urban folklore better accommodates many specific details of Salsa consciente's development and also better explains how it came to signify emerging Latino culture across Latin America as well as inside the United States.

The *consciente* part of the taxonomy refers to song texts and musical markers that poetically express political, historical, and class awareness of the shared Latino/Latin American existences, identities, and experiences: Latinidad. These collective identities/existences in turn are derived from more particular, layered understandings of being Afro-Latino, Latin American, Latino, Cuban, Nuyorican, Indigenous, oppressed, poor, immigrant, etc. Following Padilla (1985) and ethnic studies literature more generally, I define conscious Latinidad as the main axis of a collective response by Latin American migrant groups to shared conditions such as poverty and racial discrimination. This process occurred mainly in the United States, where the construction of a deterritorialized and heterogeneous Latinidad caused displacement of the "original" and specific Latin American identities associated with particular countries of origin (see Sollors 1986; Saldívar 1986, 1990; Mujcinovic 2001).

As perhaps the main cultural product of Latin American migrants in New York, and the subsequent generations of Nuyolatinos, Salsa as a product of both Latin American and New York influences cannot be understood without the concept of hybridity (see Shohat 1992; Ashcroft et al. 2001; Bhabha 1990, 1994; Rutherford 1998; Zuckermann 2004; Sinfield 1996; Hall 2002). Hybrid culture is even more important for second-generation individuals who live in one-and-a-half-generation families (Rumbaut and Ima 1988, after Thomas and Znaniecki [1958] [1918-1920]) where a continuous duality of "homeland identity" and current realities create a "third space" (Bhabha 1994). This space was eventually expressed in the textual discourses of Salsa as a reconstruction of the past based on current understandings.

In realizing the main arguments of this book, differences emerge in the theoretical approaches between this work and for example Timothy Brenann's *Secular Devotion: Afro-Latin Music and Imperial Jazz.* While Brennan develops an analysis of Salsa from the point of view of neo-African sensibilities via Cuban expressions and understands Salsa as an African-derived endeavor intrinsically centered around Cuban *son*, I understand Salsa from the perspective of hybridity insofar as I consider Salsa to be a Pan-Latino expression that moves beyond a mere re-creating of Cuban or neo-African traditions. Unlike Brennan's neo-African and mainly theoretical approach, I conceive Salsa as a cultural expression of contemporary Latinidad that was born out of the necessity to manifest a tangible set of social realities at a specific point in time. In this manner, I consider the genre not to be exclusively musical but also political, and centered on sensibilities that are intrinsically connected to being Latino and Latin American. These sensibilities function as tropes that include African, Indigenous, urban Latino perspectives, and class formation as a central axis to define the meanings of Salsa. In this sense, Brennan's African-centered approaches only serve to elaborate an argument that expresses a limited dimension of Salsa's richness. Brennan's use of the word "salsa" also presents a similar disagreement in our perspectives. While Brennan sees "salsa" "as a specific genre and a catch-all term . . . for the music that salsa borrowed from was originally referred to only by way of more specific forms . . . (Guaguancó, mozambique, mambo)" (68), I consider Salsa (with capital emphasis) to be a form of making music that is purposefully indeterminate with regard to nationality. Unlike guaguancó, mozambique, and mambo, which are styles associated specifically with Cuba, Salsa's power relies on ethnic unity, not nationalist specificity. As such, the perception of Salsa presented in this book is as much a political stance to understand Bolivarian ideals through music as it is a way of making music from an urban Latino sensibility.

My biggest disagreement with Brennan, however, concerns his analysis of Salsa's lyrics. Brennan notes: "The music is quite plainly about itself" (69). As I show throughout this book, which is greatly centered on the development of the Latino ethnic and social consciousness around Salsa's lyrics, the advancement of contemporary Latino ethnic consciousness is intrinsically related, and oftentimes spread through Salsa. While these developments of Latinidad are not to be found in every song, and though our main lyrical repertoires might differ as far as political content is concerned, Brennan's perspectives on lyrical developments seem to fall rather short of the larger picture.

Regarding the formation of Latinidad, Alonso Gallo (2002) holds that the essentializing definition of Latinidad glosses over the wealth of traditions, history, familial relationships, art, races, ethnicities, social structures, and generational differences found among the diverse Latin American populations now residing in the United States. While this statement certainly advances a point—namely, in the development of nationalistic

Hispanic-centered identities—I argue that there is a lack of comprehension of the complexities surrounding the concept of Latinidad. The first disagreement stems from the concept of hybridity—that is, creole, multiple heritages of Latinos, especially those in the United States, where besides nationalistic identities there are other layers making up the identity of being Latino that are consequently expressed in a unified manner. More important is the fact that Latinidad stems from class formation as a basic building block of a common identity. Thus, Latinidad functions at the level of social agency insofar as it allows Latinos together to resist economic and social disparities.

In this manner, I take class formation as a basic principle of understanding Latinidad. As such, the following presents a Gramscian analysis of Salsa consciente in that I analyze the music as a phenomenon that presents political tendencies tied not only to the formation of identity in general, but also to anti-hegemonic struggles. I understand, on a basic level, the appearance of Salsa consciente as a Latino response to the cultural hegemony inflicted by the mainstream popular musical culture of the United States and its imposed bourgeois musical worldview. I also expand on the cultural hegemony idea as a way to criticize colonialist culture. I argue throughout the book that Salsa consciente proposes the existence of a Latino/Latin American being, from a post/de-colonial point of view that sets aside Spain as the primary source of Latino/Latin American culture. The alternative counter-hegemonical idea, originally denied by genocide and slavery, is an identity based on African and Native pride as essential components of being Latino. Not only does Salsa consciente function at the level of African and Native identity as related to Spanish colonialism, but it also acts as the motor of the concept of the Latino Nation by massively promoting a set of anti-hegemonic ideals that came as a result of the historical role of the United States in Latin America.

In continuing Gramsci's ideas as a key concept for this book, I see his conceptualization of the intellectual as a product of its class as crucial to developing my argument. In this manner, I understand the role of the composers of Salsa consciente as "organic Latino intellectuals," who articulate through recordings, albeit often distributed by a capitalist endeavor, the language of their own culture, their experiences, and the ideals of Latinidad. This "Latino vinyl record intellectualism," I argue throughout the book, functions as a counter-hegemonical precept insofar it opposes the bourgeois ideals presented by, largely, mainstream ideologies of culture and music in the United States. Furthermore, Salsa consciente creates an educational enterprise, à la critical pedagogy, related to a renovation of the Latino consciousness, and the development of a critique of the status quo.

In line with Gramsci's ideas, it is also important to understand Paulo Freire's concept of critical consciousness (1970) as one of the theoretical arguments of my analyses. Freire's concept points to understanding the world as a place laden with sociopolitical contradictions, whereas by developing critical consciousness, we are able to confront our daily realities in order to change them. As such, Salsa consciente functions as an educational tool of conscientization that not only develops its aesthetics as grounded in entertaining dance music but also engages the listeners, largely from a lyrical perspective, and asks them to conscientize themselves in regard to history, colonialism, imperialism, communal strife, politics, discrimination, racism, etc., as well as engaging them in questioning and facing the current situations.

Another key concept that helps elucidate the different functional layers of Salsa consciente as a socio-musical phenomenon is Althusser's concept of interpellation/hailing (2006). As I have already mentioned, Salsa consciente exists beyond the mere aesthetics of entertainment and dance where most Salsa music resides. Rather than being passive, Salsa consciente develops discourse upon the expansion of critical consciousness. The lyrics of Salsa consciente, particularly those of Curet Alonso and Rubén Blades, often contain a call to action where the Latino becomes the subject of such interpellation, and thus is asked to become part of the action. This idea of Salsa consciente as a music that contains an active interpellation stands directly in opposition to Adorno's concepts of popular music (1990), where the argument relies on the idea that mass culture plays a role in the construction of passive subjects. Salsa consciente is certainly a product of mass culture, yet as we have also seen in rap and some folk music, there is an active call for the subject to defy self-centeredness as well as historic, racial, colonial, etc., ideals, and rather focus on the community, and confront the status quo and the ideologies imposed by the ruling mainstream class.

Additionally, I argue that Salsa consciente waves the banner of Latinidad above the flags of the originating nations. The resulting socio-musical discourse then is comprised of several transnational meanings and layers of motherland as well as multiple ethnic and class identities, and is filled with references to people and places that, though possibly fictitious, represent a shared Latino meta-homeland.[5] Salsa consciente accordingly shows how Latino ethnic consciousness emerged less from geographical alliances than as a composite identity, with class, postcolonial, racial, social, ancestral, Indigenous, and diasporic consciousness at its core (see Padilla 1985, Priestley 2007, Amigo 2003, Gallo 2002). This composite identity allows native Latin Americans residing outside their places of origin, as well as second-generation immigrants, to idealize and reimagine the cultural referent of "homeland." In this way, Nuyolatinos saw themselves as part of the larger milieu of a cosmopolitan city, not only as Latin Americans living in New York. As rightly noted by Baron, "Salsa music has in the last few years assumed an identity as a music of Latin New Yorkers, an identification usually considered to be superordinate to an identification with any particular Latin ethnic group" (1977, 216-217). Salsa consciente musicians helped to create this abstract identity by mingling and re-creating traditional yet innovative music that is highly recognizable as Latin American while not paying allegiance to any Latin American country in particular.[6]

In constructing an understanding of being Latino, and upholding Latinidad as the ethnic consciousness of the Latino reality, it will become clear that Latino ethnicity is a phenomenon constructed upon migration and social conflict initially in the United States. It needs to be noted nevertheless that Latinidad also exists outside the United States, though it is a relatively new phenomenon. The long historical migrations of Latin Americans to the United States serve to explain the formation of Latinidad as a phenomenon associated initially with this country. In the case of Europe, there was much less migration from Latin America, and it developed later in time. Most Latin Americans who migrated to Europe made Spain their home mainly because of the common language. However, Spain's own unstable political situation, having lived under the dictatorship of General Francisco Franco until 1975, caused Latin American migration to Spain to develop much later than its counterpart in the United States. By contrast, the formation of Latinidad in Latin America was pursued by figures such as Venezuelan Simón Bolivar and Cuban Jose Martí. Despite these ideals, the formation of a common Latin American ethnic consciousness has historically been secondary to national ideologies and superseded by nationalist divisions.

With regard to Salsa's genre classification, the music can be initially categorized as "traditional" music or "folklore," especially when considering the roots of the musical aesthetics in earlier Caribbean genres. I argue, however, that in order to assess a typology of Salsa, function should also be used to determine its genre. As such, Salsa can be considered "traditional" *Nuyolatino barrio* music insofar as much of it is learned orally and functions as a central cultural basis of the Latin American diaspora in New York. As such, Salsa's meanings need to be understood as an assertion of cultural *barrio* identities related to the position of Latinos in New York in the late 1960s and early 1970s. In this fashion, the cultural centrality of 1970s Salsa as "Latin music from the hood" presents an understanding of the music not only as a mere reimagination of Cuban music played by Puerto Ricans in New York, but as a need to culturally assert a multifaceted identity (i.e., Latino, urban, New Yorker, "hood/barrio," etc.) in a hostile environment. Salsa is ultimately an aesthetic amalgam of Latin American musics, and as such it does not aim to represent particular countries (despite the Cuban and Puerto Rican discussions of aesthetic ownership); rather its most important representational facet lies in representing urban Latino/Latin American cultural sensibilities as filtered through a Caribbean aesthetic awareness. This traditional, urban, and cosmopolitan dance music construct helps explain Salsa's rapid spread in Latin American urban centers.

It might also seem obvious to consider Salsa as popular music as the genre has, ever since the 1970s, been massively exploited for commercial profit. It should be noted, nevertheless, that the initial commodification of Salsa developed on a relatively small, grassroots scale, especially when compared to the popular music of the time. The rapid and large-scale acceptance of Salsa among an ethnic group striving for a sense of identity (popularly known and periodized as the 1970s Salsa boom) demonstrated the potential for Salsa's commercial success. "The golden age of salsa music began . . . when the record companies successfully combined . . . a spontaneous, free-wheeling, and accessible music of high quality that was also highly profitable" (Rondón 2008, 43). While in its initial form Salsa appealed greatly to Latinos and Latin Americans, to the extent that it offered a modern and popular yet traditionally rooted cultural experience, Salsa's large-scale commodification and distribution, and its involvement in the manipulations of "free enterprise" eventually caused the decline in Salsa consumption in the 1980s. In an attempt to provide a wider audience for Salsa, and to enable the music to cross over to the Anglo market—that is, subjugating Salsa to the dominant class and the largely corporate-driven music industry—Salsa was watered down by the record executives. This mass commercialization of Salsa points to the phenomenon of "standardization" in popular music as noted by Adorno, and while this standardization of Salsa eventually proved to be commercially successful with the advent of *Salsa romántica* (romantic Salsa) in the 1990s, Salsa's initial appeal, the raw barrio sentiment that made the music popular in the first place and its connectedness to political resistance were lost.

These interpretations of Salsa show that understanding Salsa exclusively from classifications such as popular or folkloric is limiting and not revealing of the true nature of this music. My proposal for cataloging the genre of Salsa is therefore based on a twofold approach that considers Salsa's traditional/folkloric nature inside the classification of popular music. As such, I classify Salsa as "Latino/Latin American urban folklore," and I utilize this hybrid classification to denote the roots of the music in Latin America. This is achieved mainly through Caribbean-folkloric forms, adding an essential pathos that reaffirms the cultural and transnational connections of the Latino diaspora in New York, and at the same time shows Salsa as popular, that is, a mass-produced, Latino urban music.

Despite the fact that Salsa has enormous relevance for a large number of people, the musical movement has often been "otherized" and deemed to reside in the lower spectrum of culture as popular music from outside the United States, devoid of major interest in the English-speaking world.

In fact, the music is habitually utilized within the popular culture of the United States to demonstrate exoticism, otherness, and the general eroticization of being Latino, oftentimes alongside stereotypical words such as *fiesta* and *caliente*. In this sense, this work also brings with it a political dimension, inviting an understanding of Salsa based on the field of humanities, which showcases the unmistakable richness of the historical and aesthetic developments that ultimately demonstrated an incredibly sophisticated level of artistic work.

Salsa's commercial reception both in the United States and in Latin America is considered by many scholars (e.g., Berríos-Miranda 1999, Cruz 1997, Rondón 2008) to have occurred on a large scale and with great impact. However, specifically quantifying this reception is incredibly difficult. The complexity of the phenomenon stems from the absence of any available and reliable sales figures of Salsa records across all music industry databases. While the impact of popular music in the United States is often measured by sales numbers, Salsa's otherness in respect to U.S. popular music deterred many of the go-to sources (RIAA, ASCAP, BMI, Downbeat polls, etc.) from keeping account of Salsa's sales during the 1970s. Salsa's impact as measured by top hits determined by airplay is also difficult to assess. Billboard did not consider Latin music a valid category until 1986, when it created "Hot Latin Tracks." Salsa's relevance in terms of commercial hits at this point, however, was relatively minimal. Not only do the sales figures and "top 100" figures provide very few resources to help quantify the phenomenon, but furthermore all of the above systems are based in the United States. As such, any quantitative data regarding Salsa's reception in Latin America is not considered in these rankings. At the same time, the measurement of Salsa's reception in Latin America is just as devoid of any significant and reliable data as its counterpart in the United States. In fact, much of the quantified rankings used today in the region are determined by local versions of Billboard, such as Billboard Mexico or Billboard Argentina.

The National Academy of Recording Arts & Sciences (NARAS) was the only entity to recognize Salsa's impact relatively early, largely thanks to the efforts of Salsa musicians themselves and their promoters in New York seeking recognition in the mainstream. Consequently, the Grammy award for "Best Latin Recording" was established in 1976. In 1984 the name of this award was changed to "Best Tropical Latin Performance," only to change again in 1992 to "Best Tropical Latin Album," then back to "Best Tropical Latin Performance" in 1995. In 2000 the award became "Best Traditional Tropical Latin Album," and in 2011 the award was dubbed once again "Best Tropical Latin Album." The year 2000 also saw the birth of the Latin Academy of Recording Arts & Sciences (LARAS) and the birth of the Latin Grammy as a separate entity from the NARAS-awarded Grammy. This history not only points to the development of Latin music's reception in the United States, including the evident role of exoticism in the terms used, but it also highlights issues of genre definition in Latin music. Throughout this work I utilize as much quantifiable data regarding Salsa's reception as I was able to uncover, and in this regard, Grammy nominations, despite all the genre definition issues, still serve greatly as a readily available means of measuring Salsa's impact.

Throughout this book I have aimed to convey the idea of a united Latin America, with New York as its northernmost city. A useful term to understand the concept is a phrase often heard in Salsa concerts: *Una sola casa*. This epithet literally means "a single house," although the phrase can be better understood in English as "we are all under the same roof" or "we all live in the same house." This epithet is used to signify the idea of the "Latino Nation" and a united Latin America. This concept has been recently utilized by Rubén Blades in the release of his (2011) live CD/DVD *Todos Vuelven*, in which the closing track is titled "Una Sola Casa" with a chorus that incites Latin American unity: "Cultures and rhythms like no other. Consciousness, Latino, you need to have. Let's join the flags, we all live in the same house." Throughout the work, I also utilize the term meta-barrio. This concept is closely related to the idea of *una sola casa* in the sense that the meta-barrio is an imaginary construct, based upon the idea of a literal barrio-neighborhood that signifies a symbolic space where all Latinos/ Latin Americans interact with each other, and Latinidad is the outcome. I argue that this concept is essential to Salsa consciente, especially in the work of Rubén Blades, not only because he links Salsa consciente to the formation of class consciousness with the meta-barrio as a semiotic construct of Latino urban marginality and class formation, but also because he describes in great detail archetypical spaces and characters that exist in this meta-barrio. Salsa consciente functions as the ultimate musico-poetic expression of the meta-barrio by expressing at the same time traits from all over Latin America and New York, developing consciousness of situations that affect Latinos and Latin Americans, and acting as an engine of class consciousness that uses the meta-barrio as an example that all Latinos and Latin Americans can relate to. Because of the implications of these semiotic conceptualizations, I theorize Salsa consciente as the sung life chronicles of the people of the meta-barrio.

Self-Reflexivity/Positionality

In going beyond the existing literature, I find myself in an advantageous position as I myself am a Latin American living in the United States, that is, a Latino. I grew up under a dictatorship in Chile where the lyrics of Rubén Blades often spoke to my everyday life. I have been a professional Salsa and Latin percussionist for over two decades, and a composer and Salsa arranger for most of that time. This facilitates my recognition of the musical features of Salsa, Salsa consciente, and the musical markers for Latino identity in general. I have personally met many of the key performers of different Salsa genres and conversed with them on these subjects, and I have maintained contacts that were useful for the fieldwork phase. Another great advantage for this research is that I am a native Spanish speaker.

There are, however, drawbacks to my position. These include, for example, bias as related to my own sociopolitical experience having grown up under a military dictatorship, as well as my position as a professional Salsa musician, although not directly within the same community; lastly, the fact of having grown up not in a Caribbean country but in South America can also pose a limitation on identifying some of the cultural trends that indicate specificity to Spanish-speaking Caribbeanness.

Methodological Considerations

Due to the mainly historical nature of the project, a fully ethnographical methodology as commonly utilized in ethnomusicology would not have sufficed. Besides the fact that my own life experience as a Salsa musician and fan informs the project, a joint approach combining fieldwork and archival research was necessary. The fieldwork portion is based mainly upon interviews and compiling of oral histories via musicians and historians as well as attending performances and rehearsals when possible. The fieldwork piece is coupled with textual and musical transcription, as well as analysis of archival material mainly in the form of, but not limited to, recorded media, album covers, and other printed materials, such as the *Latin Beat* and *Latin New York* magazines alongside previously published interviews with Salsa musicians by other scholars and journalists. The importance of archival research should not be underestimated, as arguably the bulk of the musical productions of Salsa consciente were released between the mid-1970s and the early 1990s. Fundamentally then the phenomenon as a whole demands archival analysis.

Fieldwork

My primary fieldwork methodology for this book involved attending concerts and rehearsals of selected musicians and conducting numerous and extensive interviews in New York. The interviewees were key players and historians of the Salsa movement of the 1970s as well as musicians in the New York Salsa scene of today. The interviews included conversations about definitions of Latino identity in Salsa at large, and as they relate to Salsa consciente.

In selecting my fieldwork candidates, I sought a relatively balanced sample to represent the diversity of Latinos, and to consider the different layers of Latino identity. The biggest discrepancy in my sample is that of gender, as I have only included one woman (Ariacne Trujillo) in the study.

The discrepancy stems from the role women have historically played in Salsa, where, with a few exceptions (e.g., Celia Cruz, La Lupe, and Graciela) the scene has been largely dominated by males. In recent years the afore-mentioned female artists have passed away and the music has continued to be dominated by males.[7]

For the sake of clarity, the interviewees are assigned to the following categories: people that worked directly or indirectly with Blades and/or Curet Alonso, Nuyoricans/Puerto Ricans that currently live in the United States, Cubans, Nuyolatinos, and Afro-Latinos.

People that worked directly or indirectly with Blades and/or Curet Alonso

Papo Vázquez

Ralph Irizarry

Renato Thoms

Eddie Montalvo

Cubans

Pedrito Martínez

Ariacne Trujillo

Yuniel Jiménez

Afro-Latinos

Felipe Luciano

Jose Massó

Ralph Irizarry

John Benitez

Renato Thoms

Nuyoricans/Puerto Ricans that currently live in the United States

Felipe Luciano

Jose Massó

Andy Gonzalez

John Benitez

Nuyolatinos

Jose Vázquez-Cofresí

Jhair Sala

Renato Thoms

Textual Analysis

This book includes substantial textual analysis as a means to understand the Salsa consciente discourse. These texts are taken from the original recordings and thus are considered primary sources. The analysis examines texts mainly by Rubén Blades and Catalino "Tite" Curet Alonso in search of topical issues such as creation or loss of cultural identity, presentation of social issues, and creation of metaphorical places and/or characters that express Latino/Latin American shared realities. Analyzing this type of expression presents many questions regarding nonstandard dialect and issues of signification in the Salsa consciente discourse. Therefore, the analysis aims to understand the lyrical content of the music not as standalone text, but in relation to the social and historical context upon which it was created. The pieces are analyzed as cultural products that contain ideas and positions related to context or events that might have spawned and/or affected the creation of the piece.

Musical Transcription and Analysis of Recorded Material

In order to further deepen the analysis, I transcribe key musical pieces that helped determine the Salsa consciente movement. Following the same line as the lyrical transcription, sonic markers are placed in a context that reveals how the strategies of Latino identity contained within the music were put in place.

Cross-Referenced Catalog of Recordings

In order to tackle the classification and analysis of the music, I have created a catalog of Salsa recordings that fit within the socially conscious model. The catalog is cross-referenced by several categories, including but not limited to performer, composer, style, themes discussed, changes of style, sonic markers as analyzed in the aforementioned musical transcriptions, and year issued. This catalog may enable the creation of a typological genre classification system of recorded pieces within the realm of Salsa consciente, which can be applied to objective criteria such as composition, lyrical content, arrangement, and performance style. This would enable a clear view with regard to the evolution of the genre and the content therein. It is hoped that this catalog will be made available online, and as an open source it will continue to develop over time with input from a wide range of Salsa scholars.

Chapter Outline

I have divided the book into two large sections, with the first section comprising chapters 1 and 2 dealing with the development of Salsa consciente and Latino consciousness from a mainly historical perspective. The second part of the book comprises chapters 3, 4, and 5 and develops the analysis based on two case studies of creative output from the two key figures of Salsa consciente. The first case study is based on the work of Catalino "Tite" Curet Alonso, while the second one is centered on the work of Rubén Blades.

Chapter 1 is entitled "Salsa as Class Consciousness" and explores the expansion of Latino consciousness in the United States as related to issues of class, ethnicity, and the historical development of Latino communities in New York. While the musical aspect of this section deals specifically with the elements that shaped the musical aesthetics of Salsa, the musico-historical perspective explores the social advances of what I have dubbed pre-Salsa music. The main musical referents of this chapter point to the approaches presented by Arsenio Rodriguez, the mambo craze of the 1950s and its African representations of the music, and the development of boogaloo as a result of the mix of African American and Latino music in New York. Included in this chapter are definitions of Salsa from Latino perspectives and class consciousness as essential elements of this work.

Chapter 2 is called "Salsa as the Engine of Latino Consciousness," and it analyzes relevant social circumstances and advances definitions of Latino ethnicity. Alongside this examination I analyze the changing demographics of Latinos in New York and the beginning of the role that Salsa played in transmitting a message of Latino consciousness to the Latin American markets. Regarding the social circumstances, I analyze the civil rights movement and its impact on the social consciousness of Latino immigrants in New York. This chapter also explores the dynamics of *El Barrio*/Spanish

Harlem and the South Bronx as the main Latino enclaves of the 1960s and 1970s and the development and impact of neo-Marxist social groups such as the Young Lords Party. Musically, I showcase the issues and the evolution of the current expressions of Salsa and their social emphasis through analysis of their work.

Section two of the book centers around two case studies: one investigating the work of Catalino "Tite" Curet Alonso, and the other case study focusing on Rubén Blades. The main emphasis in the second part of this book is the shift from Salsa as an orally based art "composed in performance" to Salsa consciente as a body of work based on written language. Along these lines, I analyze both Curet Alonso and Blades as composers, intellectuals, and theorists of Salsa consciente, and as ideologues of Latinidad. I consider Blades and Curet Alonso as a step further in Salsa's evolution from performers such as Héctor Lavoe, Celia Cruz, Adalberto Santiago, among others. Despite the fact that Rubén Blades is also a very accomplished performer, I center my analysis around his work as a composer, since this is where his theorization of Salsa consciente was developed. I emphasize the political aspects that both Blades and Curet Alonso explored in their respective music as an evolution of Salsa, insofar as their innovations spread into the mainstream, both rapidly and decisively.

This evolution of Salsa can be compared to other facets of popular music such as the contrast between performance and composition in the practice of jazz musicians. I utilize the examples of saxophonists Coleman Hawkins and John Coltrane. While both artists played the same instrument and were contemporaries, Hawkins established his reputation mainly as a performer, whereas Coltrane, who also began as a performer, soon began composing. Hawkins's contributions as a performer, although extraordinary, did not have the same type of impact as Coltrane's compositions did. Through his compositions, Coltrane advanced jazz's musical language enormously,[8] and he was able to move his music beyond mere sound.[9] While both Hawkins and Coltrane are fantastic performers in their own right, Coltrane's compositions can be understood as a further evolution from Hawkins's contributions in performance. In the same light, I utilize the second part of this book to analyze Blades's and Curet Alonso's contributions as Salsa composers—rather than analyzing individual performers—as they clearly present a further development in the language of Salsa.

Chapter 3 aims to classify and analyze the body of work of Puerto Rican composer Catalino "Tite" Curet Alonso as one of the main creators of Salsa consciente. Since his compositions were not performed by him, but by many different musicians, this chapter is approached thematically rather than historically, and includes lyrical and musical analyses of Curet Alonso's compositions as performed by several different artists. The main referents of this chapter are analyses of Curet's presentations of Latinidad, interpreted as a multilayered endeavor comprised of social, African, post/de-colonial, Native, and geographically unbound Latino identities. Throughout this chapter I also emphasize the tension that arises from the dialectic relation between the Salsa composer and performer, and the poetic indirections that Curet Alonso often utilized.

Chapters 4 and 5 focus specifically on the work of Rubén Blades as a composer. Throughout the chapters I analyze the development of his work into the Salsa world via Fania Records, his eventual move away from the label, and his evolution outside of it. I utilize his tenure with Fania to analyze his breakthrough work with Willie Colón and the implications that this partnership had for Salsa in general and Salsa consciente specifically. Following his greater independence, I analyze Blades's solo work so as to advance a clearer picture of his now decidedly political and Latin American endeavors. I utilize his case study in an attempt to understand his role as arguably the most important composer of Salsa consciente, and as the Latino musician whose work has functioned as the principal engine in the development and transmission of Latino consciousness.

Acknowledgments

The writing of this book would not have been possible without the help of many people. I am forever grateful to everyone who helped me see the process through. I dedicate this work in the most heartfelt way to my amazing wife Ellen, and my son Victor. Ellen saw the process of this book all the way through and was by my side all along, cheering me, supporting me, discussing the issues of the work, and helping me continue when the going got rough. I could not have done this without her by my side. Ellen: I love you and I am forever grateful to have you in my life. Thank you. Victor: Te quiero! Gracias por llegar a nuestras vidas. Besos, Papá.

Both of my parents, Drs. Irene Agurto Timoner and Vicente Espinoza Espinoza, were big inspirations for this work. I thank them for instilling discipline and the love of knowledge in me. Gracias. I am also grateful to my grandparents, mi Nana y mi Tata, y mi tia Ceci por todo lo que me han dado. My family in Cuba, who always encourages me to continue working hard: Joseito, Olga Lidia, Sergito, tio Sergio, Erick, Chayanne, Carlitos, Osniel, El Babi, y toda la gente de Aña Ilú Kan. To my United States family, the

Rondinas, who have so beautifully received me in this country, thank you. Additionally, a huge thank you to my friends Amanda Ruzza and Aaron Thurston who so graciously allowed me to stay at their places in New York while doing research for this book.

I would also like to express my deep appreciation and gratitude to my colleague and dear friend Dr. Victor Manfredi. His mentorship and guidance through the process were invaluable. I feel truly fortunate to have worked with such a knowledgeable, passionate, and caring person. Vito, I am very grateful to have sat at your kitchen table, and for our many meals, the coffee, and, more than anything, our talks. Thank you. To Drs. Brita Heimarck, Victor Coelho, James Iffland, and Marié Abe, thank you for the guidance and thought-provoking suggestions along the way. I also give great thanks to the people who helped me edit this work: Ian Copestake and Rubén Martinez. Rubén, thank you for your patience and dedication, and for the opportunity to publish my work.

I specially need thank all the performers, producers, engineers, arrangers, etc., who participated, directly or indirectly, in the recordings that I used as primary sources. You made the music happen. I have done my best to credit everyone I could find listed in the records. I have attached a list, as complete as I could manage, of everyone involved in the appendices. Additionally, the limited scope of this work only allowed for a limited amount of people to be included so, to anyone who was part of the Salsa consciente movement in any shape or form: A heartfelt thank you for your contributions and your music.

To all the musicians and Salsa historians who I interviewed for this work: You guys are amazing! Thank you! Every person I reached out to was fantastic to work with, knowledgeable, and incredibly generous with their time. To Renato Thoms, Jhair Sala, Jose Vázquez-Cofresí, Andy Gonzalez, John Benitez, Pedrito Martínez, Ariacne Trujillo, Yuniel Jiménez, Edwin Perez, Papo Vázquez, Ralph Irizarry, Jose Massó, and the whole Orquesta Salsa con Conciencia: Thank you for sharing your experiences and ideas with me. A special thank you to Eddie Montalvo, who, aside from sharing his story, treated this broke student to a fantastic lunch after our interview. Special and truly heartfelt thanks to Felipe Luciano, who gave me an incredible amount of firsthand "lived" knowledge and breakdown of the whole Salsa consciente movement. His thorough understanding and critical analysis of the subject were crucial throughout the research process.

Finally, I thank Rubén Blades and Catalino "Tite" Curet Alonso for their amazing musical contributions. This book would not exist if I had not heard their amazing music in the first place. I thank music, la música, for she inspires me every day. I also thank Latin America, mi bella América Latina; even though we are now far apart, you are in my thoughts every day. I never forget you and I miss you.

Performing Consciencia: Salsa as a Chronicle of El Pueblo

2. *We want self-determination for all Latinos.* Our Latin Brothers and Sisters, inside and outside the [U]nited [S]tates, are oppressed by amerikkkan business. The Chicano people built the Southwest, and we support their right to control their lives and their land. The people of Santo Domingo continue to fight against gringo domination and its puppet generals. The armed liberation struggles in Latin America are part of the war of Latinos against imperialism. Que Viva La Raza!
—From the Young Lords Party 13-Point Program and Platform, 1969

While much of the Salsa boom of the 1970s was not centered around social themes, there is a clear musical stream featuring a degree of social consciousness that was part of Salsa's discourse at large. Toward the end of the 1960s, musicians who would eventually participate in the upcoming boom, such as Eddie Palmieri, Ray Barretto, and Cheo Feliciano, directly included themes of social justice in their music. Whereas the ideals expressed in their music helped germinate the seeds of the movement that eventually would be known as Salsa consciente, their discourse needs to be understood from music and ideals that came before them, and at times developed parallel to their own compositions. Therefore, in order to comprehend the rise of Salsa consciente and its eventual development, culminating in the full discourses of musicians Catalino "Tite" Curet Alonso and Rubén Blades, it is fundamental to contextualize and recognize the soil from which arose Salsa as an aesthetic concept and consciente as a sociopolitical stream of Latino ethnic consciousness. In the subsequent two chapters, I develop my work regarding the ideals and contextualization of

■ 1

the building blocks of Latinidad as related to the music. In this manner, I advance definitions of consciousness in relation to being Latino, and how this consciousness manifested before and in the earlier stages of Salsa.

In the following two chapters, I center some of my analysis around Latin music from New York before Salsa became known as Salsa. I refer to this music as *Pre-Salsa*. I address the contextualization of the music alongside understanding and defining the basic concepts and developments of Latinidad at the time. As such, I tie the realities, largely as social studies, to the large Puerto Rican migration to New York following the end of World War II, the development of the urban realities of El Barrio/Spanish Harlem, the civil rights movement, the outcome for Latinos in the United States of the socialist revolution in Cuba, and the general revolutionary feelings of the times. To these concepts, I add ways to understand definitions of Salsa as related to the development of Latino identity.

The central topic of chapter 1 is largely of racial consciousness. I address the discussion of race and racial consciousness not as a standalone topic related to the civil rights movement, but also as the first level of Latino ethnic consciousness.[1] In this manner, I seek to show the ways in which *Pre-Salsa* music addresses issues of race. I utilize racial consciousness as a primary building block of Latinidad since the conceptualizations of race, being Black, and Africa, as part of the Latino ethos, are the earliest ones to be showcased in the music. I utilize as a key axis the works of Tito Puente, Machito and his Afro-Cubans, Tito Rodriguez, Rafael Cortijo, Joe Cuba, and Arsenio Rodriguez as early representatives of what would eventually become Salsa, as a means to understand the ways that the trope of race was being discussed in the music. It is important to note, however, that the trope of race at this stage was largely understood in relation to the binary division of Black and White, and made no mention of Indigenous people. It is only with the appearance of Catalino "Tite" Curet Alonso that the concept of Indigenous as part of the Latino ethnic construction is showcased.

Another concept that helps us appreciate these developments frames Salsa as a people-centered endeavor as opposed to a nationalist-centered inquiry. It is in this frame where being one with the people, not Dominican, not Puerto Rican, not Cuban, but rather part of The People, what in Spanish is referred to as being part of *El Pueblo*, becomes a crucial trope.[2] It is in this trope that we can define Salsa as a music of resistance, a counter-hegemonical music developed largely in a grassroots fashion and with the need to express social realities beyond entertainment. This music was developed "on the streets" of Latin New York as opposed to the heavily produced mainstream music of the United States. We can also analyze this counter-hegemonic dialectic in geographical terms wherein Salsa is music from El Barrio/Spanish Harlem, and the South Bronx, both minority-centered communities and socially displaced areas of New York, as opposed to mainstream American pop music developed in and for an audience who would be largely centered in the more affluent Manhattan.

Continuing the push to understand Latino ethnic consciousness, I develop chapter 2 as a way to grasp the advance from racial consciousness as a primary level of Latinidad to the development of class consciousness as a second level in the development of Salsa consciente. As such, and having already assumed racial concerns as part of the Latino ethos at large, Salsa consciente begins near the end of the 1960s to address the development of class consciousness, poverty, displacement, and the general disenfranchisement of Latinos. The socio-physical context upon which Salsa continues to develop then becomes a vital element in the construction of the consciente discourse. In order to understand these ideals, I analyze the social circumstances that eventually led to the activism of the Young Lords Party as part of the efforts of Latinos in New York City, largely in Harlem and the South Bronx, to develop self-determination as a means to advance their communities. It would be a highly safe bet to assume that the soundtrack to these activities would have included Salsa. This is largely confirmed by the presence of poet/activist Felipe Luciano, one of the key informants of this book, active member of the Young Lords Party as well as an emcee for many Salsa shows during the time discussed.

Within the late 1960s context, I also analyze the work of Willie Colón and Hector Lavoe. While the iconic duo did not fully develop a socially conscious body of work, their presence as part of The People/*El Pueblo*, and their image as hustlers and street-smart heroes, as noted in their album covers, clearly expressed the realities of a Latino working-class group of people

"hustling" daily to survive. The critical artist in this pre-boom period, however, was Eddie Palmieri, who was keenly aware of the social realities of
Latinos and directly began to address these issues in his music. The release
of his album *Justicia* (Justice) in 1969, which includes the track of the same
name, directly addresses economic injustice and class awareness as part
of the discussion. As a follow-up to *Justicia*, Palmieri released *Vámonos Pa'l
Monte*, where, aside from his masterful sonic experimentations, he continued to address social injustice as part of his work.

Palmieri's success with this material and the subsequent Salsa boom
that propelled the Fania All Stars to stardom, largely due to the success of
the movie *Our Latin Thing* featuring the All Stars as street heroes, in many
ways both allowed and at the same time forced Salsa to continue to emphasize, at least on a primary level, socially conscious material. This idea
became highly successful as not only did it resonate with many everyday
realities for Latinos and Latin Americans, but the social message was intertwined with an entertaining, and more lighthearted, dance-centered set of
music.

Aside from the literal advances made in the works analyzed in the
following section, it is key to consider the concept of Salsa in these two
chapters as a created-in-performance endeavor. In understanding that
most of the developments of Latino ethnic consciousness in Salsa music
were lyrical as opposed to instrumental, we see that a large majority of
the advances in the music, as understood from social justice perspectives,
happened with the appearance of the composer, and not the performer, as
the primary developer of Salsa's consciousness. While many performers did
develop the concepts that I have discussed here, the manifestation of their
work was centered around their charisma and connection with the audience while performing, and not necessarily on the lyrics. In this manner,
understanding that singers such as Hector Lavoe and Pete El Conde—who,
as master stage improvisers with a large amount of street credibility that
in the long run failed to sustain a socially centered output but developed
their careers as entertainers, often sang music composed for them—helps
center the discussion of section two of the book, where I address the works
of Catalino "Tite" Curet Alonso and Rubén Blades from the point of view

of composition as song in literary form. In many ways we understand the developments of Salsa consciente as emerging from a "street" oral tradition, where the master singer might touch upon social issues, shifting toward a literary/composer-centered music where the intent is directed at promoting a higher level of social consciousness.

Additionally, in understanding that the late 1960s was an era of mass consumption in the United States during which Salsa was being positioned as a sung chronicle of Latino life, it is not surprising that the wide distribution of vinyl records eventually started to reach a larger audience beyond Latin New York. Salsa began to achieve popularity within Latin America, mainly in the Spanish-speaking circum-Caribbean, and while addressing the social realities of Latin New York, there was a broader connection via discussions of race and class mixed with entertainment as expressed from Nuyolatino experiences that were paralleled in many equally marginalized, racially and socially displaced areas of Latin America. It is in this connection where the music begins to form the third level of Latinidad: Trans-Latino ethnic consciousness. I address this development in chapters 3, 4, and 5 as a continuation of the foundations laid in the following two chapters.

[handwritten annotation: PRIMARILY ABOUT ALLE AS INDICATED ON page 2]

Salsa as Class Consciousness

Many People will say that Salsa is street music. Well, I was not born in a mansion, and most of us here come from humble beginnings—from parents who came here as immigrants braving a whole new world in order to build a new foundation. In many ways Salsa is synonymous with that foundation, because Salsa is not the music itself, but the spirit behind the music. The spirit that moves us to dance, sing and go on in spite of all the obstacles.

—Izzy Sanabria (1979, 29)

Arriving at a clear definition of Salsa consciente is a complex task and requires breaking down the concept into its two core elements: Salsa and consciousness/conscience. For the purposes of this book I define Salsa consciente as Latin dance music produced mostly in New York, and characterized by texts that combine poetic structures with a Latino/Latin American-centered political, racial, historical, and social consciousness.

Defining Salsa

It is widely accepted that Salsa's musical aesthetics originated largely from the Cuban *son*, *son montuno*, *mambo*, and *guaracha* styles (see Waxer 2002b, Steward 2000, Duany 1984, García 2006). These sets of musical aesthetics were then reimagined and hybridized in New York, mainly by Nuyoricans (New York Puerto Ricans) with the often unacknowledged, additional participation of other Latin American nationals. Thus, most discussions regarding the development of Salsa have been dedicated to questions of origins, ownership, and national associations as the primary identity markers. Previous debates tried to determine whether the music is an extension/reworking of the Cuban genres such as the *son, guaracha, mambo,* and *son montuno* of the 1940s and 1950s (Acosta 1997, 2004a; García 2006; Manuel 1994), or a genre mainly developed by Puerto Ricans in New York (Negron 2006; Duany 1984). This specifically Cuban/Puerto Rican manner of performance as conceived in a New York framework has been conveyed as "Nuyorican Salsa," and has largely become the symbol of a musical Latinidad in the United States. In this way the sensibilities of Puerto Ricans in New York have been treated as the primary way to understand the signifiers of Salsa.

It is with this understanding of Salsa as tied mainly to nationalistic identities, and therefore as a product that shapes a subset of nationally centered cultural identifications, that I disagree with the general trends found in Salsa literature.[1] I situate Salsa at the center of the discussion and understand it from a neo-Marxist point of view as a crucial element in the Latino sociocultural and economic resistance and struggles in the United States and Latin America, and posit that the current readings of Salsa have failed to understand a crucial aspect of the music: The People, *El Pueblo* their everyday struggles, and their realization of such struggles as intrinsically linked to socially constructed contexts that pushed for the appearance of Salsa as a critical cultural expression of being Latino/Latin American. As such, equating Salsa with Puerto Ricanness or Cubanness is an incomplete proposition since I consider Salsa to be essentially a hybridized expression that owes much but not all to nationality, and instead needs to be considered as an intrinsic mode of expression based on Latino/Latin American urban realities stemming from postcolonial and imperialistic binary oppositions, that is, center/periphery conceptions as understood from history, class, race/ethnicity, and the politics of the modern world. I argue that these modes of expression are not exclusive to nationality and, in fact, traverse it. Therefore, I conceive of Salsa as the product of historically specific material and social conditions, not a mere passive reflection in artistic form of limited geographical content. This understanding allows Salsa to be analyzed as a multi/transcultural Latino/Latin American phenomenon that is continental in size, spreading over various nation states. It is not exclusive to New York, Puerto Rico, or Cuba, but belongs to Latin America as a whole, with New York being the northernmost city in a semiotic conception of Latin America.

This conception of Salsa, however, does not deny the importance of nationality in the musical movement. On the contrary, nationalistic alliances play a large role in Salsa, and the contributions of those nationalities should and will be acknowledged in what follows. I argue, however, that there is an unacknowledged level of understanding in Salsa that plays a significant role both in the music and in the cultural significations associated with it. I therefore claim that reading Salsa as the product of an exclusive Cuban and/or Puerto Rican perspective robs the music of one of its biggest assets: a multicultural affirmation expressed as a soundscape that could arguably only happen in New York City. I posit that these nation-centered approaches are ultimately incomplete, since Salsa, and by extension Salsa consciente, as both a social and musical movement are intrinsically tied to the larger social movements of the 1960s and 1970s that incorporated both the Latin American population and its diaspora in New York, not to mention the participation of many non–Puerto Rican and non-Cuban musicians in the zeniths of Salsa. Consequently, I analyze Salsa as a cultural creation from below, and I postulate that the best means of understanding the music is as part of Latino/Latin American urban folklore. This definition of Salsa presents a view of the music that, in agreement with the revolutionary movements of the 1960s and 1970s, reflects the experiences of Spanish-speaking Latinos in New York City regardless of nationality, as the original center of Salsa's success, and presents the music as the catalyst for the social evolutions of Latinos in New York. Over time, Salsa also acted as a mediator of a transnational socio-musical phenomenon that eventually expanded all over Latin America.

Romero (2002, 12) defines Salsa as "an urban socio-cultural movement, synthesized in a musical expression created and developed by Caribbean emigrants and some North American musicians identifying with Latino pathos and seduced by the rhythms of Cuba and Puerto Rico." This definition gives a multicultural sentiment to the assessment of the often nation-centered discussions regarding a definition of the music. Even though it moves the discussion toward a sociocultural reading of the phenomenon, Romero's definition does not develop the exploration of the Latino/Latin American social sensibilities associated with Salsa as a means of understanding the signifiers associated with the music.

Drawing on the cultural conceptions of Romero (2002) and the sociological ideas of Padilla (1990), I conceive of Salsa as an expression of Latino urban folklore, with its center and disputed birth site in New York City. It is here where Salsa in general and Salsa consciente specifically were developed to a very high level regardless of the often discussed Cuban/Puerto Rican geographical ownership of the style. Duany argues that "in fact, the genre's [Salsa] center of diffusion, in terms of commercial production and distribution, has not been San Juan as much as New York City" (1984, 186). This study thus aims to advance an understanding not of the nationality, or nationalities, of Salsa as a movement, but of Salsa as a signifier of a transnational and transcultural Latino/Latin American identity based on conceptualizations of Salsa's message of a shared Latino/Latin American consciousness rather than on geographical alliances.

This view is supported by artists such as Rubén Blades, Catalino "Tite" Curet Alonso, and various others, who in many songs disprove a solely nationalistic reading of Salsa and present the music as an ethnically related Latino/Latin American endeavor not bound to one particular nationality. This is not to say that nationalistic alliances do not belong in analyses of Salsa. On the contrary, they actually clarify a big part of Salsa's ethnic milieu. Yet, the large impact of Salsa in Latin America shows that nation-based identifications lack a sufficient comprehension of the nature of Salsa as a transnational communicator of contemporary Latino/Latin American issues related to ethnicity, class, and politics apart from national understandings of these issues. In this case, then, I suggest a broader conceptualization of Salsa's origins and argue that Nuyolatino urban folklore better accommodates many specific details of Salsa, and by extension Salsa consciente's development. This approach, connecting oral culture to the urban-based social, political, and racial milieu of Latino and Latin Americans, presents a clearer explanation of how the music came to signify Latino culture and developed transnational connections with Latin America.

The next logical question would be to ask how this consciousness formed and was expressed by the music. In order to offer a complete answer, it first needs to be understood that Salsa is a dance-centered music that united working-class Latino immigrants with their fellow New Yorkers of other ethnicities, especially Blacks, Italians, and Jews. In analyzing Salsa as oral folklore I argue that the music was able to spread virally, in the dance halls, rather than requiring formal instruction in school, which is the case with written culture. This phenomenon, coupled with the existence of a huge roster of jazz players in the city, also meant that performance reached and maintained an incredibly high standard, despite the economic marginality of everyone concerned. In a parallel manner, the emergence of radio and long-playing albums made the phenomenon a paying endeavor outside of the dancehalls, which gave more scope to individual creativity. It needs to be said, however, that although the musicians involved were able to earn a basic income, only an elite lived from royalties, while at the same time the music industry exploited the marginality of the musicians, reaping record profits and paying only measly salaries to the performers.

Becoming Salsa

While the popularity of Cuban music in the city played a major role in defining Salsa in terms of aesthetics, with Tito Puente clinging to the Cuban essence of the music and famously stating that the only Salsa (sauce) that exists is "tomato sauce" (Acosta 2004a, 7), it should be understood that the continuity of Cuban music as an exclusively Cuban product in New York City was affected to a large degree by the 1959 Cuban revolution and the subsequent blockade imposed on Cuba. These events marked a clear rupture in the role of Cuban music as the main informant of Latino culture in the United States at this point, mainly because of the physical unavailability of Cuban musicians in New York City.

The Cuban revolution unfolded toward the end of what was known as the *mambo* craze of the 1950s in New York with the Palladium Ballroom as its center, with profound consequences for the Latin music scene in the city. The precept of Cuban music being the only Latin music in the city was now not only hard to find but quickly became associated with Communism. This shift in the understanding of Latin music happened prior to the existence of Salsa per se, yet it is of great significance in the development of the movement. The fact that Cuban music had become something beyond mere entertainment, as it was now linked to an ideology, presented a political conundrum for musicians to be associated with a type of music that represented Communism. Moreover, it could be argued that because of the negative political associations that Cuba carried, and the diversity of Latinos in New York performing and participating in the music, the categorization of the music on the radio and street soon stopped being Cuban music and became "Latin Music." Arguably, then, the political concerns of the United States toward Cuba at the time caused the association of the music with Cuban national heritage to fade, as the sound was now performed by non-Cubans and approached from a stylistic, rather than nationalistic, point of view—that is, *mambo*, *charanga*, *guaracha*, *cha cha cha*, and eventually, as an umbrella term, Salsa.

While this phenomenon was developing in New York, Cuba's totalitarian Marxist-centered policies began to affect the music on the island as well, when the official policy declared that music should serve the revolution's ideals and project the Cuban revolutionary philosophies to the world. While this promptly meant the rise of the *Nueva trova* movement, with figures such as Silvio Rodriguez and Pablo Milanés at the forefront developing excellent lyrics with music serving mostly as a backdrop to the words, the typically Afrocentric popular music associated with Cuba, such as the *son*-based music of Chapottín y sus Estrellas and Arsenio Rodríguez, was set aside as low culture that did not serve revolutionary ideologies.

At the same time in New York, Cuban musicians such as Machito and his Afro-Cubans became engulfed in a "time warp" where the sound of the *mambo* was still relevant and informed the burgeoning new Latino music, yet it did not appeal to the new generations, either aesthetically or socially, as it failed to reflect their new urban and social realities. It should be noted, insofar as Machito and the Afro-Cubans are concerned, that regardless of the political ideologies that the band might have had, a possible return to

Cuba by Machito and his musical director, Mario Bauzá, would have meant musical suicide, as their jazz-tinged music would have been potentially constructed as imperialistic and anti-revolutionary.

In order to consider the other nationalist center of Salsa—namely, Puerto Rico—it is necessary to develop a framework of analysis that recognizes Puerto Rico's colonial status with regard to the United States. The result of the colonial approach placed Puerto Ricans not only as the historically dominant Latino majority in New York, but also as a nation in constant search of its long-denied identity. Moreover, understanding the position of Puerto Rico in New York at this historical juncture also presents the concept of an urban ethno-linguistic group of people that is not isolated from other Spanish speakers with whom they live together, and with whom they share the inheritance of a wider Latin American culture. There is then a natural development with regard to Puerto Ricans utilizing what was initially Cuban music as a representational tool, especially since Cuban culture at this point did not have a voice in the United States. Economically it is crucial to understand that the popularity associated with the *mambo* provided an income for a group of people that proved to be the most destitute in New York City, thus making Latin music performance a profitable venture for Puerto Ricans. In this manner, by a natural evolution of the creative processes of an expressive culture in search of an identity to express both the meta-homeland and the new urban and cosmopolitan folkloric realities of Latinos, Salsa's appearance as a consequence of this historical context appears to be an inevitable fact. Furthermore, in recognizing the place of the Puerto Rican diaspora at the crux of the development of Salsa, it can be understood that, as a Latino cultural product initially formed from Cuban aesthetics, Salsa fulfilled the role of a Puerto Rican national linguistic identity as a codified language that contained enough traits of the Puerto Rican/ Latino meta-homeland and Nuyolatino realities to be considered their own. In order to further comprehend the status of Puerto Ricans in New York at the turn of the 1960s, however, it is necessary to consider at least a basic timeline of the arrival of Puerto Ricans to the city.

The history of Puerto Ricans in New York dates back to the nineteenth century. Following the Spanish American War of 1898 and the advancement of the 1917 Jones-Shafroth Act that made Puerto Ricans U.S. citizens, Puerto Ricans began to migrate to the United States in significant numbers. Following the Great Depression, World War II, rising unemployment in the island, and the advent of air travel, the 1950s saw a large surge of immigrants from Puerto Rico to the United States, with New York as one of the primary destinations:

> From the mid-1930s to the mid-1960s, U.S. corporate, export-oriented agriculture in the island (sugar and tobacco) went into crisis and decline. This process was accompanied by massive unemployment and a distinct shift on the island toward export-oriented, light, labor-intensive, machine-based industry; the uneven imposition of welfare-state reforms; and a mass market for low income housing and individual mechanized transportation. . . . The reincorporation of Puerto Ricans within the restructured world-economy in this manner created the circumstances that led many manual day laborers, landless peasants, and devastated small-property owners to leave the island in unprecedented numbers. The migrants who left the island at this time moved into the dilapidated tenements vacated by Italians, Jews, and Poles in the northeastern U.S. seaboard and Chicago during the 1940s and 1950s. (Santiago-Valles and Jiménez-Muñoz 2004, 90)

The area of East Harlem between 95th Street and Fifth Avenue, and limited by the Harlem River, has been historically known for its immigrant communities. Included in this zone, the area surrounding 110th and Lexington Avenue has historically been known as Spanish Harlem, having been settled by Puerto Rican migrants following the First World War. This area became a hotspot for newly arrived Puerto Rican immigrants largely due to the already established social networks between Spanish Harlem and the Island of Puerto Rico. Spanish Harlem soon began to grow beyond Lexington and 110th Street and established itself as a primarily Puerto Rican neighborhood. The expansion went beyond East Harlem as Puerto Ricans quickly settled to a large extent also in the neighboring South Bronx. As Puerto Rican immigration continued to expand, the urban definition of East Harlem changed, and eventually the area became known as El Barrio (The Neighborhood), the largest Puerto Rican enclave in the United States.[2] Regarding the sheer numbers in this migration, Santiago-Valles and Jiménez-Muñoz (2004, 89) indicated that

> There were already almost 900,000 Puerto Ricans on the U.S. mainland by 1960, which amounted to a 200 percent increase when compared to island migrants identified by the 1950 census as living in the United States. According to this same 1960 census, over 600,000 Puerto Ricans in the United States had been born in the island, and this was 172 percent larger than the number of U.S. residents who had been island born in 1950. Almost 300,000 Puerto Ricans in the United States in 1960 were of parents born in Puerto Rico, which represented a 262 percent increase from the figures for 1950 (tabulations based on: USBC 1963; USBC 1973).

Following the postwar migration, many of the new immigrants ended up working jobs in the service industry, and this class of worker became associated with Puerto Ricans. Fitzpatrick (1971, 60) indicated that "they dominate the hotel and restaurant trades to such an extent that these businesses would be helpless without them." The low wages associated with these types of jobs, coupled with the overcrowded living conditions of the large numbers in the underserved public housing of El Barrio and the South Bronx created the living conditions of a ghetto, to the extent that Puerto Ricans throughout the 1960s proved to be the most destitute segment of the entire New York City population (Fitzpatrick 1971, 59-60).

Despite the fact that Puerto Ricans are citizens of the United States, they were essentially considered no different from any other immigrants. The result of the U.S. colonialist policy in Puerto Rico (euphemistically referred to as Commonwealth) created a natural social experiment that resulted in a large migration of U.S. citizens, of which a large majority did not speak English, did not share the cultural traits of the mainland, and were treated as second-class citizens in their own country.

While the Puerto Rican communities of New York made up the largest Latino segment, there were also other groups of Latinos that were absorbed into the strong identity of Puerto Ricans in the city. Demographically speaking, Gurak and Fitzpatrick (1982, 922) indicated that "the Puerto Rican population increased from 612,574 in 1960 to 846,731 in 1970 (U.S. Bureau of the Census 1973). Perhaps of greater significance, the 1970 census found 1,278,593 individuals of Spanish language background." These numbers show that in 1970 there were 431,862 officially counted—as undocumented immigrants probably preferred not to be counted—non-Puerto Rican Latinos in New York City. Roughly one out of every three Latinos in the city in 1970 was not Puerto Rican. Fitzpatrick and Gurak (1979, 923) indicated that "increasingly, 'Hispanic' in New York City refers to Dominicans, Colombians, Ecuadorians, Cubans, and other immigrants and their descendants from South and Central American countries." Sociologically speaking, the assimilation of Puerto Ricans with other Latinos was shown to be an important trait as demonstrated by the same study that analyzed marriage records among the "Hispanic" population of New York (Fitzpatrick and Gurak 1979, 923-924). "Of the 27,712 Hispanics included in these marriages, 55.8% were Puerto Ricans, 18.8% were South Americans, 13.1% were Dominicans, 8.1% were Mexicans or Central Americans, and 4.2% were Cubans." These basic descriptive statistics clearly indicate the diversity of the broad category "Hispanic."

Besides demographics, Latino diversity in the city has since the early stages of immigration made strides culturally. From jazz's "Spanish tinge" to Salsa there are myriad musical trends that had significant, albeit often exoticized and eroticized, cultural relevance. The 1920s and 1930s saw the emergence of Argentine tango music in the United States, as well as the "*rumba* craze" spearheaded by Cuban-born Don Aspiazú and his hit "El Manisero" (the peanut vendor), followed by the appearances of the also Cuban-born "Desi Arnaz and his conga taking Broadway by storm in 1939" (Roberts 1979, 70), Waldorf Astoria resident band leader and Catalan-born (yet considered part of the Latin bandwagon) Xavier Cugat, and Brazilian-Portuguese Carmen Miranda. The 1940s continued to show a clear presence of Latino culture in music with the inclusion of Cuban-born Luciano "Chano" Pozo in Dizzy Gillespie's band, eventually giving birth to Cubop alongside the work of Mario Bauzá and Machito. Puerto Rican trombonist Juan Tizol, composer of the now-famous jazz standards "Caravan" and "Perdido," was part of Duke Ellington's band for over fifteen years, and Puerto Rican-born pianist and composer Noro Morales also enjoyed widespread popularity at the time, rivaling Machito's popularity until the arrival of the 1950s "*mambo craze*."[3] Last but not least, it is necessary to mention Cuban-born *tres* player and composer Arsenio Rodriguez, who upon migrating to the United States in 1952 arguably became the musician who had the greatest aesthetic influence on Salsa.[4]

As I have already mentioned, key Salsa performers such as Panamanians Rubén Blades and Victor Paz, Venezuelan Oscar d'Leon, and Dominicans Héctor "Bomberito" Zarzuela, Jose Alberto "El Canario," and Johnny Pacheco (who could be called the "architect" of Salsa because of his role within the movement) also played extremely important roles in the development of the music. As I argue throughout this book, not enough attention has been paid to the range of their nationalities, as they have often been grouped and associated with the Puerto Rican population of New York.

Not only were Latinos culturally involved in music, they also made an impact in sports. The New York Cubans, for example, was a baseball team that played the Negro leagues in the 1930s and had players from Mexico, the Dominican Republic, Puerto Rico, and Cuba. In addition, Burgos (2001, 74) indicates that "Latinos appeared on each of the city's Major League teams before the breaking of baseball's color line in 1947: the New York Yankees, the New York Giants, and the Brooklyn Dodgers . . . For many, their interactions aided the process whereby they became more than Cubans, Puerto Ricans, or Dominicans; it facilitated their becoming Latino."

The comingling of these groups as demonstrated by Fitzpatrick and Gurak (1972) and their adaptation to being "Latinized" as remarked by Burgos (2001) indicates the fluid nature of Latinos and Latino interactions in the city. In terms of Salsa, this Latino diversity, and the flow of interactions among Spanish-speaking groups makes it necessary to remark that the consumption and identification of Salsa in New York City has never been restricted to either Cubans or Puerto Ricans but is linked to the larger Nuyolatino population (Baron 1977, Blum 1978). Thus, it can be deduced that the cultural products of such a combination express to varying degrees traits from all of the "Hispanic" groups residing in the city. Despite this diversity, and the fact that the cultural presence of Latin America until the 1950s was mainly dominated by the Cuban side of the equation, New York City's Latino population has largely been associated almost exclusively with the Puerto Rican nationality. This fact as well as the strength found in "becoming part" Puerto Rican as a member of the demographic majority has often made all Nuyolatinos "Puerto Ricans" whether they want to be or not. Luciano (2013) indicated that "if you stay in this culture for more than five years, you become Puerto Rican. I've seen it happen to Mexicans, Dominicans, Italians, Jews . . . they in a strange way become Puerto Rican."

My point here is that Nuyolatinos of all nationalities have often found refuge from the hardships of immigration by associating some traits of their original cultures with what were initially Puerto Rican and Nuyorican cultural traits, as in the domains of food and music. While Puerto Ricans certainly paved the way for Latinos in the city, and as such their place at the top of the historical New York migration pyramid is rightfully assigned, I argue that the diversity of Latinos in the city not only shows the existence of differing stories, but makes the understanding of Puerto Rican/Nuyorican consciousness in New York City a totemic example of unacknowledged Latino ethnic consciousness.

The Musical Aesthetics of Salsa

As stated previously, aesthetically Salsa takes much of its language from Cuban and Puerto Rican music. Since this terminology will recur throughout this book, it is necessary to develop at least a basic understanding of what the musical forms and elements that have become part of the standard language of Salsa sound like. Accordingly, I advance here a series of musical annotations and short analyses regarding the basic aesthetics of Salsa. I should clarify that this musical exploration is not intended as a complete guide to the musical range of Salsa. There are many books and studies that highlight the use of these elements in its traditional forms and in its hybrid Salsa arrangements.[5] Instead, this section is intended as a primer for the reader to understand the terminology used in this book. As I stated earlier, Salsa's transnational and transcultural character is at times expressed sonically; therefore throughout this work I include additional transcriptions as a tool to advance understanding of specific musical signifiers that appear in particular compositions.

THE CLAVE

Clave translates in Spanish literally as password or passcode, and it is indeed the password to understanding Cuban music. The clave holds incredible importance in the performance of Salsa, and is really what aesthetically holds the music together. While a clave, the instrument, is ultimately a percussion instrument, this section is focused on the *concept* of clave as the organizing musical system that rules over all of the performers involved. In Salsa performance, clave is usually played in the same manner as it is in Cuban *son* music. Rumba clave, although similar, is not really used in Salsa.[6]

Clave is a two-measure rhythm that can be expressed in either a "straight" or "reversed" direction. This idea of clave direction is often referred to as 3-2 (straight) or 2-3 (reversed) in reference to the number of strokes in each measure, often referred to as sides (3 side and 2 side). The direction of the clave is ultimately related to the melodic alignment of the song and its relationship to the clave, not the drums. The rest of the rhythm section adjust their rhythmic patterns to accompany either clave pattern according to the song's requirement. Clave direction has been and will continue to be the subject of countless debates among Salsa musicians. Suffice it to say, I do not wish to add to the confusion, merely to clarify the basic concept as it relates to the genre of Salsa.

Figure 1. *Son* clave in 3–2 direction.

Figure 2. *Son* clave in 2–3 direction.

Inherent to clave direction is a sense of tension and release. The 3 side, being more syncopated than the 2 side, often marks the idea of tension; therefore it is common to find upbeats and dominant harmony on this side. The 2 side, on the other hand, is often associated with release; therefore it is more common to find downbeats and tonic harmony on this side. These are most certainly not strict rules, merely tendencies, and the reader will discover many exceptions to this principle.

THE PERCUSSION SECTION

THE TIMBALES

The timbales accompany the head (*cuerpo* is the term used in Spanish) of the song by marking a rhythm called *cascara* (literally shell) performed by striking the side (shell) of the drums with a stick while the left hand often supports the bass lines on the lower-pitched drum.

Figure 3. Timbales *cáscara* in 3–2 clave direction.

Figure 4. Timbales *cáscara* in 2–3 clave direction.

During the *mambo* (pre-composed horn sections) and call-and-response (chorus) sections, the timbales switch from the side of the drums to the bell in a pattern often referred to as *mambo* bell or *contra campana* (counter bell). The left hand continues to support the bass lines.

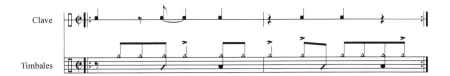

Figure 5. Timbales *mambo* bell in 3–2 clave direction.

Figure 6. Timbales *mambo* bell in 2–3 clave direction.

THE *BONGÓ*

The *bongó* player accompanies the head of the song with a basic pattern called *martillo* (literally hammer). This pattern is only a single bar in length, therefore it does not imply clave direction. The bongo player, however, is responsible for ornamenting the percussion section by utilizing ad-lib improvisations and accents, which must be aligned with the clave. In this case, I present only the basic accompanying pattern to the instrument.[7]

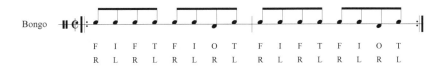

Figure 7. Basic *bongó martillo*.

As part of the performance of the bongo, the percussionist is also responsible for switching to a bell, referred to as bongo bell, during the call-and-response sections. This part is often called *campaneo*, literally "belling." Unlike the drum accompaniment, this pattern is two measures in length and subject to clave direction.

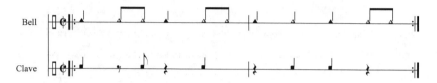

Figure 8. *Campaneo* in 3–2 clave direction.

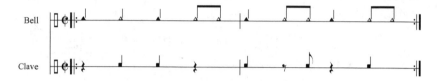

Figure 9. *Campaneo* in 2–3 clave direction.

THE CONGA DRUMS

The role of the conga drums within the Salsa rhythm section consists in setting a steady stream of subdivisions upon which the rest of the rhythm section develops a series of syncopated patterns. This base is often referred to as *tumbao* or *marcha* (literally march). During the head of the song, the conga player often plays only one drum in a single measure. During the call-and- response sections, the performer switches to a clave-oriented pattern on two drums.[8]

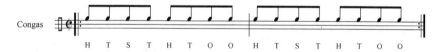

Figure 10. Basic conga *marcha* used during the *cuerpo* (head) of the song.

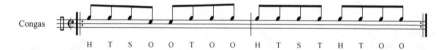

Figure 11. Basic conga *marcha* used during the chorus of the song (3–2 clave).

Figure 12. Basic conga *marcha* used during the chorus of the song (2–3 clave).

THE PUERTO RICAN *BOMBA SICÁ*

In addition to the Cuban-based percussion patterns, New York Salsa often switches to a Puerto Rican style called *bomba sicá*. This style of Afro-Puerto Rican music was popularized by Puerto Rican musician Rafael Cortijo, and it plays an important role in New York Salsa, as *bomba sicá* often marks Puerto Rican pride during an aesthetically Cuban-centered performance.

The instruments of the *bomba sicá* include the *cuá*, traditionally a piece of bamboo played with sticks, and the *buleador* or *barril* (literally barrel), a drum akin to the conga but shorter and wider. In Salsa performance, the *cuá* is often played by the timbales player substituting what was originally a piece of bamboo with a wood block mounted alongside the bells. The *buleador* part is often performed by the conga player on the lower-pitched drum.

This rhythm, being first Puerto Rican, and second a single measure in length, is not constructed around the Cuban-based concept of clave.

Figure 13. *Bomba sicá*: Basic *buleador* and *cuá*.

THE AFRO-CUBAN *BEMBÉ*

The last rhythm that is commonly utilized in Salsa performance is one derived from Afro-Cuban folklore called *bembé*. There are a great number of regional variations to this rhythm, yet the form that I show here is the one that is most commonly utilized in Salsa. In performance, the bell part is typically played by the timbales player, while the conga player utilizes several variations over the basic form shown here.

This is a ternary rhythm that is used much less frequently than the former examples, and is often used, however, as a signifier of Africanness. Even though there are clave implications to this rhythm, as it is two measures in length, it is generally performed in the manner described.[9]

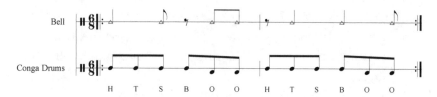

Figure 14. Basic *bembé* bell and conga parts.

BASS LINES

The connection between rhythm and harmony in the bass is one of the biggest demonstrations of the ever-present amalgam of African and European music that constitutes Latin music. The bass displays an African aesthetic through its utilization of syncopated rhythms usually associated with drumming, yet performed by the bass, a European instrument that lays a tempered tonal center.

Salsa bass lines are based mainly on a single rhythm—a rhythm that in Cuba and the Latino music scene of New York is referred to as *tresillo* (literally triplet). Even though the figure is not in reality a triplet, the figure does contain three notes per measure, and is often interpreted as "in between" a strict triplet and the actual written figure. It is, however, standard practice for arrangers to write the figure as shown in the following examples. The antecedents of these bass lines in Salsa date to the use of *tresillo*-based lines that appear in the styles of the *habanera*, the *tango*, and the *son*.

Regarding clave direction, this rhythm is a single measure in length, and therefore does not imply a clave direction. In the case of the bass lines, the clave is often implied by harmonic motion.

Figure 15. Basic *tresillo* rhythm.

The following examples show several variations utilized in Salsa. While these bass lines represent much of the African component of *son*, and to a large extent became the backbone of Salsa music, they have been employed too generically to analyze them today as a point of racial consciousness. I show them here to delineate some of the more relevant musical elements of what eventually became Salsa.

Figure 16. Basic *tresillo* form on bass.

Figure 17. Basic *tresillo* with octave embellishment.

Figure 18. *Habanera*-style *tresillo.*

Figure 19. *Tango*-style *tresillo.*

Figure 20. *Son*-style *tresillo.*

There are two more *tresillo*-based variations that are typically employed and have become part of the Salsa bass language. First the *bolero,* produced by not playing the syncopation of beat 2 (and of beat 2):

Figure 21. *Bolero* basic bass line.

Second, the *guaracha,* produced by the addition of beat 2 as an ornamentation to the original *tresillo* syncopation:

Figure 22. *Guaracha* basic bass line.

All of these lines have been and are still highly significant to Latin music produced in New York. They are, in fact, the standard bass lines of Salsa. They are all one repeated bar in length, thus allowing only for a short number of variations.[10]

THE PIANO IN SALSA

The piano in Salsa functions much like an additional drummer in the way it marks ostinatos with limited variations. These ostinatos are often referred to as *tumbaos*, *montunos*, or *guajeos*, terms that are interchangeable and mostly dependent on the region where the word is used. More specifically, *guajeo* refers to a syncopated accompanying ostinato that was originally interpreted by the *tres* (Cuban guitar) in *son* music and later by the strings in danzón groups such as Arcaño y sus Maravillas. These ostinati eventually made their way from the *tres* to the strings, then to the saxophones in the Cuban big band era, and eventually to the piano. The *guajeo* that has become one of the most standard accompaniments in Salsa is probably the one played in the *danzón* entitled "Mambo," which was composed by Orestes Lopez in 1938.

Figure 23. String *guajeo* from the *danzón* "Mambo."

As can be seen by the order of downbeats and upbeats, this idea is presented in 2-3 clave direction. Reversing the order of the measures would convert this *guajeo* to 3-2 clave direction.

Musically, the idea of this particular *guajeo* and its many variations dominated the Salsa of the 1970s eventually becoming the standard piano accompaniment of Salsa. The following example shows one of the many possible variations:

Figure 24. Modern piano *guajeo* example in 3-2 clave.

Figure 25. Modern piano *guajeo* example in 2–3 clave.

In actual performance, however, the rhythm sections of Salsa perform a remarkable number of variations, based on either harmonic or rhythmic language. As a sample of this interaction, I include a more realistic score of what a contemporary piano and bass section might perform. In this example, the piano uses several rhythmic variations to the original "Mambo" *guajeo* template, as well as combining this rhythmic language with chord changes. The bass line is based on a combination of the *son* and *guaracha* rhythmic models while navigating the chord changes:

Figure 26. Sample piano and bass accompaniments for Salsa in current practice (2–3 clave).

As a final note to this musical description, I should add that all these examples are nothing more than basic annotations of generic forms as employed in contemporary Salsa practices. Salsa musicians in performance do not necessarily abide by these strict patterns, as they constantly execute variations to enliven the performance. This mode of performance is what Moore (2010) has described as "controlled improvisation," where the basic units of musical language are practiced alongside a number of variations and then utilized interchangeably during presentations. I strongly encourage the reader to listen to a Salsa performance and experience these examples executed by professional musicians.

Latin Music Consciousness before Salsa

As a parallel to my sociologically centered analysis of Latinos in New York, I aim in this section to look at the Latin music produced in New York before the release of Willie Colón's *El Malo* in 1967 by Fania Records, arguably the first recording of Salsa. Doing so allows me to underline possible discourses that might have hinted at a development of social consciousness among Nuyolatinos. Even though I start the bulk of the overview presented here with the *mambo* craze of the 1940s, it is important to note that Latin music has been part of the musical milieu of the United States for a very long time. Indeed, Roberts (1979, vii) stated that

> Over the past century, Latin music has been the greatest outside influence on the popular music styles of the United States, and by a very wide margin indeed . . . not only does the standard repertory contain a significant representation of tunes of Latin American origin or inspiration, but the whole rhythmic basis of U.S. popular music has become to some extent Latinized.

Some of the earlier appearances of Latin music in the United States include the Cuban *habanera*, the Argentinian *tango*, and also the Cuban *rumba*, which was actually *son* yet had its name changed and was sometimes misspelled *rhumba*. All of these styles had specific dances associated with them, and they were all adopted in large cities in the United States. The *tango*, and the *rumba* specifically were much more popular than the *habanera*, and actually caused what is now referred to as the *tango* and *rumba* dance crazes. These crazes of the 1920s and 1930s helped establish the ever-enduring exoticized and eroticized images of Latinos/as that are still popular to this day in the United States (see Hall 1996, 2002; Roberts 1979).

The late 1940s and 1950s saw the development and subsequent explosion of the *mambo* and its respective dance craze in the United States. While the creation of the *mambo* has for a long time been a topic of discussion, it is not within the scope of this study to delve into the origins of the style.[11] However, it is crucial to understand the development and enormous subsequent influence of 1950s *mambo* on Salsa, a decade Rondón (2008) refers to as "Salsa zero." From the rhythmic aesthetics, to the dance, orchestrations, and the arrangements, the legacy of *mambo* is of extreme importance. Even today, *mambo* orchestras (generally fifteen or more musicians) retain a certain amount of popularity as exemplified by the 2013 Grammy award given to the Pacific Mambo Orchestra in the Best Tropical Album category. Indeed, *mambo* orchestras in several large cities in the United States are still playing today and touring around the world.

Historically, some of the most prominent participants who assisted in developing the *mambo* include the following: Dámaso Pérez Prado, Orestes Lopez, Arsenio Rodríguez, Rene Hernández, Israel "Cachao" Lopez, Bebo Valdés, Frank Grillo "Machito," Mario Bauzá, Tito Puente, and Tito Rodríguez (see Acosta 2004a, Cano 2009). All of these artists contributed to distilling *mambo* from its earliest forms to the incarnations of both the 1940s-1950s craze and the revival of today.

In New York specifically, Machito, Tito Puente, and Tito Rodriguez, often referred to as the big three of *mambo*, enjoyed the fame brought by the *mambo* dance nights at the now famous Palladium Ballroom of 53rd St. and Broadway. At the same time that the excesses of the dances of Cuban Pete and the appearance of celebrities filled the Palladium, El Barrio and the South Bronx were beginning to fill up with Latino immigrants looking to escape the hardships of daily life. Despite the large success of the *mambo* in New York, the music was not one that aimed to develop social consciousness on a large scale. Instead, *mambo* was meant to be danced to as a means of release.

Prior to the 1959 Cuban revolution, New York and Cuba had a mutual relationship of musical exchange. As a matter of fact, New York-based jazz musicians would often visit the island and Cuban musicians regularly traveled to New York. A well-known story involves percussionist Luciano "Chano" Pozo and his inclusion of the conga drums and Abakua chants in the work of Dizzy Gillespie in the 1940s (Moreno 2004, 94), which arguably ignited the Latin Jazz movement. The connection between them, and possibly the creator of Latin Jazz, was the Cuban trumpeter, clarinetist, and composer Mario Bauzá, who migrated to New York in 1930 (Moreno 2004, 84).

Besides connecting Gillespie and Pozo, in the early 1940s Bauzá, alongside his brother-in-law Frank "Machito" Grillo, put together a *mambo* orchestra that rose to fame and headed the *mambo* craze. Signaling their racial pride, Bauzá and Machito's orchestra was cleverly named "Machito and his Afro-Cubans." The key issue here was the inclusion of the term "Afro" as this indicated a clear nod to the yet unrecognized African heritage of the music. This was a very conscious move on the part of Bauzá, as Moreno (2004, 87) confirms:

> Bauzá again observed the lack of representation of Black Latin musicians in music he considered unthinkable without their contribution. "Every time I seen it," he observed in Musica, "the Latin bands was lily-white or something similar to that. Musicians of my color, they had no opportunity in those bands." The urgent desire for representation and the struggle for musico expressive recognition and self-regulated economic options began with an analysis that no longer viewed the existing asymmetries in the binary terms of U.S. racism: "I said, 'but these people . . . they ain't with Black and they ain't with the other one, where are they? Nowhere! So I said, 'I gotta organize a band.' That's how I organized the Machito band."

Despite the specific intent behind the formation of Machito and his Afro-Cubans, their repertoire did not do much to support the initial statement. While their formation did indeed include many Black men, the political positioning of the band, probably for economic and booking purposes, was not geared toward creating a wider social consciousness. It did, however, include coded references to Santería as well as other Afro-Cuban-based religious practices, with some titles including names such as "Canto Karabali," in reference to the Abakua in Cuba; "Chango ta bení," a Santería reference; "Ebo," including references to Santería; and the track called "Zambia." While the music did indeed at times include Afrocentric elements, they were, however, always filtered through a Cuban lens. Machito had already included references to Santería in earlier songs such as "Mi padrino me manda," recorded between 1939 and 1940 in New York with the son-based Cuarteto Caney. However, Cuarteto Caney did not have the type of impact that the Afro-Cubans did. The popularity of the latter allowed for the possibility of including a subset of racial codifications that allowed the African component to be partially represented while still filling the ballrooms. While these codifications are largely African, as they were derived directly from the surviving African cultural forms in Cuba, the most important identity trope in the case of the Afro-Cubans was that of being Cuban, not African or Black.

In the case of Tito Puente, his work within the *mambo* craze included rhythmic elements of African descent such as the utilization of *bembé* rhythms, the occasional reference to Santería practices by including a traditional chant, or references to African language in tunes such as "Ariñañara" and "Babarabatiri." Yet these were not the most relevant or popular cuts in his oeuvre. By a large margin, Puente's music was built around popular dance music and was not intended to develop the African element as a racial or social statement, but rather to emphasize a sense of exoticism that could be seen in the work of many other artists that fell prey to the discovery of Africanness in Latin America, especially in Cuba. An example of this exoticism is noted in the 1960 release of the LP *Tambó*, which includes song titles such as "Dance of the Headhunters," "Call of the Jungle Birds," "The Ceremony of Tambó," "Ritual Drum Dance," "Witch Doctor's Nightmare," and "Voodoo Dance at Midnight."[12]

However, there is an album by Puente entitled *Top Percussion*, recorded in 1957, that added Cuban drummers Julito Collazo, Mongo Santamaria, Francisco Aguabella, and United States-born Willie Bobo to Puente's ensemble, a record that features authentic Santería-based songs as well as traditional drumming in the style of *guiro*, *iyesá*, and *bembé* in the same manner that would be done ceremonially in Cuba. The Santería section is only on side A of the album and appears to be led by the Cuban components of the band, since there are no timbales (Puente's main instrument) on that side of the recording. Side B opens with a timbal solo by Puente and is then followed by composed percussion pieces of a secular nature accompanied by bass.

Tito Rodriguez developed the same type of strategy that Puente did. While the majority of his music is based on Cuban popular music without many social or racial hints, he did include a few songs in his repertoire that include verses "in tongue" as processed by the Cuban music aesthetics. Among these songs we find "Chen-cher en Guma," based on a *Palo* (Congo) song entitled "yenyere guma," as well as others such as "Boco boco" (originally made famous by Chano Pozo) and "Yambere."

As a sum total of the *mambo* craze and the role of both Puente and Rodriguez within it, Nuyorican poet, activist, and Salsa personality Felipe Luciano (2013) pointed out that

> We had instances of people, like Puente [who] did not really venture into political criticism, neither did Tito Rodríguez, they were interested in the dancing public, and the dancing public was not asking them to do that, there wasn't the need to do that, because being a factory worker, what you want to do is escape, and this music was about escape, it was rhythmic, it was powerful, it was jazz oriented, it was modern enough to be accepted by the new generations of Puerto Ricans being born here, and traditional enough to be accepted by the older ones who were born on the islands.

The idea of introducing "Africanisms" or brief references to African culture within the music was explored by these artists, but the depth of their utterances did not go far beyond some traits of identification within the mainly Cuban community of Santería practitioners in New York. The inclusion, however, of Santería, *bembé* rhythms, and allusions to other religious Afro-Cuban practices in the musical setting of the *mambo* constitutes an extremely codified appearance of an African sensibility that was only understood by a very limited minority. Julito Collazo estimated that "in 1955, there were approximately twenty-five people in New York City who were believers in the Orisha tradition" (in Moreno Vega 1995, 202).

The main musical and social ideas expressed within the works that fueled the *mambo* craze showed a set of practices grounded almost exclusively in a Cuban point of view as a beacon of the true essence of Latin music. Despite the fact that both Puente and Rodriguez were of Puerto Rican descent, at this point there was no clear push to develop a specifically Puerto Rican or broadly based Latino approach to the music. The almost exclusively adopted method characteristic of the era was derived from the already popular *mambo* and/or mainly Cuban popular-based styles. As such, and as suggested by Frith (1996), the codifications inherent in the *mambo* craze directed the Latino exploration of the music almost unilaterally toward expressing a Cuban identity. While there was a New York musical sense to the *mambo* of the 1950s, since the music contained a great deal of jazz influences, and the orchestras often shared the stage with the burgeoning bebop movement of Birdland on 52nd St. and Broadway, the Latin exploration of the music was arguably exclusively Cuban as the main source of musical "truth," despite the nationality of Puente and Rodriguez. While Puerto Ricans in the city did embrace the Cuban music to a great extent, up until this point the expressions of Latinidad were essentialized in a Cuban totemic practice in the same way that Puerto Rico did later with Salsa.

ARSENIO RODRIGUEZ

While the Africanized exclamations in the work of the big three were not really directed toward creating a socialized Black man, or a drive toward a Latino consciousness, the work of another artist, Arsenio Rodriguez, presents a clear move toward discussing issues of African identity that were not expressed as traits of exoticism or Cuban identity. Born in Matanzas, Cuba, in 1911, Arsenio Rodriguez was without question one of the greatest innovators of the twentieth century with regard to Cuban music. He literally revolutionized Cuban popular music and by extension "created" much of the modern Salsa sound. According to Moore (2013), Rodriguez moved to New York City in 1952 and continued to pursue his career in the United States until his death in 1970.[13] The musical innovations of Arsenio

Rodriguez include the introduction of the bass riff into popular music and the renovation of the *conjunto* ensemble as we know it today to include piano, congas, and two trumpets. All of these factors were extreme departures from the norm at the time and significantly influenced the music of the Puerto Rican and Cuban communities of East Harlem and the South Bronx, and continued to exert an impact on the Salsa boom of the 1970s in New York City (García 2006, 1-2).

Besides being ahead of his time musically, Rodriguez also developed early on a strong African sensibility in his music by including Afrocentric songs and rhythms in his repertoire. I consider his work to be the link that joins the folkloric aspects of Afro-Cuban music with the approach of popular music. This is clearly exemplified in songs such as the 1949 recording of "Me boté de guano," filled as it is with references to Afro-Cuban lore of the Abakua group of Cuba, or the 1937 release of "Bruca Maniguá," in which Rodriguez juxtaposes Ki-Congo language with Spanish in what is referred to as *bozal*, and utilizes a rhythm called *afro* that is possibly derived from a Yoruba-based batá rhythm.

The inclusion of Afrocentric aesthetics in his music, though incredibly relevant, is not the most important aspect for the purposes of this book. Rodriguez not only utilized Afrocentric aesthetics but he was also a proud Black man, and in his music, we find several instances in which he makes a stand on racial issues. Despite the importance of his lyrics, this is a topic that remains underanalyzed, though García clearly indicates that Arsenio's lyrics contained "coded critiques to slavery and its legacy of racism" (2006, 2).[14] As an example of these critiques, García shows that in Arsenio's composition "Aquí como allá," recorded on November 9, 1950, "Arsenio clearly understood and commented on the pervasiveness of racism, making no distinction in the plight of Black people based on cultural, national or historical boundaries" (2006, 8-9). "Aquí como allá" ("It's the same here as it is there") is a song that not only denounces racism, but shows Rodriguez as someone well aware of the tribulations of all Black people by interrelating the struggles of post-slavery societies around the world that remained largely segregated by naming Africa, Brazil, Haiti, New York, Argentina, Mexico, and Venezuela (see the translation of "Aquí como allá" as performed by Arsenio Rodríguez). The song is thus incredibly significant, not only because of its remarkable content but because it was recorded years before the explosion in the 1960s of the significance of the civil rights movement, Black Power, and Pan-African consciousness.

"AQUÍ COMO ALLÁ" AS PERFORMED BY ARSENIO RODRÍGUEZ

En África, en el Brasil	In Africa, as in Brazil
Igual en Cuba como en Haití	The same in Cuba as in Haiti
Igual al sur que en Nueva York	The same in the south as in New York
El Negro canta su dolor	The Black man sings his pain
Ay dios, ay dios	Oh god, oh god
En La Argentina pue' pasar	In Argentina it may happen
En México poquito más	In Mexico a little more
En Venezuela se burlan	in Venezuela they mock
Ay que condena, que pesar	Oh, what a sentence, what sorrow
Ay dios, ay dios	Oh god, oh god
El Negro canta su canción,	The Black man sings his song
lleno de angustia y de dolor	filled with anguish and pain
Mirando que todo está igual	Looking at everything being the same
Que para mí ya está peor	That for me is already worse
Coro: Cantan los Negros su dolor	**Chorus:** Black people sing their pain
…	…
Aquí como allá ya están llorando	The same here as there they are crying
Allá como aquí están mirando	The same there as here they are looking[15]

While in 1950 Rodriguez was already tying his African identity to that of all Black people in the world, by 1960 he had recorded in New York "Yo nací del Africa" (I was born of Africa) for his LP *Cumbanchando con Arsenio*. The lyrics express a deep sentiment of African identity within Rodriguez. As García (2006, 12) points out, Rodriguez "signifies on the trope of Africa in the title 'Yo nací del Africa' (I Was Born of Africa), in which he affirms his African identity as having been 'born' from the legacy of colonialism, slavery, and the ideology of white racial supremacy." The song's first part questions his national and ethnic identity by suggesting African places and ethnicities that might represent his place of origin. The second part of the verse rejects the Spanish side of his ethnicity by negating a series of surnames, including his own, stating, "I am not Rodriguez." The third part of the verse aims to reclaim his African ethnicity using Congolese surnames, as García (2006, 12) indicates:

> Arsenio does more than merely claim Africa and the Congo as his homeland. In fact, he reclaims the tropes of Africa and the Congo, which historically stood for cultural and racial inferiority and backwardness, and redeploys them as viable and enviable entities of identity. He expresses this sentiment by signifying on the Republic of the Congo's independence in 1960 from Belgian colonial rule when he lists Kasavubu and Lumumba—Joseph Kasavubu was the first president (1960-65) of the Republic of the Congo, and Patrice Lumumba was its first prime minister (1960-61)—as his possible "real" names.

In closing the song, Rodriguez finally dedicates his declamation to Africa and the Congo with the chorus repeating the word Africa, as the response poetically confirms Rodriguez's idealized homeland. Idealized as Africa may be in the lyrics, this song is incredibly relevant in the narrative of Salsa consciente not only because of the racial content and Rodriguez's Black pride, but because of Rodriguez's undisputed influence on Salsa. Given his standing, it is almost indisputable that the musicians of the soon-to-be realized Salsa movement were listening to Rodriguez's affirmations.

"YO NACÍ DEL ÁFRICA" AS PERFORMED BY ARSENIO RODRÍGUEZ

Yo nací del África	I was born of Africa
¡Sí!	Yes!
Coro: Tal vez	**Chorus:** Maybe
Tal vez sea del Congo	Maybe I am from the Congo
Tal vez sea de Ampanga	Maybe I am from Ampanga
Tal vez del Rio Congo	Maybe from the Congo River
Tal vez sea Musungo	Maybe I am Musungo
Tal vez sea Congo Real	Maybe I am Royal Congo

Tal vez sea de Ampala	Maybe I am from Ampala
Tal vez sea Abakua	Maybe I am Abakua
Coro: ¡No!	**Chorus:** No!
Yo no soy Rodríguez	I am not Rodríguez
Yo no soy Travieso	I am not Travieso
Yo no soy Herrera	I am not Herrera
Yo no soy Fernández	I am not Fernandez
Yo no soy Barroso	I am not Barroso
Yo no soy Peraza	I am not Peraza
Yo no soy García	I am not Garcia
Yo no soy Morales	I am not Morales
Coro: Tal vez	**Chorus:** Maybe
Tal vez sea Lomoto	Maybe I am Lomoto
Tal vez sea Lumumba	Maybe I am Lumumba
Tal vez Kasavubu	Maybe I am Kasavubu
Yo nací del África	I was born of Africa
¡Sí!	Yes!
Coro: África	**Chorus:** Africa
Eres mi tierra	You are my homeland
Mi tierra linda	My beautiful homeland
Yo soy del Congo	I am from the Congo
Yo soy del Congo	I am from the Congo
Tú eres mi tierra	You are my homeland
Mi tierra linda	My beautiful homeland[16]

In addition to the aforementioned pieces of music, many more examples could be used to illustrate the politicized rhetoric of Rodriguez's work. But while this is not the place to delve exclusively into Rodriguez's oeuvre, García (2006, 23) points out a very relevant fact for this exploration:

> While living in New York City in the early 1960s, Arsenio composed two songs in which he reflected on the continued injustices that Blacks were suffering. In "La democracia" (Democracy) he asks, "Si ya las cosas han cambiado / y hay derechos de igualdad / ¿por qué yo soy discriminado? /

si todo el mundo somos iguales / ¿la democracia dónde está? / nos falta mucho pa' llegar" (If things have changed / and there's equal rights / then why am I discriminated against? / for everyone is equal / where's the democracy? / we have a long way to go).

While García ties the song to Blackness issues, in his transcription of the lyrics there is no explicit reference to being Black. There is the word "democracy," though, in the title of the song, which can be read, as García does, as denoting racial problems, but it can also be understood as a denunciation of injustice in general and not only regarding being Black. There is also a mention of discrimination in the song, yet there is no resolution to indicate the basis of such discrimination. Since this song was composed in the 1960s in New York City, the injustice and discrimination mentioned could easily be read not only as a discrimination of class as well as ethnicity against Black people, but as a statement denouncing the living conditions of Latinos in El Barrio and the South Bronx at the time. This reading potentially places Rodriguez as "the father" of the socially conscious Latino dance music produced in New York. The song, however, was never recorded, and it is only available via museum archives. Thus, while it could be seen to have great significance within the Salsa consciente movement, its impact is limited by the fact that most people have not been able to listen to this song.

RAFAEL CORTIJO

While Cuban-born Arsenio Rodriguez was claiming his Blackness through music, the Afro-Puerto Rican side of the music was also developing. In this category it is important to mention probably the most racially conscious Puerto Rican musician prior to the appearance of Catalino Curet Alonso, the father of modern Puerto Rican music, Rafael Cortijo. Although I do not intend to discuss Cortijo's work in detail here, his influence on Salsa, much like Arsenio Rodriguez's, is enormous.[17] His creative use of Puerto Rican musical forms within a modern sensibility was the sound that arguably defined the Puerto Rican components of New York Salsa still to come. Early in his career, Cortijo began utilizing the traditionally Afro-Puerto Rican rhythms of *bomba*, particularly that of the *bomba sicá*, as a basic cell from which to construct modern popular Puerto Rican music. Within his use of the *bomba*, as an African-derived form, Cortijo produced a particular racial signifier that allowed many people to appreciate Afro-Puerto Rican folklore as a valid form of music. Luciano (2013) pointed out that Cortijo

> was revolutionary in two ways: He was an incredible player and focused his attention and highlighted bomba and plena but he was also Black. [In the 1960s] Cortijo was beginning to rise up, and people were beginning to see the forms of bomba and plena as being valid. Prior to that it was always mambo, or trio, or aguinaldo or country music, but suddenly bomba and plena become parallel in our people's consciousness.

Within Cortijo's early oeuvre, there is a particularly poignant song where, engulfed in a semi-comical delivery by Ismael Rivera, the song references racism and negritude in a form unlike the *mambos* of Puente, Rodriguez, and Machito. The main difference here lies in the fact that the language of choice is Spanish, and the primary focus rests upon the idea of being Black. Composed by Bobby Capó, the song is entitled "El Negro Bembón" (The Black man with big lips). Released in 1960, the song was possibly inspired by Cuban poet Nicolas Guillén's verses of the same name included in his book *Motivos de son*, originally written in 1930, and also possibly linked to the 1940s song "Bemba Colorá" composed by José Claro Fumero and made famous by Celia Cruz during the Salsa boom.

"EL NEGRO BEMBÓN" AS PERFORMED BY ISMAEL RIVERA AND RAFAEL CORTIJO

The verse of the song discusses what would now be considered a hate crime, where a Black man with big lips is killed for no other reason than the way he looks. The lyrics indicate:

Coro:	Chorus:
Mataron al Negro bembón,	The big-lipped Black man was killed,
Mataron al Negro bembón	The big-lipped Black man was killed
Hoy se llora noche y día	Today we cry night and day

Porque al Negrito bembón	Because the little Black man with big lips
Todo el mundo lo quería	Was loved by everyone
Porque al Negrito bembón	Because the little Black man with big lips
Todo el mundo lo quería.	Was loved by everyone.[18]

The first chorus of the song is actually the response of the Black police officer to the killer after learning the reason for the murder: "That is not a reason" (to kill someone).

Y llegó la policía	And the police arrived
Y arrestaron al matón	And arrested the killer
…	…
Y saben la pregunta que le hizo al matón	And do you know the question he asked the killer?
¿Por qué lo mató? Diga usted la razón	Why did you kill him? Tell me the reason
Y saben la respuesta que le dio el matón?	And do you know the answer the killer gave?
"Yo lo maté por ser tan bembón"	"I killed him because his lips were so big"
El guardia escondió la bemba, y le dijo:	The guard hid his lips and told him:
Coro: Eso no es razón.	**Chorus:** That is not a reason
Pregones:	**Ad-libs:**
Ay dios para matar al bembón.	Oh god to kill the one with big lips.
…	…
Bembón, para matar al bembón	Big-lipped, to kill the one with big lips

While the first set of lyrics establishes the reason, the second chorus gives no solution to the issue and only tells the listener to hide their lips so as not to look so Black. Another possible reading of this song pointed out by Luciano (2013) is that of the song as a satire of internal racism with the killer personifying one's own prejudices and the internal racism that tries to "kill" the Blackness by simply denying it and, in this case, hiding the big lips.

Segundo Coro:	Second Chorus:
Esconde la bemba que ahí viene el matón.	Hide the lips, the killer is coming.
. . .	. . .
Esconde la bemba	Hide the lips
Esconde, que esconde la bemba	Hide, hide the lips
Mira, mira que viene el matón	Look, look, the killer is coming

This is only an example of Cortijo's work, but he continued to forge a path for the advancement of Black people in Puerto Rico, where his band of mainly Black men became very popular. Cortijo's Combo appeared in many movies and was the house band for the TV show *La Taberna India*. While my research focus is based in New York City, given the fluid nature of Puerto Rican immigration into New York, it is relevant to address the appearance of racial issues from the perspective of an artist who influenced Salsa to a very large extent, despite the fact that he did not produce the bulk of his work in that city.

By 1965, the significance of the Black Power movement was beginning to make its presence felt in Latin music. Released that year, for example, was Palmieri's "El Tema del Apollo" (The Theme of the Apollo), a title referencing the famous African American Harlem Theater, which included the following utterance by singer Ismael Quintana: "El tema del Apollo, pa' que gocen los niches!" (The theme of the Apollo for the Black people to enjoy). This marker is a clear example of the Latino/African American market crossover, and the New York-based understanding of the race/class relationships that eventually played a role in developing the amalgamating discourse that had such a strong impact on Salsa consciente:

> Slowly the chants and the political philosophy of Blacks begin to seep into Puerto Rican culture. Palmieri wrote in 1965 El tema del Apollo (Pa' que gocen los niches) in other words, we are celebrating them and saying come on let's party with us. This is rare . . . So Eddie Palmieri is developing for the first time whether he knew it or not a not only Puerto Rican market but a Black market, as is Ray Barretto, and Willie Colón who is developing

a gangster image and more and more Blacks are being attracted to it.
(Luciano 2013)

Up to this point, and including Palmieri, popular Latin music in New York was almost exclusively built out of Cuban components. The musical elements and trends set by the *rumba* craze and reexplored and modernized in *mambo*, alongside the work of Arsenio Rodriguez, were still the main framework upon which audiences danced and musicians made a living. However, the arrival in the early 1960s of boogaloo—or as spelled by the Latino communities of New York, *bugalú*—marks the first expression of popular music by the Latino community of New York that does not attempt to replicate traditional Cuban styles.

LATINO SOUL AND *BUGALÚ*

The boogaloo is a hybrid comprised of Latin music and rhythm and blues. According to Kempton (2005), the term boogaloo reflects an insider designation used to refer to music in the African American communities and what is nowadays often known as soul or R&B music. The music I am referring to, however, has often been dubbed Latin boogaloo. As such, I suggest that in its hybridized and ethnically determined form, boogaloo of the Latino variety (or my preferred term *El bugalú*) is a mutt in the best possible sense of the word. This style is in essence New York, as it is definitely not pure, nor does it attempt to be, and it certainly has attitude.

Socially, *bugalú* played an important role in integrating communities as it spoke to Latinos and Afro-Americans alike. As such it provided an identity for the young Latino and African American societies and bridged certain gaps by reflecting on the realities of daily living rather than ethnicity in the street, and the struggles of marginalized life—in other words, the everyday realities of El Pueblo, The People.

The Latino musical point of reference of the *bugalú* was still the circum-Caribbean filtered through New York, especially the *son montuno* and the *cha cha cha*. But the biggest appeal of the music to the youth of the day lay in the combination of Latin music and R&B. This aspect was hip and distinct enough from *mambo* to appeal to the new generation. This music was born out of the combined experiences of the neighboring African American and Latino communities in New York, and the overlap of the musical market, concerning which Flores (2004) specifies that Latinos and African Americans used to share stages. In addition, there was the influence of Black Power as a unifying social force in marginalized communities.

This new Latino generation, the sons and daughters of those who experienced the Great Migration, were either bilingual, did not speak Spanish, or fluently used Spanglish as a preferred means of communication. These are thus native New Yorkers of Latino descent, true Nuyolatinos, and as such signify equally the music of New York—or perhaps more specifically that of Harlem and the Bronx—and Latin Music. *Bugalú* expresses this sentiment in the best possible way, while embracing at the same time the music of Aretha Franklin, Isaac Hayes's *Shaft*, Marvin Gaye, Tito Puente, Arsenio Rodriguez, and Cortijo. As a clear reflection of this hybridity, much of *bugalú*'s lyrics were actually in English, and thus allowed for a strong market crossover. Aparicio (2004, 355) refers to the idea of biculturalism within Latino communities.

> Given the history of migration, displacement, and marginalization that many Latinos have faced in the United States, forms of expressive culture such as popular music, visual arts, performance arts, film, and literature have served as important sites for exploring bicultural identity, debates on representation, and the cultural agency and role in U.S. history of people of Latin America.

Perhaps the most successful story of this market crossover is that of Afro-Filipino Joe Bataan, bandleader, composer, and former gang leader raised in El Barrio. Bataan created a sensibility within his music that was appealing to both Latinos and African Americans. His albums included, as many *bugalú* artists did, lyrics both in English and Spanish, and eventually he dubbed his style "Latin soul," and even coined the term "salsoul," a mixture of Salsa and soul. Style notwithstanding, Bataan was ultimately able to capture the New York street feel of the times, and even though his lyrics were not specifically designed to raise social consciousness, in keeping with the discourse of the time, Bataan proposed an agenda pointing to the idea of power to The People, glorifying the ghetto, and the general rebelliousness of the Spanish Harlem community.

Although Bataan was a major contributor to *bugalú*, his lyrics failed to deliver a fully developed socially involved contemporary message; yet his tracks included titles such as "Young, Gifted and Brown" and "Riot!" Despite this, Bataan was able to develop archetypical street characters with tracks such as "Ordinary Guy," and the Spanish version, "Muchacho Ordinario," and "Subway Joe," a trope that was eventually repeated in Salsa consciente. Perhaps the most poignant image of late 1960s Bataan was the cover art and title of his 1968 release entitled *Riot!* where a street fight with knives, bottles, and guns is depicted while Bataan calmly sits in the middle of the scene.[19]

Another important artist who developed his work within the confines of *bugalú* was Joe Cuba and his sextet. This group featured future Salsa star Cheo Feliciano at the very beginning of his career. By 1966 the band released the album *Wanted Dead or Alive (Bang! Bang! Push, Push, Push)*, containing their biggest hit entitled "Bang Bang," which crossed over and "made it to the U.S. national hit parade" (Rondón 2008, 26). In the same year, the band released another album entitled *Estamos Haciendo Algo Bien! (We Must Be Doing Something Right!)*. This release contained the expected *bugalú* sound, via the song "El Pito (I'll never go back to Georgia)," which included the already well-known Dizzy Gillespie utterance "I'll never go back to Georgia," as well as the anticipated lyrics in English and Spanish. There is, however, a socially significant track on the record called "Y tu abuela dónde está?" (And your grandmother, where is she?).

This track, which is based on a poem of the same name by Puerto Rican poet Fortunato Vizcarrondo, speaks of the self-racism and denial of African heritage prevalent among Latinos. While the lyrics are different from the original poem, and have been re-placed in New York, the message still remains the same: *No matter how you try to hide it, you have African in you*. This statement is placed in context both in the original poem and in the 1966 song by asking where your grandmother is, so as to denote that by looking at the past, and whether you like it or not, you will not be able to deny your heritage. In the contemporary version there is a spoken section that references the idea of "society," denoting high society. The full sentence is: "Don't you go thinking that you have snuck in as white in [high] society." Not only is this a comment on the self-whitening of Latinos, but it identifies high society as a place where dominance is exercised by white people.

"¿Y TU ABUELA DÓNDE ESTÁ?" AS PERFORMED BY THE JOE CUBA SEXTET

Mi pana, sacó un poquito de color

My friend had just a little color (was light skinned)

El viejo aparenta ser medio rubio

The old man feigns being kind of blonde

Cuando andas por las calles de New York

When you walk the streets of New York

La pandilla te grita:

The gang yells:

"¿Y que cocolo"?

"What's up cocolo"?[20]

Y por eso yo pregunto

That is why I ask you

"¿Y tu abuela dónde está"?

And your grandmother, where is she?

...

...

Coro: ¿Y tu abuela dónde está?

Chorus: And your grandmother, where is she?

...

...

Hablado:

Spoken:

...

...

Oyeme, oye lo que te voy a decir, atiende esto:

Listen to me, listen to what I'm going to tell you, pay attention:

"Aunque la gente te aplaude

"Even if people clap for you

Y se agita de verdad

And shakes for you

Y te aceptan porque tienes mucha Salsa en realidad.

And accept you because you really have real Salsa.

No por eso te equivoques

Don't be mistaken because of that

Ni te vayas a engañar

Don't go fooling yourself

No pienses que te has colao

Don't you go thinking that you have snuck

De blanco en la sociedad"

As a white into society"

...

...

Coro: ¿Y tu abuela dónde está?

Chorus: And your grandmother, where is she?[21]

While the establishment of Latin music (i.e., *mambo* musicians) did not like *bugalú* because they felt it was stealing their work, *bugalú* had a great impact on the new generation. The music was drastically different, and did not require the type of musical training needed to perform in a *mambo* orchestra. This was music from the street, built from the ground up. The Latin music establishment, however, felt that they were losing out both in terms of the purity—that is, the "truth" represented by Cuban music—in the ability to charge more for performances, and in market sales. In addition to that, the advancement of Black Power was still controversial and therefore they questioned whether Latin musicians should associate themselves with the Afro-American market. Luciano states that by 1967, when

> Joe Cuba is at the pinnacle of his career . . . Puerto Ricans were [still] reluctant to identify with Black power because their handlers, many of them Jewish and Italian did not want to enter into the controversy of Black power because they didn't believe in it . . . they thought it would hurt market sales." (Luciano 2013)

Shortly thereafter, the established models of distribution and the performance/recording market monopoly established by Fania Records, along with the pressure applied by Latin music purists in the early 1970s, displaced *bugalú* from the public eye and into oblivion.

FROM ETHNICITY TO CLASS

As indicated by the musico-historical analysis of this chapter, the seeds of what came to be known as Salsa and Salsa consciente were sown (to paraphrase Blades) in movements spread sporadically through time by Latinos. The grounds upon which the songs' themes were based were, however, varied. Yet the seeds of what later became a steady movement were already beginning to germinate. I have suggested how these developments were connected beyond the exclusive focus of nationality, and as intrinsically linked to The People. Up to this point, many of the themes discussed were still part of songs that were primarily aimed at entertaining audiences and serving as an escape from the daily hardships of the urban ghetto rather than developing a clear discourse relating to any kind of social movement. I have also shown how the music was beginning to function as a transnational and transcultural mediator of social phenomena and operated as a subset of popular culture that was not produced for mere entertainment, but crafted from below as the result of a social context and of historically specific material and social conditions. Luciano (2013) indicates, however, that the appearance of socially conscious themes in Latin dance music at this point

> were all exceptions to the rule because at that time our people were coming here [New York] in droves and what they wanted was entertainment, not education at that point, they wanted entertainment, they needed to move away from the travails of daily existence.

Of the themes explored in this chapter, the most relevant is that of race/ethnicity, via negritude, as this topic played a significant role in the advancement of the consciousness of marginalized communities following the 1964 Civil Rights Act and the Black Power movement. A particular temporal exception to this is certainly the music of Arsenio Rodriguez in which his articulation of Black pride was one that appeared quite early in the timeline of what became Salsa.

Regarding the conceptualization and discussion of race as socially constructed in Salsa, it is necessary to remark that the music had thus far failed to recognize racial concerns beyond a Black and White division, thus categorizing and limiting the discussion only to a binary mode of expression that did not yet present a complete view of Latinidad. The idea of a racial identity in Salsa that included the Native population of the Americas was one that took longer to arrive despite its obvious importance in understanding the identities of Latin Americans. Accounting for the fact that the Spanish-speaking Caribbean is the main informant of the aesthetic impulses of Salsa, this omission is related to the near extermination of the Native population in the Caribbean at the hands of the Spanish conquistadors. As we shall see in the chapter dedicated to him, it is only with the appearance and crucial participation of composer Catalino "Tite"

Curet Alonso in the Salsa movement that Indigenous themes begin to be explored. While at this point the efforts at promoting a Latino consciousness were almost exclusively dedicated to exploring African concerns, the second half of the 1960s saw the germination of what soon after became known as Salsa, and which saw the expansion of a larger and more refined Latino ethnic consciousness that included not only race or ethnicity but also class in its discourse.

CHAPTER TWO

Salsa as the Engine of Latino Consciousness

3. *We want liberation of all third world people.* Just as Latins first slaved under [S]pain and the yanquis, Black people, Indians, and Asians slaved to build the wealth of this country. For 400 years they have fought for freedom and dignity against racist Babylon (decadent empire). Third World people have led the fight for freedom. All the colored and oppressed peoples of the world are one nation under oppression. No Puerto Rican Is Free Until All People Are Free!

—From the Young Lords Party 13-Point Program and Platform, 1969

In the previous chapter, I presented a definition of *Salsa* and analyzed the social implications of the pre-Salsa musical movements. As I have shown, the social concerns of pre-Salsa music were geared mostly toward race/ethnicity issues. I understand this stage as the first level in the development of a Latino consciousness. In acknowledging the position of Latinos in the 1950s and early 1960s, one naturally leans toward accepting African heritage as one of the main contributors to the concept of Latino ethnicity, thanks mainly to the civil rights movement and Pan-Africanism. By the mid-1960s, however, there was a large advance in the understanding of being Latino and the development of Latino ethnic consciousness due to the incorporation of class issues. I thus conceive of this development in Latino consciousness as a second level, which, having already adopted racial/ethnic concerns as one of its main components, was becoming increasingly clear at the turn of the 1960s. This was especially true due to the roles played by the declaration of the Cuban revolution as a socialist endeavor, the general revolutionary feeling of the 1960s, the civil rights movement, and the social conditions of Latinos in New York City in expanding the Nuy-olatino community's social consciousness. Throughout this chapter, and as a mirror to chapter 1, I analyze the development of class consciousness and the music as intertwined with the previous concepts of race/ethnicity. I thus utilize this section to further understand Latino ethnic consciousness and aim to explain the development of the social context as inseparable from the development of the music.

In particular in this chapter I argue that, to develop a proper reading of the levels and frameworks of Latino consciousness/conscience in Salsa, one must consider the context, the distinct yet connected levels of textuality expressed in the lyrics, and any sonic markers. I also maintain that the construction of Latino consciousness within Salsa consciente needs to be understood within the framework of Latinidad as a marker of class consciousness.

Latinidad and Being Latino

[handwritten: REDEFINE LATINIDAD WITHOUT SCHOLARSHIP]

As a central argument, I contend that the conscience/consciousness denoted in Salsa consciente reflects a shared Latino social existence, in which Salsa music is experienced with a heightened social awareness. I refer to this phenomenon as Latinidad, which should be sociologically understood as a collective response by Spanish/Spanglish-speaking migrant groups to shared conditions, such as poverty and racial discrimination. I theorize that Latinidad is a concept that needs to be comprehended as socially constructed with a prevalent role given to issues of class and race/ethnicity, which are common to all Latinos/Latin Americans, regardless of nationality.

The concept of Latinidad in general, however, presents a potential conflict when considering the hegemonizing and homogenizing issue of classifying Latinos as only one group, regardless of nationality. Alonso Gallo (2002) indicates this in the following observations:

> *Latinidad* is an unstable concept, much like that of postmodern identity. We need to assume from the outset that an essentializing definition of

[handwritten: OUTDATED]

what being Latino is denies the wealth of traditions, history, familial relationships, art, races, ethnicities, social structures, generational differences, etc., all of which characterize the wide varieties of Latin Americans who are nowadays part of U.S. society. Critics and intellectuals use the term *Latinidad* acknowledging the heterogeneous nature of the Hispanic group in the U.S. as well as the different degrees found in their process of transculturation. (242, note 11)

The construction of a concept such as Latinidad is quite complex, as it opens the door to a displacement of the "original" national identity to a deterritorialized and heterogenic "new" Latino ethnicity based on shared social realities as a result of migration. This socially constructed phenomenon is very important in the structure of Salsa consciente, as much of its textual and musical discourse takes advantage of the hybrid points that culturally define diasporic populations as unique and distinct from their current and original (though perhaps imagined) homelands. This diasporic discourse is achieved by overlooking nationalist identities, which Tammelleo (2011) refers to as National Hispanic identities, and I refer to as Latin American, for a larger non-nationalist yet socially conscious discourse of Latinidad. Understanding Latino ethnic consciousness as a product of a nationally disjointed, yet linguistically and socially related urban group points not to national alliances, but to a sociological reading of composite ethnic and social identities shaped and informed by the diasporic concept of the Latino meta-homeland as a "place" that holds the commonalities of Latinos, transcending nationality.

Expanding on Padilla's thoughts, I posit that there is an unexplored link between being Latino and the idea of national Hispanic identities as expressed in Salsa's alliance with and success in Latin America. Padilla's primary understanding of Latinidad is based on linguistic alliances, migration, and situational social relations in the United States (1989); this concept can be understood as a primary stage of Latino ethnic consciousness. The secondary, unexplored stage of Latinidad, however, develops in the form of a transnational Latin American alliance. I argue that Salsa, due to its large popularity in Latin America, is the main engine of this secondary stage of consciousness. The music acts as a mediator of Latinidad and spreads Latino consciousness back to Latin America via oral culture. This link of consciousness is connected not to migration, as the primary stage was, but to the awareness of social issues, class struggles, and racial issues as a defining fact in the intersecting of Latino/Latin American music and consciousness. This idea ties Latinos and Latin Americans not by country or reimagined homelands, but as people linked by social resistance, marginalization, and racial concerns in different countries under different governments. Therefore, it is no coincidence that Salsa consciente as a transnational Latino/Latin American musical movement develops a large part of its discourse in relation to these particular topics. Whereas musicians such as Pete "El Conde" Rodriguez sing about Black pride, or Cheo Feliciano sings about the hardships of a construction worker, there is a significant connection built upon language, a common historical past, ethnic makeup, and a shared situation of oppression, marginalization, poverty, and social consciousness—that is, not national differences or alliances, but rather the shared social adversities of Latinos and Latin Americans, whether in New York, Caracas, or Medellín.

With regard to the transmission of Salsa culture in Latin America, I posit that this phenomenon is linked to the arrival of the 1960s' society of mass consumption in the United States and the development of the record industry beyond radio and into the mass production of vinyl records as a highly marketable commodity. Through these phenomena, Salsa became quickly distributed transnationally to other Spanish-speaking markets. Thus, the development of recording technology became central to the transformation of this primarily oral culture into a Latin American transnational sensation. In this sense, the appearance of the Latino recording industry, and its mass distribution systems, can be compared to the idea of print capitalism (Anderson 2006), with the distribution systems of the imagined communities based on vinyl recordings, rather than print, produced in the capitalistic center of Salsa: New York.

Although the distribution and performance of Salsa outside of New York was initially directed to the Spanish-speaking countries of the circum-Caribbean—mainly Puerto Rico, Venezuela, Panama, and Colombia as the major consumers of Salsa outside the United States—the reception of the music in every Latin American country was not equal. The popularity of the music in the Spanish-speaking Caribbean, however, propelled the expansion of a massive distribution system that reached virtually every Spanish-speaking country in the region. Despite the national divisions, the distribution of Salsa consciente in Latin America allowed for the ideals of Latinidad to be quickly disseminated. These ideals, as presented in the music, were developed specifically upon non-nationalistic ideologies. This nonspecificity allowed for the union of the struggles to be understood as an analogical hegemon (Dussel 2008), encompassing the daily hardships of living in Latin America under a set of ideals that spoke of, and to, the shared situational identities of every country.

As I have suggested, within the sociological conception of Latinidad as a shared struggle, Salsa consciente advances a discourse with an identity marker that develops into tropes based on the idea of the united struggles of the Latino meta-homeland. This identity marker formed by the collective union of the everyday struggles of Latinos and Latin Americans as related to the general disenfranchisement of the population is one that I follow Santos Febres (1997) in calling the Pueblo identity marker.

Understanding the Concept of El Pueblo

El Pueblo is a concept that often gets translated into English as "the people." The concept of El Pueblo in Spanish, however, requires a more detailed explanation, especially to tease out a proper understanding of the significance of the concept in song. For this book, I translate the concept as "The People." I utilize the capitalization to give added emphasis to the translation and as an indicator and reminder of the revolutionary ideals embodied by the Salsa consciente movement.

The use of El Pueblo as a neo-Marxist political term in Latin America incorporates differential claims under one guise (Laclau 2005), even though they might be opposed in principle. These claims are ultimately organized in a universal manner:

Through mutual information, dialogue, translation of proposals, and shared militant praxis, these movements slowly and progressively constitute an analogical hegemon, which to some degree includes all demands . . . the need arises for a category that can encompass the unity of all the movements, classes, sectors, etc., in political struggle. And so the people is that strictly political category (since it is not properly sociological or economic) that appears as absolutely essential, despite its ambiguity (and indeed this ambiguity does not result from misunderstanding but rather from inevitable complexity) . . . In this reformulation, the people is transformed into a collective political actor rather than being merely a substantial and fetishized "historical subject." The people appears in critical political conjunctures when it achieves explicit consciousness as the analogical hegemon of all demands, from which it defines strategy and tactics, thereby becoming an actor and constructing history on the basis of a new foundation. As many social movements note: "Power is constructed from below!" (Dussel 2008, 72-75)

Santos Febres (1997) suggests that Puerto Ricanness is not Salsa's key signifier, but rather the performance of Pueblo, or peopleness. I posit that it is in this performance of The People/for The People where Salsa, and by extension Salsa consciente, becomes a distinct genre from the Cuban *son* and the Nuyorican perspectives exclusively. This hybrid construction of diasporic Latino identities, represented by Salsa consciente as a transnational/translatino medium, creates a cohesive non-nationalistic social dialogue, united by the common struggles of The People.

I thus argue that the fact that Salsa developed initially not as a commodity, although it quickly became one, but as a cultural manifestation from and for The People was the primary catalyst of Salsa's success in New York and also of Salsa consciente's transnational success in Latin America as the engine of social consciousness. In analyzing the case of New York's Salsa, it can be seen that the marginalized development of Salsa—and its musicians as "street heroes," culture bearers, and performers of a Latino reality—accounted for Salsa's quick acceptance by The People. The case of Latin America is, in essence, an extension of Nuyolatino realities, which evince marginalization and poverty. The association of the music with the working class in New York, and its presentation as such, with no pretense, resonated very strongly in Latin America, where the "ghetto" realities depicted in New York's Barrio-based Salsa were being replicated in the Latin American urban centers. Not only was the idea of the working class essential to understanding the connection of Salsa consciente with Latin America, but the analogical hegemon, as described by Dussel (2008), of El Pueblo in Salsa consciente united the general, everyday struggles of the Latin American Pueblo under the same guise.

Salsa consciente ultimately presents a discourse that has at its core the concept of social justice. The music does not pledge to exclusively be Latino or Latin American; Salsa consciente's first allegiance is to The People, El Pueblo. Because Salsa develops from the everyday contexts of The People, Salsa consciente, as a subgenre of Salsa, ultimately advances a discourse that differentiates it specifically from what could be constructed as ethnic-centered Salsa, political Salsa, or racial Salsa, although all of these concepts are ultimately integrated as part of the everyday struggles of The People. Salsa, the musical expression of Nuyolatinos, one of the most historically disenfranchised groups of people in New York, by its own nature expresses social consciousness, identifying specifically with the Spanish-speaking working class, a marginalized and racially discriminated-against subset of the city, who came to be known as El Pueblo, The People, that is, Latinos in the city.

Nuyolatino Social Studies

Following the 1959 Cuban revolution, its declaration as a socialist revolution, and the subsequent formation of guerillas in Latin America who aimed to imitate the Cuban example, Latinos in New York began to question their place within U.S. society. By the 1960s, El Barrio and the South Bronx were in the midst of an urban crisis and had turned into a ghetto with a set of living conditions that were essentially inhumane. At the same time, Latinos were being treated as second-class citizens and were violently repressed by the police. Soon thereafter, the 1970s saw the South Bronx become the site of an arson epidemic, where "between 1970-1979 more than 30,000 fires were set deliberately in the South Bronx" (Hemenway, Wolf, and Lang 1986, 17). Tied to the living conditions, the underground economic sphere ballooned as Latinos of nationalities other than Puerto Rican were not able to work legally; thus, they were often taken advantage of and paid even lower wages. Although the welfare system was not one designed to aid these communities as a whole, it was particularly ineffective for Latinos of nationalities other than Puerto Rican due to their immigration status.

This large urban community constituted a labor force that continued to be seen as socially inferior. The impact of a socialist revolution in neighboring Cuba and the subsequent global shifts in consciousness catapulted a Latino ethnic consciousness into view, spearheaded by a shared sense of oppression, poverty, and linguistic commonalities. The discrimination faced by Latinos eventually exploded into riots in East Harlem in 1967, following the shooting of a civilian by the police. After three days of violence, the riots also spread to Puerto Rican neighborhoods in the South Bronx. In total, four Puerto Ricans were killed, all with the same type of bullets (.38 caliber) used in police guns (Fernandez 2004).

The social resentment of the Nuyolatino community provided a figurative and literal battleground where class consciousness led to the emergence of neo-Marxist social movements. Groups such as the Young Lords Party (YLP) demanded decent living conditions and raised a militant voice for the empowerment of Puerto Ricans and other Latinos/as in the United States. Regarding these social movements, Santiago-Valles and Jiménez-Muñóz stated:

> This was the type of effort that resulted in the uneven emergence of social welfare and job programs (including vocational training), as well as civil-rights reforms, for Puerto Rican barrios in the United States. In New York City, similar developments during the late 1960s and early 1970s materialized as militant and antiracist trade unionism, especially in public sectors such as hospitals and sanitation, and a leftist nationalist revival (Puerto Rican Student Union, Young Lords Party, Movimiento de Izquierda Nacional Puertorriqueña-El Comité, Partido Socialista Puertorriqueño, et al.),

and demands for the community control of schools (Ocean Hill-Browns-ville, Two Bridges). In addition, New York Puerto Ricans began resisting the destructive elements of urban renewal and demanding rent controls. But the movement also included mobilizations for welfare rights, greater access to health services and higher education—such as the struggle for open admissions within the City University of New York (CUNY)—and socioculturally affirmative educational programs (such as bilingual sec-ondary education and Puerto Rican studies college programs).(2004,102)

Salsa musician Rubén Blades (in Blades 1983) made the following observation:

In the 70's there was much ambiance in the city, there was the beginning of a consciousness process of the American-Latino, it was a consequence of the Civil Rights Movement of the 60's: the protest against the Vietnam war, the marches of Alabama, Montgomery by Martin Luther King, the re-birth of the feeling of the Black man towards his rights, all of these things that were transmitted to the American-Latino who still today belongs to the most laggard minority in the economic advancement of this country. In fact, the indexes of unemployment and lacks of the Latinoamerican are much higher than the average of Black people, because the person that has migrated here in general maintains his/her nationality and therefore can-not take refuge in social welfare programs. At that time, the "Young Lords" movement put together by Puerto Ricans was born, and that affected other areas of the American-Latino ways of living, they began through music to embrace their origins, to rescue their own identity.

As the 1960s came to a close, grassroots movements had begun to orga-nize and make political and social strides. These groups played a large role in the formation of the social consciousness that fueled the mobilizations of Latinos:

The political organizing of the Black Panther Party provided a model for grassroots social mobilization that captured the imagination of budding radicals, especially among groups with a history of racial oppression in the United States. These radical groups helped orchestrate militant protests of the poor that addressed community issues and simultaneously advanced a broader political movement. By fomenting local change, they aimed to rebuild society anew. (Fernandez 2004, 3-4)

As a result of the social anger of the New York Latino communities, organized social movements began to surface. Among these, the YLP emerged as a Puerto Rican nationalist entity that was related to the advancement of the communities in New York as well as to the cause of independence of the island of Puerto Rico. The majority status of Puerto Ricans within the Latino community of New York caused the YLP to become the leading voice of Latino activism as a whole in the city. This activism, Puerto Rican-centered as it might have been, played a large role in the advancement of the Latino communities of El Barrio and the South Bronx.

The YLP was originally established in Chicago in the mid-1960s and eventually spawned a branch in New York City in 1969. Formed by a group of mainland-born Puerto Ricans, the YLP was a self-identified socialist movement akin to the Black Panthers. The movement aimed at the advancement, liberation, and self-determination of the Puerto Rican communities of New York and the island (Fernandez 2004). It began to develop community-based efforts that included, for example, mobile vaccinations for Latinos in El Barrio and the cleaning of streets of their communities. The latter, however, turned into the garbage offensive of 1969:

The garbage offensive emerged in late June/early July 1969, when *El Barrio* was dirty and the city sanitation department was ignoring the needs of the neighborhood. To address the problem, the YLO (a small group at this time, composed of a handful of members) began quite simply by arriving every Sunday to clean up the garbage. On July 27, one day after officially becoming the New York chapter of the Young Lords Organization, and two weeks after starting to clean the streets, the first point of social discord surfaced when some members attempted unsuccessfully to procure new supplies (brooms, cans, etc.) from the local sanitation department. It was at this point that the YLO came face to face with the bureaucracy of the liberal capitalist system and subsequently advanced a revolt in *El Barrio*. The YLO, together with a variety of community members who had been helping them pick up garbage, took heaped trash collections and placed them in several busy intersections, blocking significantly the traffic coming into and going out of Manhattan. The tactical placement of garbage peaked on August 17 when hundreds of Barrio Boricuas expanded their rebellion to include overturning cars, lighting fire to the trash, and assaulting police property. The Sunday garbage offensives continued until September 2, with Lords and other community members engaged actively in dissent. YLO Minister of Information, Pablo "Yoruba" Guzmán, recounts, "We would hit and run, block to block, talking and spreading politics as we went, dodging the slow-moving pigs sent to crush any beginning Boricua movement for freedom. The garbage offensive united us through struggle" (Enck-Wanzer 2006, 175).

The YLP guerrilla-type efforts presented a model within the New York Latino communities that paralleled the ideals proposed by the Black Panthers but within a Puerto Rican framework. The main contribution that the YLP gives to this book is that of elevating the social-justice and self-determination components within the Latino communities of New York at the time of the Salsa explosion. These social justice efforts ultimately influenced the very same people who were the audience and musicians of Salsa, thus making it inevitable that such types of sociopolitical discourse would eventually be incorporated into the music. Though most of the members of the YLP did not participate directly in the Salsa scene, one of their main members, poet and activist Felipe Luciano, played an extensive role within the bourgeoning Salsa movement, both as guest to read socially and racially charged poetry and, often, as master of ceremonies for Salsa shows. I interviewed Luciano at length, and he is one of the main primary sources for this book due to his involvement in both the YLP and the Salsa movement.

Regarding the philosophies proposed by the YLP, a strong emphasis was placed on the idea of class consciousness as a crucial marker for the Latino communities of the city; but the issue of race/ethnicity was still one of great contention. The push of the civil rights movement as an advancement of the neighboring African American communities had a large impact in El Barrio and the South Bronx. Luciano (2013) describes the context in the following terms:

> In the 60's the Black power movement began to push Puerto Ricans, it certainly pushed me. I was in the Black power movement before I was in the Puerto Rican movement with a group called The Last Poets, so I started reading poetry and teaching Black Nationalism and Black power to students, and Puerto Ricans came over to the loft that I was in called the Eastland, and said: why don't you come to East Harlem?

Despite the importance of African culture for Latin Americans and Latinos in general, the idea of Black pride has been a complex issue for a long time in these communities. The Puerto Rican generation that migrated to New York in the '40s and '50s were somewhat ambivalent regarding their heritage, especially if they were light-skinned. Culturally, within the realms of Puerto Rican racial signification, having a drop of Black blood did not mean that the person was Black. Having one drop of White blood, however, did make them White. Thus, the preferred identity associated with being Puerto Rican was more Spanish/White and less, or not at all, Black. This denial of African heritage in the Puerto Rican ethnic makeup developed into an internal racism within these communities that led to a self-understanding of Latinos as a separate race rather than an ethnic categorization that included African heritage.[1] Due to the historical dominance of Whites in Latin American society, the immigrant Puerto Ricans associated a negative connotation with being identified as Black, which, upon their arrival, caused a level of antipathy toward African Americans in the United States. According to Luciano (2013),

> Most Puerto Ricans saw being Puerto Rican as a race. It was easier for them to delude themselves into thinking that they would get better treatment, that they would be afforded better treatment if they were perceived as honorary Whites, and so it did matter how Black they were. They were different than African Americans because they were Puerto Rican. One

could understand their reluctance to accept the title of Black when you look at the treatment that was accorded [to] Black Americans in this country. I mean they were the pariahs.

It was only in the 1960s that Latinos began to see social struggles as a broader element of society that was not unique to their communities. Insofar as these struggles were shared by the neighboring African American communities and not just related to the economic and social status of Latinos, the advancement of Black Power played a significant role in the social development of Latinos as part of a discourse of marginalization that included race/ethnicity as well as class. In this environment, the existence of Afro-Puerto Rican music, such as *bomba,* began to be accepted as something to be proud of, as it meant both racial and nationalistic pride:

> I think our people began to soften their attitude, soften their internal racism and it was able to emerge. It does not mean that institutionally anything changed. We still don't have a Black Puerto Rican governor and I don't think for a long time [we] will because of our own internal racism. But at least we are willing to look at the possibility of African rhythms and being proud of them.

By the late 1960s, the views of Latinos had begun to change dramatically, race/ethnicity and class consciousness were beginning to be discussed more openly, and The People were beginning to reflect these shifts in consciousness. As I have shown thus far, the appearance of ethnic, social, and racial consciousness of Latinos in New York required a slow development that allowed for a more complete depuration of the concepts. As far as the music was concerned, Salsa as a genre and Salsa consciente as part of the larger Latino cultural pathos had not yet arrived onto the main stage, but it was beginning to develop as a solid movement. As I will show in the next section of this chapter, while the sound of the *bugalú* (boogaloo) with its bilingual lyrics was beginning to fade and Salsa was beginning to dominate the Latin music scene of New York, the consciousness of Latinos was becoming an important part of the music.

Consciousness in Salsa

With regard to the appearance of social consciousness in Salsa and pre-Salsa music, issues of race and ethnicity had already begun to be addressed via codified Afro-Cuban references in the *mambo* craze, more literally in the works of Arsenio Rodríguez and Rafael Cortijo, and during the *bugalú* era. I will continue to trace the development of Salsa by analyzing the music that followed the founding of Fania Records by Dominican musician Johnny Pacheco and Italian American lawyer Jerry Masucci in 1964 and the subsequent 1967 release of Willie Colón's album *El Malo* on the same label. I choose this instance because I consider it to be the moment that Fania Records became a synonym for Salsa, and Salsa as a unique movement began. For the uninitiated reader, it should be noted that Fania Records became the company that developed the blueprint of the 1970s' Salsa explosion and pioneered the sound, distribution, and marketing of Salsa to an extent that no one could have foreseen. Even though many other New York-based record labels, such as Alegre, Cotique, Discuba, Inca, Mardi Gras, Speed, Tico, Vaya, and WS Latino, had been releasing Latin music long-plays and 45RPMs in the U.S. market, Fania eventually purchased all of these companies and the rights to their music catalogs, effectively creating a monopoly.

It is worth noting, before I delve into the music, that there are many word-of-mouth accounts that speak of unethical practices on the part of Fania as a company. I refer to these practices in order for the reader to understand how the politics of the business of Salsa was handled. This is relevant to this book, as it exemplifies the power of the ruling class (Fania's executives) over the artists and composers as the working class of Salsa. As an example of these practices, Fania's copyright-handling strategies took full advantage of the 1962 Cuban embargo. Where many of Fania's albums utilized music written by Cuban composers, the compositions appear listed in the albums as D.R.: *derechos reservados* (reserved rights). Due to the political and cultural embargo of Cuba, composer credits and, therefore, royalties were never given to their rightful owners. By withholding copyright dues, this practice created a large amount of revenue for the record label. Another example of Fania's practices was the company's treatment of musicians.

There are word-of-mouth accounts that speak of Fania's owner, Jerry Masucci, becoming a millionaire while the musicians were being paid token amounts and not being told the actual number of records sold. In fact, as part of the fieldwork of this book, I interviewed several of the musicians who participated in some of the most crucial recordings released by the company. One of these musicians, trombonist Papo Vázquez, confirmed this in a personal communication in 2013 stating that he was paid $200 for his participation in Blades/Colón's *Siembra*, which was released in 1978 and sold in the millions.

Ethical considerations aside, Fania Records managed to produce an astounding number of albums and artists who completely defined the sound of Salsa. The company eventually formed its most successful group in 1968 by combining the leaders and singers of several different groups from its artist roster. The group was called *The Fania All Stars*, and I analyze their work later in this chapter. Regarding the beginnings of the firm, founder and musician Johnny Pacheco recounts (in Padura Fuentes 1999) that the company started by hiring the young talents who were either not signed to any company yet or unhappy with their current record label. One of the young talents they hired was teenage trombonist Willie Colón. Colón became, without a doubt, one of the most influential Salsa musicians ever. He popularized and remade the sound of Salsa many times over, and his work with singer Héctor Lavoe is, to this day, held in the highest esteem by Salsa connoisseurs. Colón was crucial in the expansion of Salsa consciente, as he was the one to give singer Rubén Blades an opportunity to showcase his fully developed, socially conscious discourse to what had become a worldwide audience. The Blades development, however, happened about ten years after Colón's debut with Fania.

WILLIE COLÓN

Colón, a third-generation Nuyorican, was born in the South Bronx in 1950. He is known primarily as a trombone player, though he is also a composer, producer, and singer. He released his first record with Fania when he was only seventeen years old. The recording, *El Malo* (The Bad One), was released in 1967. This recording featured Hector Lavoe as the lead singer on several tracks, and quickly catapulted both of them to fame. The recording, released at the height of what became known as the Latin boogaloo craze, contained a Cuban-centered sound filtered through New York as well as English-language *bugalús*, such as "Willie Baby," "Skinny Papa," and "Willie Whopper." At the same time, there is a clear trope that marks a Puerto Rican identity, probably influenced by the appearance of island-born Lavoe. This identity is clearly exemplified by the song "Borínquen" (the Native name of Puerto Rico), where Lavoe declares that *Borínquen* is calling him. Musically, there is also a very relevant signifier in the title track, "El Malo": the use of the rhythm of *bomba sicá*, just as Rafael Cortijo did about a decade before. This time, however, the signifier is related to being Puerto Rican, and not to Black pride. Although this is not the first appearance of Puerto Rican bomba in Salsa, the song signaled a clear Nuyolatino identification with and trope of Latinidad, as it utilized the Cuban sonic template of *guaracha* in contrast to the *bomba* without losing either its Puerto Rican or Nuyolatino identities.

By 1968, Colón released *The Hustler*, reinforcing his suave yet "tough guy" street image. The cover of the album expanded this look by portraying a scene that was based on the 1961 movie *The Hustler*, starring Paul Newman. The band was shown, with Colón front and center, sharply dressed, smoking cigars, and "hustling" pool. The concept of the antihero, as developed in the movie, played a large role in determining the image of Colón for years to come, where he was portrayed as a "bad guy." This image was utilized by making a statement that compared class struggles and the resistance to being culturally dominated by "high society" to toughness and being one with The People.

The Hustler featured Lavoe as the exclusive singer of the band for the first time, thus fully abandoning any English lyrics. There is, however, still the instrumental, English-titled track "The Hustler" that perhaps was carried over from the previous album's success. The release of this album marked the beginning of the departure from the *bugalú*, as evidenced first by the lack of English lyrics so expected of *bugalú* releases, and specifically by the track "Eso Se Baila Así," which, despite retaining some *bugalú* flavor in the musical part by its use of the backbeat, included a chorus that declared *bugalú no va conmigo* (boogaloo does not go with me).

Regarding the identity factor of the album, the lyrics do not specifically refer to any type of racial or social issues, and the music is based mostly on New York–filtered, Cuban-based structures, including *guaracha, son montuno, bolero, guajira, guaguancó,* and *son.* Despite the lack of Puerto Rican or other Latin American musical structures, one important aspect of this period of the Colón/Lavoe effort lies not only in affirming their nationalistic identities as Puerto Rican/Nuyolatinos, but in the idea of being or having "street."[2] This "street" concept was affirmed by their image and performance attitude as tough street-life-educated musicians, and not by the literal content of their music. The projected attitude showcased the fact that their music, despite being based on Cuban structures, contained a strong, urban Latino component and strongly identified their stand with the working class, The People, El Pueblo.

Colón and Lavoe's 1969 album release, *Guisando Doing a Job,* now included Lavoe as an essential part of the band and showed him for the first time on the cover. The album's popularity pointed to Salsa as a movement that was beginning to peak, with the Colón/Lavoe duo in one of the coveted top spots. The album cover shows the development of the "tough guy" image previously endorsed by Colón, depicting the duo as gangsters who are taking money from a safe, with Colón holding a gun while Lavoe counts cash. This image plays to the sensibility of the times, where being tough and "streetwise" indicated a degree of urban recognition or savoir-faire.

Although thematically the album did not really include traits that could be considered part of a socially engaged discourse, the song "Guisando" portrays the idea of the antihero by developing a song built on the misadventures of a purse snatcher. Musically, the album is centered on the tried-and-true Cuban-based musical styles, yet it also features the song "Oiga Señor," which is sung in the Puerto Rican style of *bomba sicá.*

The next two albums released by Colón and Lavoe, *Cosa Nuestra* (1970) and *The Big Break* (1971), continued to explore the image of a tough street guy. The cover of *Cosa Nuestra,* a play on words with the idea of *Cosa Nostra,* the Italian Mafia, perhaps connoting the image of a Latino "Salsa mafia," shows Colón standing next to a corpse with a rock tied to its feet and Colón armed with his trombone. All of this happens in front of the Hudson River, as though he is ready to dispose of the corpse, mafia-style.

Salsa was almost at its peak at the time of *Cosa Nuestra*, with Colón utilizing a mainly Cuban-centered framework for the music, with the notable exception of what is perhaps the most interesting track of the album: "Che Che Colé." Rhythmically, this track is significant in the fact that it utilized an obscure Puerto Rican rhythm called *gangá*. The use of this rhythm is reminiscent of Rafael Cortijo's negritude statements, as it utilizes Afrocentric (as opposed to Cuban-centric) percussion layering like the one featured in such tracks as Cortijo's 1968 "Sorongo."[3] In the same manner, Colón's arrangement of "Che Che Colé" showed a very deliberate attempt to sound non-Cuban. Although the rhythmic arrangement of this song could have easily been done over Cuban *son* structures, there was a very distinct choice to not utilize Cuban music as a template. This is demonstrated by the lack of *timbales* and bongo, and in the addition of a triangle and a shaker (*cabasa*) in the percussion section. The rhythms performed by the percussion section deliberately moved away from the *tresillo*-based lines that had become ever present in Cuban-derived Salsa. As such, the rhythmic layering utilized in this song, coupled with the half-note/downbeat centered bass line, is more reminiscent of popular African music rather than Cuban music. Although it is not possible to show the rhythm's exact precedence in relationship to Africa, these choices were probably deliberate on the part of Colón to emphasize, as the lyrical analysis that follows will show, the African-based lyrics that, in fact, indicate, "This rhythm is African."

The song also incorporates a piano ostinato as its basic motif that moves away from the Cuban-centered *guajeos* derived from the aforementioned *danzón* titled "Mambo." In this way, the combination of the ostinato with the half-note bass line and the *gangá* rhythm avoids a Cuban feeling, even though it utilizes a very typical *son montuno* chord progression (I-IV-V-IV in either major or minor keys). Because *gangá* is a relatively obscure rhythm, and many similar-sounding rhythms are found in Latin America, the music sounds as though it could have been developed in almost any Latin American country. This type of non-Cuban-sounding device is highly relevant, as it denoted a unique approach to a Pan-Latino musical language

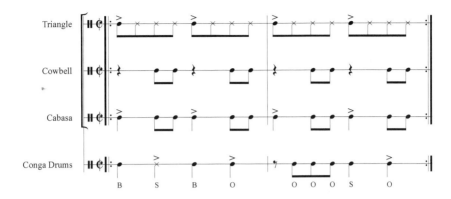

Figure 1. *Ritmo gangá* as performed in "Che Che Colé."

Figure 2. Piano ostinato utilized in "Che Che Colé."

that spoke of sensibilities that go beyond the Cuban-centric views of Salsa and embraced the people of Latin America within the significations of Salsa.

Lyrically, "Che Che Colé" is an exception to all of Colón's previous work in several ways. First, as Lavoe indicates in the lyrics, the song incorporates an African style, possibly accounting for the more African-sounding use of the *gangá* rhythm.[4] Not only does Lavoe's delivery mention African music, but the chorus of the song is based on a Ghanaian children's song titled "Tse tse kule." I show this song in its original form, as transcribed by Agawu (1995, 14).

Although the original Ghanaian song functions as a call and response in the Ewe language, Lavoe's version utilizes the chorus in Ewe with a response in Spanish. Not only has the song denoted the African element of the music and dance in the lyrics and musical choices, but it also extends a Pan-Latino arm by including Venezuela and Panama in the lyrics. This is extremely significant, as it is probably the first mention of Latin American countries other than Cuba and Puerto Rico within a popular New York Salsa

Figure 3. "Tse tse kule": Ghanaian children's song, as transcribed by Agawu.

track. This broader appeal, supported by the non-Cuban flavor of the music, denotes not only the popularity and consequent distribution of Salsa as popular dance music in various Latin American countries, but also an early Pan-Latino appearance through explicit references to the shared trope of Africa.

"CHE CHE COLÉ" AS PERFORMED BY WILLIE COLÓN AND HÉCTOR LAVOE

Vamos todos a bailar	Let's all dance
Al estilo Africano	African style
...	...
Para que goces ahora,	So you can enjoy now,
Africano es el bembé.	African is my bembé.
Coro:	**Chorus:**
Che che colé, (Que bueno e')	Che che colé, (How good it is)
Che che cofiza, (Muerto e' la risa)	Che che cofiza, (Laughing so much)
Coqui saranga (Ahí viene la malanga)	Coqui saranga (Here comes the taro root)
Caca chilanga, (Viene de Katanga)	Caca chilanga, (Comes from Katanga)

Ayeiyeee, (A ver e' tú lo ve)	Ayeiyeee, (Let's see, hey you can see it)
Oye tú sentado allá	Hey you sitting there,
Pareces Venezolano	You look like you are Venezuelan
Ven aquí vamo' a bailar	Come over here and let's dance
Que todos somos hermanos.	We are all brothers.
Lo bailan en Venezuela,	It is danced in Venezuela,
Lo bailan en Panamá.	It is danced in Panama.
Este ritmo es Africano	This rhythm is African
Y donde quiera va a acabar.	And it's the bomb everywhere.
Coro:	**Chorus:**
Che che colé, (Que bueno e')	Che che colé, (How good it is)
Che che cofiza, (Muerto e' la risa)	Che che cofriza, (Laughing so much)
Coqui saranga, (Ahí viene la malanga)	Coqui saranga, (Here comes the taro root)
Caca chilanga, (Viene de Katanga)	Caca chilanga, (Comes from Katanga)
Ayeiyeee, (A ver e' tú lo ve)	Ayeiyeee, (Let's see, hey you can see it)[5]

Torres Torres, in his review of the album for the Fania website, noted that the song

opened the doors of Panama, France, Colombia, Venezuela and Perú to them. The value of Willie and Héctor substantially improved thanks to the success of "Che Che Colé" and soon we would find them competing for "top billing" in the clubs of Manhattan, the Bronx and Queens with the likes of Eddie Palmieri's La Perfecta, the Lebrón Brothers, Frankie Dante & La Flamboyán and other bands of the time.

The following year, Colon and Lavoe released *The Big Break–La Gran Fuga*. The cover of this album explored the same type of sensibility noted in *Cosa Nuestra*. The image of the tough guy is portrayed on the cover by showing Colón—aka "El Malo" (The Hustler)—in a mug shot as if being sought by the FBI. Colón's repeated use of this mafia/bad guy image in his work is crucial in understanding Salsa's original principles. The roughness depicted on the covers represented Colón's approach to Salsa as a music of resistance and of anti-hegemonic ideals, where the value of urban Latino resilience, despite the social circumstances and class oppression, is held high. In this sense, the urban Nuyolatino concept of being "bad" is partially related to the antihero imagery of African American Blaxploitation movies, such as *Shaft* (1971) and *Sweet Sweetback's Baadasssss Song* (1971). In the Latino part of the equation, this bad-boy image was equated with urban credibility and anti-hegemonic resistance as it showed the life of "the common man" doing what was needed to survive in the "concrete jungle" and defeating the odds of a system that was designed to make him fail. As such, Colón's bad-boy/mafia image quickly placed him as an antihero for urban Latinos, while, at the same time, the idea of *Cosa Nuestra* (our *Latin* thing or *the Latino mob*, after the Italian Cosa Nostra) or Colón being "wanted by the FBI" represented the unification, glorification, and strength to deal with the struggles of contemporary Latino urban life.

Thematically, the most important development in Colón's *The Big Break–La Gran Fuga* album is the inclusion of a "follow-up" to the success of "Che Che Colé," titled "Ghana'e," even though this track did not get as much recognition as its earlier counterpart did. There is also a continuation of the Pan-Latino sensitivity seen in two separate tracks. The first is a song called "Pa' Colombia," written by Tite Curet Alonso, which lyrically avoids delivering social content, as it only exalts the beauty of five different Colombian cities. The second is a song titled "Panameña," which exalts the beauty of Panamanian and Dominican women over a Nuyoricanized *danzón* rhythm, followed by the inclusion of the beauty of Puerto Rican women supported by the Puerto Rican style of *aguinaldo*. Although the thematic content of the latter two songs is not particularly geared toward advancing a Latino unity discourse, they do present an important inclusion of a larger Latin American sensibility, demonstrating the distribution and importance of Salsa in Venezuela, Colombia, Panama, and the Dominican Republic as centers of Salsa consumption. "Pa' Colombia" and "Panameña" also signify the inclusion of the circum-Caribbean in a Nuyolatino-produced discourse. In compositional terms, it is also worth noting the appearance of Curet Alonso.

It is important to remark that the construction of the tough/street image that is so prevalent in the Colón/Lavoe collaboration is directly tied to the conceptualization of masculinity within Latino society, and the expected role of women in Latino societies of the times. While the number of female artists during this time period in Salsa is very limited, they were led by three Cuban-born singers: Graciela, La Lupe, and Celia Cruz. While Graciela commanded a fantastic stage presence, was in fact a phenomenal singer, and could have easily been part of the Salsa movement, most of her output precedes by about a decade those of La Lupe and Celia Cruz, and Graciela's work is almost exclusively known for her collaboration with Machito and the Afro-Cubans during the *mambo* era. Without a doubt, however, Celia Cruz soon became the most popular female Salsa artist of all time, and the only one of the three that actively recorded and performed for Fania Records. Her artistic image, however, was not one built upon the idea of toughness and "street," but instead her Cuban nationality was exploited, whether consciously by Cruz or not, as a source of authenticity in the performance of a set of musical styles that derived directly from Cuba. Also, due to her incredible stage presence and performance abilities, Cruz's work did not require a great degree of validation from the audience. Cruz's performance style came directly from the source, as she grew up singing Cuban music and absorbed all its influences completely unfiltered. While La Lupe was also Cuban and had gained a great reputation singing in New York slightly before and also actively during Cruz's rise to fame, her instability during performances, tied to rumored addiction concerns, prompted Fania Records to favor Cruz as their female star. La Lupe, besides being the person who introduced one of the main composers of Salsa and Salsa consciente to the world, Catalino "Tite" Curet Alonso, also gave a clear demonstration of the aforementioned street principles. Her performances included a certain degree of grittiness and roughness that lacked the refinement of Cruz. It is certainly conjecture whether her "unladylike" behavior might have prompted the Latino audience, with its stereotypical rigid macho structures and strict and socially constructed images of what a female should be/do, to lose interest in her. But there was a subsequent decline in her popularity that may have also led to Fania executives deciding to not promote her to the level of Cruz, and ultimately to terminate her contract with the label.[6]

By the close of the 1960s, the cultural setting of New York and the sociopolitical movements of the times had begun to press Latino musicians to reflect the urban realities of their daily lives. Thus, social consciousness became a component of the New York Latin music scene. The initial push of the Black Power movement, the example set by Arsenio Rodriguez and Rafael Cortijo, the union of Black and Latino culture as exemplified by the boogaloo, and the urban realities depicted by Colón had begun to create a clear path for the discourse of Salsa consciente as a movement to come.

RAY BARRETTO

In 1969, Ray Barretto produced the album *Together* for Fania Records, in which he included a nod to Venezuela in the song "No Olvido a Caracas" (I do not forget Caracas) as well as the racially minded song "¿De dónde vengo?" (Where do I come from?). The latter seems innocent enough in its introduction by developing the story of Adam and Eve. The end of the verse, however, twists the song into a pursuit of racial identity, in which singer Adalberto Santiago asks, "If Adam and Eve were White, then why is my skin Black?" The chorus of the song then continues the negritude plot by questioning the hegemonic religious discourse of denying Blackness in the form of a question: "(If Adam and Eve were White, then) where do I come from?"

"¿DE DÓNDE VENGO?" AS PERFORMED BY RAY BARRETTO'S BAND

Dicen que en el mundo	They say that in the world
No había habitantes	There were no inhabitants
Tan solo un edén glorioso y brillante	Only a bright and glorious Eden
Y un día al edén Dios vida le dio	And one day God gave life to Eden
Y de barro y de polvo un hombre sacó.	And from the mud and dust he made a man.
...	...
Fueron como hermanos	They were like siblings
Hasta que Eva comió de una manzana	Until Eve ate from an apple
Y el pecado nació	And sin was born
Tuvieron sus hijos y el mundo se llenó	They had their children and the world was filled

Pero no me explico de adonde vengo yo	But did not explain to me where I come from
Yo vi en el teatro la muerte y pasión	I saw in the theater the death and passion (of Christ)
Mas no vi un Negrito en ninguna ocasión	But I did not see a Black person on any occasion
Si blanco fue Adán y Eva también,	If Adam was White and so was Eve
Entonces ¿por qué es Negra mi piel?	Then, why is my skin Black?
Coro: ¿De adonde vengo?	**Chorus:** Where do I come from?
Ay yo lo quiero saber	Hey, I want to know
...	...
Yo sé que soy Niche, yo sé que soy Niche caballero	I know I am Black, I know I am Black, man
Oye, mira, ¿de dónde yo vengo?	Listen, look, where do I come from?
Si blanco fue Adán y Eva también	If Adam was White and so was Eve
Entonces ¿por qué es Negra mi piel?	Then, why is my skin Black?
Ehh, yo lo quiero, lo quiero saber	I want to know
...	...
Oye Eva fue Blanca y ¿por qué es Negra mi piel?	Listen, Eve was White, and why is my skin Black?
...	...
Eh, yo soy un Niche con sabor, papá	Hey, I am a Black man with flavor, daddy[7]

Up to this point, the most common advances of a socially engaged Latin music had been related to issues of race/ethnicity that stemmed mainly from the impulse given by the Black Power movement and paralleled African American music with the arrival in 1968 of James Brown's *I'm Black and I'm Proud*. Nevertheless, by 1969, as Luciano (2013) states,

the social protest movement forces the musicians to look anew at their space and their place in history. At this point there are military dictatorships all over South America. Mexico's '68 kills 300 students, Brazil is under military dictatorship, Chile not yet but they are ready to kill Allende, Paraguay [has] Stroessner, Uruguay, and those not under military dictatorship are run by corrupt oligarchies. At the same time Paris is hav-ing its riots and Japan is going to the red army.

EDDIE PALMIERI

It was then, in 1969, that pianist and composer Eddie Palmieri released the album *Justicia* (Justice). It is in this album that a socially conscious discourse that went beyond the idea of race/ethnicity as the main struggle is achieved. The title track, with lyrics written by singer Ismael Quintana, unites the social struggles of Puerto Ricans and Blacks and makes mention of "the unfortunate ones" as an acknowledgment of class consciousness and the marginalization of both these groups. The conceptualization of Salsa consciente at this point is really in a prototypical stage, yet this is arguably the first instance where a popular Salsa track includes rhetoric based specifically on class awareness. The concept of class consciousness is not only one of the most relevant topics of Salsa consciente in general, but also one that achieved great relevance within the work of Curet Alonso, specifically.

Regarding the song, Ismael Quintana (2001, 2004), the writer of the lyrics, elaborated as follows:

> The idea of that song was Eddie's [Palmieri], and had to do with the frus-tration of the world's situation—political, economic, etc., . . . especially in our Latin American countries and we thought that by means of our music, that Eddie composed and for which I wrote the lyrics, we were sending a message. I tried to do it [the lyrics] very carefully so as not to offend anybody, because there were some artists that did many things and were boycotted, they were not played in other countries. They were offending governments and such. I always tried to be very diplomatic in my lyrics.

"JUSTICIA" AS PERFORMED BY EDDIE PALMIERI

Justicia tendrán,	Justice they will have,
Justicia verán en el mundo,	Justice will be seen in the world,
Los desafortunados.	The unfortunate ones.

Con el canto del tambor	With the song of the drum
Del tambor la justicia yo reclamo	With the drum, justice I demand
Justicia tendrán,	Justice they will have,
Justicia verán, el mundo	Justice will be seen in the world,
Y los discriminados,	And the ones discriminated against,
Recompensa ellos tendrán	They will be rewarded
No serán, no serán perjudicados	They will not be, will not be wronged
Si no hubiera tiranía,	If there was no tyranny,
Todos fuéramos hermanos	We would all be brothers
Dulce paz y armonía	Sweet peace and harmony
Alegría, tú lo veras.	Joy, you would see.
Justicia tendrán,	Justice they will have,
Justicia verán el mundo,	Justice they will see in the world,
Y lo que deseamos	And what we want
Con el canto 'e mi tambo	With the song of my drum
Oye mi tambo,	Listen, to my drum
La justicia yo reclamo	Justice I demand
Coro: Ay cuando llegará la justicia?	**Chorus:** Oh, when will justice arrive?
Cuando llegará, cuándo llegará?	Oh, when will it arrive, when will it arrive?
Justicia pa' los boricuas y los Niches	Justice for Puerto Ricans and Blacks
Mi tambor reclama justicia	My drum demands justice
Que lleguen, que lleguen, que lleguen las buenas noticias	Let them come, let them come, let the good news arrive
Tanta tiranía, tanta tiranía, tanta tiranía	So much tyranny, so much tyranny, so much tyranny
Justicia, que yo reclamo justicia	Justice, I demand justice
Interludio instrumental	**Instrumental interlude**
Segundo coro: La justicia	**Second chorus:** Justice
Tu verás mi socio	You will see my brother
Voy a ponerte a guarachar	I will make you enjoy yourself
Y cuando llegue ese día,	And when that day comes,
To' será felicidad	Everything will be happiness
Justicia tendremos	We will have justice
Justicia pa'l Niche	Justice for the Black man

Justicia para el Boricua	Justice for the Puerto Rican
Boricua pa' ti, Boricua pa' ti.	Puerto Rican for you, for you, for you.[8]

By 1971, Barretto had produced two albums with titles that hinted at the idea of *Salsa consciente*: *Power* (1970) and *The Message* (1971), although, in terms of their content, they ultimately failed to deliver substantial advancements regarding social consciousness. Palmieri, however, in 1971 produced his now-famous album *Vámonos Pa'l Monte*, which includes the well-known song of the same name. A track on the album that sought to elevate Latino consciousness is "Revolt La Libertad Lógico" (Revolt Freedom Logically).

This track, much like "Justicia," demonstrates the rising awareness of sociopolitical issues within Latino consciousness as presented through Salsa. In this track, there is no direct mention of racial issues, as had been the case thus far, nor is there an incorporation of a nationalistic tone by mentioning Puerto Rico. There are, however, two particular instances of social emphasis besides the title that invite listeners to "revolt for freedom." The first instance concerns the concept of being mistreated due to ethnic conflict, stated by the line "This is where I was born." This sentence specifically questions the place in society of Nuyoricans and Nuyolatinos, who, despite having been born in the United States, were often treated as immigrants and, thus, not "allowed" to share the same rights and privileges as the dominant White classes.

The second instance concerns the concept of being a slave to the capitalistic system, found in the line "Economically, your slave." The first sentence refers to discrimination and feelings of being treated as second-class citizens, an experience faced daily by Latinos vis-à-vis the dominant White majority. This second line plays off the idea of being an economic slave to the implied system, that is, the higher class, and the lack of mobility and economic opportunities for the Latino communities. As can be seen, the idea of class consciousness had become an important part of Salsa's discourse. This utterance places the concept I alluded to earlier, namely, the idea of Nuyolatino, as a crucial label that determines a hybrid identity (New York and Latino, including Afro-Latino) within a subset of the population who, despite having been born in New York, were being treated as immigrants, and consequently as inferior. Within the same concept, the title of the song ("Revolt La Libertad Lógico") also evokes the previously mentioned hybrid identity by including both English and Spanish in the same sentence. This song in particular is highly relevant, as it showcases, fairly early within the development of Salsa consciente, not only a geographically unbound concept of being Latino, but also two of the most crucial determinants of the movement: Latinidad and Pueblo.

"REVOLT LA LIBERTAD LÓGICO" AS PERFORMED BY EDDIE PALMIERI

Coro: No, no, no, no me trates así

Chorus: Don't, don't, don't, don't treat me like that

La libertad, caballero, no me la quites a mi

Freedom, my man, don't take it from me

Pero que mira, pero mira, pero mira que también yo soy humano y fue aquí donde nací

Look, look, look, I too am human and this is where I was born

La libertad tú ves, La libertad tú ves, caballero no me la quites, no me la quites a mi

Freedom you see, freedom you see, man, don't take it, don't take it from me

Económicamente, económicamente esclavo de ti

Economically, economically your slave

Esclavo de ti, esclavo de ti, esclavo de ti caballero, pero que va, tu no me engañas a mi

Your slave, your slave, your slave man but come on you don't fool me

Tú no me engañas, ¡eh! tú no me engañas, tú no me engañas,

You don't fool me, hey! You don't fool me, you don't fool me,

Interludio instrumental

Instrumental interlude

Segundo coro (sobre la seccion instrumental):

Second chorus (over instrumental section):

La libertad, lógico

Freedom, logically

Tercer coro: No me trates así

Third chorus: Don't treat me like that

Mira que fue aquí donde nací

Look, here is where I was born

¡Eh! Tu no me engañas a mi

Hey! You don't fool me

¡Eh! tu no me engañas, tu no me engañas, tu no me engañas, tu no me engañas, caballero

Hey! You don't fool me, you don't fool me you don't fool me, you don't fool me, man

¡Eh! la libertad, caballero

Hey! Freedom, man

¡Eh! no me la quites a mi	Hey! Don't take it from me
Económicamente	Economically
Esclavo	Slave[9]

In 1972, Palmieri produced a live album that was recorded while he performed at Sing Sing Prison, titled *Live at Sing Sing, Volume 1*.[10] The very fact that Palmieri recorded the album while performing at this prison emphasizes his social commitment. The most important track of the album, however, is not a musical performance by Palmieri, but instead features the participation of Young Lords member, poet, Latino activist, and one of the key sources of this book, Felipe Luciano, reciting his poem "Jíbaro, My Pretty Nigger."[11] This recitation is particularly poignant, intense, and profound, and thus very much in the style of classic Luciano. The poem entices Puerto Ricans (under the guise of *Jíbaro*) to embrace their African heritage at the same level as that of being Puerto Rican. Although the use of "nigger" might be considered offensive, the qualifier "pretty" questions this assumption and places Luciano, a proud Black man himself, speaking directly to his fellow Black Puerto Ricans (his "niggers"), asking them to embrace their Afro-Puerto Rican heritage. The album was a great success both commercially and in the spread of its explicit social message.

FANIA RECORDS AND THE FANIA ALL STARS

The Fania All Stars (FAS) was an ensemble created in 1968 to showcase the talents of the lead singers and bandleaders of Fania Records's roster. Their popularity, however, rose in 1971, when the ensemble played a now well-known concert at the Cheetah Club that helped turn Salsa into a worldwide phenomenon. From this concert, four records were produced, and the film *Our Latin Thing* (*Nuestra Cosa*), featuring large segments of the concert, was released in 1972.

The scenes depicted in the film reinforced Salsa's commitment to The People by including many images of the Latino communities of El Barrio and the South Bronx. Other excerpts included musical numbers from the performance and rehearsals that led up to the show. The film quickly made stars of all the musicians, especially the singers, and the popularity of the endeavor beyond New York launched a Salsa craze that had FAS touring Latin America and the world almost immediately. The impact of the film led to massive sales and great recognition for the Fania All Stars as ambassadors of Salsa. Berríos-Miranda (2004) noted the following:

> First through the film of this show, and later through countless recordings and concerts, salsa gave form and recognition to the culture of the barrio. This recognition, affirmed by salsa's international acclaim (as measured in record sales and international tours by the Fania All Stars to Latin America, Africa, Australia, and Japan) challenged an oppressive value system that ignored the worth of barrio culture. (165)

The imagery of the film set in El Barrio and the South Bronx allowed enough commonality within the discourse for audiences to recognize the Fania musicians as Latino "street heroes." It is with this crucial trope of El Pueblo that Salsa was turned into an extremely powerful tool "of the people and for the people." The film thus marks the realization of Salsa's potent ability to influence or integrate The People, a powerful relationship that had been developing since the 1960s and that eventually played an extremely important role within the discourse of Salsa consciente. Sociologically, however, the content of the music and the lyrics of the Fania All Stars' performance were not particularly focused on the elevation of Latino social consciousness. Yet, the recognition of the FAS as street heroes and the popularity of the film helped to spread not only the popularity of Salsa, but also the "replicable" idea of Latino heroes who come from the ghetto. This recognition, coupled with the popularity of the music, largely due to the advent of mechanical reproduction in the form of vinyl records and the subsequent distribution of the music in both New York and Latin America, triggered a very strong sense of Latino identity, regardless of whether the people were in New York or Latin America.

By 1973, *Salsa* and *Fania* had become interchangeable terms, and the popularity of the Fania All Stars was undeniable. On August 23, the Fania All Stars played to a sold-out crowd of 40,000 mainly Latino fans at Yankee Stadium. Salsa had become *the* music of the New York Latino community.

The concert, however, ended when the audience breached the security barriers and overtook the stage. The concert was replicated in Puerto Rico in November of the same year. The concerts were recorded and released in 1975 under the title *Fania All Stars Live at Yankee Stadium.* Though inaccurately titled, as much of the material was actually recorded at the Puerto Rico concert, the album became a great success and garnered a Grammy nomination in 1976.

By the time the Yankee Stadium/Puerto Rico concerts were held, the intermingling of ethnicities that made up New York was reflected within the Fania All Stars lineup. Although the majority of the participants were of Puerto Rican heritage, there were a significant number of other Latinos as well as non-Latinos in the ensemble. From the Fania release, the following musicians fulfilled the Nuyolatino criteria: Johnny Pacheco, the creator and musical director of the Fania All Stars, was Dominican; Víctor Paz on trumpet was from Panama; and the special guests, Celia Cruz, Ramon "Mongo" Santamaría, and singer Justo Betancourt, were all Cuban. Non-Latinos included Barry Rogers and Lewis Kahn on trombone, as well as Larry Harlow on piano.

By comparing the personnel of the Yankee Stadium and Puerto Rico concerts to the famous 1971 Cheetah concert, often referred to as the "launch" of the Fania All Stars, one can note that the 1973 version of FAS had a more ethnically diverse range of personnel. In 1971, the only non–Puerto Rican musicians were Dominicans Johnny Pacheco on flute/musical direction and Héctor "Bomberito" Zarzuela on trumpet; Cuban-born Orestes Vilató on timbales; and New York natives Barry Rogers on trombone, Larry Spencer on trumpet, and Larry Harlow on piano.

In terms of the lyrical and social content, it is important to compare the repertoire of these two concerts, as the 1971 Cheetah concert boasts only one piece, "Anacaona," that could be considered socially conscious. This piece, written by Catalino "Tite" Curet Alonso and performed by Cheo Feliciano, touches on the seldom-discussed racial identity of Native/Indigenous Americans, a trait often forgotten in the Caribbean, due mainly to the near-total extermination of Natives by the Spanish conquistadors. However, the Yankee Stadium/Puerto Rico concert took what is perhaps the biggest step yet toward Salsa as a measure of Latino consciousness, and potentially the keystone of Salsa consciente, by including Curet Alonso's song "Pueblo Latino," sung by Pete "El Conde" Rodriguez.[12]

This piece was released prior to the debut of Rubén Blades as a Fania artist, and despite the nods to a socially based discourse by many others, including Blades singing about guerrillas in "Juan Gonzalez" (in the 1970 release *From Panama to New York*),[13] "Pueblo Latino" marks the first time that such a straightforward discourse of Latinidad, Latino unity, and the significance of Pueblo were presented to such a widespread audience. The popularity of the Fania All Stars, combined with the social awareness prompted by the civil rights movement, meant this was the first occasion that Salsa played such an explicit and active role in furthering the Latino community's consciousness movement.

The song speaks literally of Latino unity by calling for Latinos of any neighborhood or city to unite. With this song, Curet Alonso lyrically argued that through unity, the strengths that join Latinos would be heightened, and Latinos would move away from unhappiness. The chorus of the song, however, indicates a gloomy view of the situation of Latinos in 1973, in the line "If I am to continue as is, I'd rather die." Notably, the song was re-recorded by the well-known contemporary Salsa group Spanish Harlem Orchestra in 2002. The song's overall arrangement, though refreshed, was kept formally similar to the aesthetically Cuban-based original recording, as the Spanish Harlem Orchestra aims at re-creating the Salsa sound of the 1970s, often labeled *Salsa Dura* (Hard Salsa). The lyrics, delivered in 2002 by Herman Olivera, however, differ from the original as the chorus says: *Pueblo Latino vamos a unirnos por siempre* (Latino people, let's join as one forever). The original song became one of the best-known songs by the Fania All Stars, and the fact that the song has been re-recorded and is often performed during concerts of lesser-known Salsa groups underlines the relevance of the lyrics, even by today's standards.

"PUEBLO LATINO" AS PERFORMED BY THE FANIA ALL STARS

Pueblo Latino de cualquier ciudad	Latino People of any city
Ha llegado la hora de la unidad	The time of unity has come

Ha sonado la hora del estrechón de manos

The time has come to shake hands

Como protección

As protection

Pueblo Latino de cualquier barrio

Latino People of any neighborhood

De cualquier ciudad

Of any city

(**Coro**) De cualquier ciudad

(**Chorus**) of any city

Tu hora ha sonado, ¡únete!

Your time has come, unite!

(**Coro**) ¡Únete!

(**Chorus**) Unite!

Porque en la unidad es que está la fuerza monumental

Because in unity lies strength monumental

Que nos puede salvar de la infelicidad

That can save us from unhappiness

Que nos puede salvar de la infelicidad

That can save us from unhappiness

Pueblo latino de cualquier ciudad o barrio

Latino People of any city or neighborhood

Únete,

Unite,

Que ha llegado la hora de estrecharnos las manos

The time to shake hands has come

Como protección,

As protection

Como protección.

As protection

Coro: Pa' seguir así, prefiero la muerte

Chorus: If I am to continue as is I'd rather die

Ay! Únanse por favor, querido publico oyente

Oh! Unite please, dear audience

...

...

Ay, viviremos y lucharemos sin miedo hasta la muerte

Oh, we will live and fight with no fear until death

Oye, trátame como hermano y yo podre corresponderte

Listen, treat me as a brother and I shall treat you the same

...

...

Oye, prefiero la muerte, prefiero la muerte

Listen, I prefer death, I prefer death

Interludio instrumental

Instrumental interlude

Hablado: ¡Oye! Agárrate, que en la unión está la fuerza

Spoken: Listen! Hold on that in unity we find strength

Coro: Pa' seguir así, prefiero la muerte

Chorus: If I am to continue as is I'd rather die

Oye, prefiero la muerte, prefiero la muerte	Listen, I prefer death, I prefer death,
…	…
Medio coro:[14] Prefiero la muerte	**Half chorus:** I prefer death
Hablado (durante el Solo de Barry Rogers):	**Spoken** (during Barry Rogers' Solo):
…	…
(El Conde) Guapea Barry! El pueblo Latino Americano te quiere con cariño	(El Conde) Work it Barry! The Latin American people love you
Hablado (durante el Solo de Victor Paz):	**Spoken** (during Victor Paz's Solo):
(El Conde) Guapea Victor Paz que en la unión está la fuerza	(El Conde) Work it Victor Paz. In unity we find strength
Coro: Pa' seguir así, prefiero la muerte	**Chorus:** If I am to continue as is, I'd rather die
¡Eehh! Piensen bien en la unión y nada podrá detenerte	Eehh! Think deeply about unity and nothing will stop you
Oye, prefiero, prefiero la muerte, prefiero la muerte	Listen, I prefer death, I prefer death
Hablado: Pueblo Latino, nos unimos o nos lleva la miseria	**Spoken:** Latino People, we either join forces or misery will take us[15]

Musically speaking, the arrangement of the song draws heavily on the rhythmic and formal structures of the Cuban *son* and *guaracha*. Larry Harlow, on piano, for the most part rhythmically plays the string *guajeo* taken from Orestes Lopez's *danzón* titled "Mambo." The main difference between the piano of this recording and that of the aforementioned *guajeo* is the use of extended harmonies. In this case, the main difference is the use of dominant 7(13) and dominant altered chords, often harmonized by the horn section. It should be noted that, harmonically speaking, the use of these types of extended harmonies is one of the biggest differences between the Cuban *son* and Salsa. The bass lines and percussion parts are nevertheless still based on the standard Cuban *son* accompanying patterns.

Overall, the musical aesthetic choices of *Pueblo Latino* as performed by the Fania All Stars do little to support the delivery of such profound lyrics. There is, however, a difference between the version as performed by the All Star ensemble and the regular band of Pete "El Conde" Rodriguez. During the performance of the song, El Conde's band includes Puerto Rican *bomba* as a contrast to the Cuban-centered accompaniment. Given the content of the lyrics, however, especially the lack of mention of racial issues, the inclusion of the *bomba* points to a marker of nationalistic Puerto Ricanness rather than a marker of Blackness. This musical shift did not seem to be relevant to the Fania All Stars, as their music was nevertheless wildly popular among Latino communities. In retrospect, the delivery of a tested set of dance music still afforded them the opportunity to convey a small amount of Salsa consciente-type messages without losing their fan base. This formula, as a commercial ethos, worked for most Salsa artists: a very well-executed set of mostly Cuban-based, and often Cuban-composed, dance music, containing lyrics that often spoke of humorous situations, love, life in the city, or longing for the idealized homeland, alongside a small number of songs that contain some type of social message, many of them written by Curet Alonso.

Condiciones que existen (The Reigning Conditions)

Throughout this chapter, I have attempted to convey the movement of Salsa from the point of view of Latino class consciousness. In terms of the development of this Latino consciousness, El Barrio, and by extension the Latino communities of the South Bronx, experienced a set of living conditions that saw the barrio as a place of poverty, marginalization, and class struggle. At the same time, El Barrio/South Bronx can be viewed as an extension of the struggles of Latin America within the hegemonic dominance of the United States. In the case of El Barrio/South Bronx, it is productive to analyze the local identity based not only on a social construction of class, but also in relation to Latino "nationalism" and a sense of anti-system rebellion that developed from the shared conditions of poverty, disenfranchisement, and oppression as a "nation," or rather, the extension of particular nations via diasporic sensibilities (Padilla 1985). This sense of exclusion and resistance to the hegemony of the United States as formulated in New York can be analyzed as an extension of the resistance to the historical role of dominance exerted by the United States in Latin America. This issue is exemplified not only by the colonialist approach of the United States toward Puerto Rico but also by cases such as the "Banana Wars," including the 1912 occupation of Nicaragua, the 1916 occupation of the Dominican Republic, the series of United States-sponsored coups in 1954 in Guatemala, 1964 in Brazil, and 1973 in Chile; the embargo toward Cuba in 1962; the Panamanian Martyrs' Days riots of 1964; and the occupation of the Dominican Republic in 1965. The role of immigration, marginalization, and general social resistance then united the different nationalities under the flag of Latino ethnic consciousness, Latinidad. Aparicio (2004) elaborates on this with the following:

> The historical and colonial relations of power that have characterized U.S.-Latin American relationships need to be considered in understanding the role of expressive cultures among Latinos in the United States. They have been displaced by the historical and economic forces of colonialism, capitalism, industrialization, and, most recently, the globalized economy. This displacement is experienced not only physically and geographically, as in the case of Puerto Rican migration or Mexican and Central American immigration, but also psychologically and culturally, as in the case of native-born Latinos and Latinas. U.S. schools and other dominant social, educational, political, and cultural institutions undermine culturally different behavior and traditions in the name of assimilation and Americanization. Thus, young Latinos have been dispossessed, to varying degrees, of their cultural heritage, be it language, rituals, cultural memories, or other forms through which all people reaffirm their social and cultural selves. In this context, expressive cultures play multiple roles. The arts are not only entertainment, but also expressions through which U.S. Latinos, both as performers and as audience, can reconnect—either symbolically or through their bodies and senses—to their traditional cultures of origin, to their heritages and languages. Expressive cultures have offered Latinos in the United States a space for collective identification and self-recognition in the larger context of their invisibility within the dominant society. (355–356)

As such, the Latino communities of El Barrio and the South Bronx present a hybrid identity, that is, Latino and New Yorker (see Ashcroft et al. 2001; Bhabha 1990, 1994; Hall 2002; Rutherford 1998; Shohat 1992; Sinfield 1996; Zuckermann 2004). These communities are part of the multicultural milieu of New York and add to the ever-expanding cultural diversity of the city, but at the same time, they are a presence that socially can be considered an extension of Latin America, placing New York semiotically as the northernmost "Latin American city." Thus, El Barrio and the South Bronx denote both an inclusion of Latino culture in the United States as well as a resistance to the dominance of U.S. culture, despite Latin Americans' immersion in that culture in their daily lives. The people of El Barrio/South Bronx presented, at the same time, traits of New York, of various regions of Latin America, and of being Latino, that is, as immigrants. It is only natural, then, that the cultural products of this mix contain, as the affirmation of a Nuyolatino identity, all of these elements. With the second-generation immigrants, that is, New York-born Latinos, this hybrid identity becomes even clearer (Rumbaut and Ima 1988, after Thomas and Znaniecki 1958 [1918–1920]).

The civil unrest and transformations of the 1960s also marked El Barrio/South Bronx as a place where the postmodern concept of the "third space" of discourse (Bhabha 1994) became clear. It is in this "third space" where not only Puerto Rican and Latin American culture coexisted, but now where Nuyoricans, Nuyolatinos, African Americans, Black Latinos, a ghetto/oppression culture, and a metropolitan sense of identity became part of a new cultural identity that is geographically unbound, yet tied to Latino, Latin American nationalist, and New York qualities. This metropolitan sense of identity, which is often referred to as being a "native New Yorker," is also strongly determined by class struggles and social consciousness, which, in turn, serve as an important interpretive lens for understanding the resulting cultural products of this time and place.

Salsa, then, as the soundscape of the Latino communities of El Barrio and the South Bronx, soon became a music of resistance. Whereas the *mambo* of the 1940s and 1950s exemplified the commodification of places such as the Palladium, with its large bands and institutionally educated musicians, Salsa and its post-*mambo* antecedents were the polar opposite. The norm was street-educated musicians, smaller groups, and small clubs—often referred to as the *cuchifrito* circuit. This resistance is clearly reflected in Colón and Lavoe's earlier albums, where the covers depict toughness and grit in a mafia style. These artists wanted to shake off the image of Desi Arnaz singing "Babalú" in *I Love Lucy*; Tito Puente fully dressed in a shiny suit, leading a big band that conformed to the standards of high society; or the watered-down sound and image of Xavier Cugat playing at the Waldorf Astoria. This music was not for a high society that wanted shirt ruffles on their arms; this was the music for and from the people of the toughest barrios, that is, El Pueblo.

Musically speaking, this early Salsa period, especially as expressed in the Colón/Lavoe collaboration, is fairly rough. Although, to many, this roughness might be considered a deficiency due to the lack of training of the musicians, it represents the attitude of Salsa vis-à-vis what might be construed as the music of the bourgeoisie (Aparicio and White in Rondón 2008). I argue that this roughness is ultimately one of the primary factors that appealed to the working-class Nuyolatinos, and which marks, as Santos Febres (1997) also asserts, the development of the performance of *Pueblo*, a people-based performance. This performance of *Pueblo* is grounded in an idea of class-consciousness, as it exemplifies the marginalization and disenfranchisement of Latinos in the United States. This is in line with Frith (1996, 109), who believes that the music not only reflects the people, but it constructs the experience. In this case, not only did the grittiness of Salsa reflect the living situations of Latino communities in the city, but at the same time, this rough image also exalted the virtues of the toughness and resilience of Latinos in a "don't mess with us" statement.

Rather than creating music as an endeavor for pure entertainment, Colón and Lavoe, and many other Salsa musicians of the same period, used music as a necessary means to reflect and help ease the hardship of the barrios of New York and Latin America, thus making Salsa a clear vehicle for delivering true Pueblo credibility to the working classes. In this manner, Salsa picked up the already-popular musical elements of the Cuban sound, added a number of Puerto Rican-based elements, filtered them through a

New York sensibility that included Black Power and urban toughness, and included a large dose of "street" in the mix.

The music presents, in a very clear manner, a level of attitude that gives the musicians this type of urban credibility, which, coupled with vinyl record distribution and the dance appeal of this music, is ultimately one of the biggest factors that account for the success of Salsa in Latin America. Whereas the living conditions of the Nuyolatino working class were replicated in the barrios of Latin America, the music, by extension, though perhaps unknowingly at first, identified the Latin American barrio people as part of the intrinsically "street" background of Salsa.

Salsa's success, both musically and in terms of Latin American/Latino ethnic identity, fits within the sociological precept that the Latino ethnic identity develops from the cultural and structural similarities of two or more Spanish-speaking groups and often in response to common experiences of social inequality. In the case of Padilla (1985), however, this concept is based on the idea of migration and the connection of two nationalities in the United States. In the case of Salsa, the music produced in the Latino ghettos of New York speaks to the same sensibilities found in the ghettos of Latin America. Thus, the idea of class consciousness, whether expressed in the lyrical content of Salsa or in the grittiness of the music, develops through identities that respond to the same division of labor market and economic power structures, fueled primarily by social and economic conditions, into the haves and the have-nots, in both Latin America and the United States.

Sociologically speaking, Salsa consciente is an expression of conditions, such as poverty and racial discrimination, common to both Latin Americans and Latinos. These associations, which have the capacity to assert identity beyond nationalistic ideals, coupled with the large distribution networks of Fania and the obvious appeal of a dance-oriented music, had begun to drive a very strong following for Salsa in Latin America, especially in the circum-Caribbean, as this is the main source of musical inspiration for the music, thus laying the groundwork for the soon-to-come social consciousness of Salsa. Whereas the Nuyolatino population was almost entirely marginalized and quickly identified with Salsa based on the common language and experiences of marginalization, Latin America's identification with Salsa initially happened specifically within the working classes. This fact is intrinsically related to the grittiness of the music and Salsa's discussion of issues of class and race/ethnicity. Although these markers of marginalization and "street" credibility resonated profoundly within this segment of the population, Salsa's popularity did not initially appeal to the dominant, often White, and more educated upper classes of Latin America. This segment of the population preferred rock and pop music (Rondón 2008). It is only with the appearance of highly-educated musicians such as Blades and his brand of "intellectual" Salsa that the lower-class identification began to be shaken from Salsa, and the music quickly gained validity across all sectors of society.

Literizing Salsa: The Compositions of Catalino "Tite" Curet Alonso and Rubén Blades

Can we make our lyrics speak of what I call first dimensional reality for our people? Can our lyrics make sense? We are not asking for leftist lyrics; we are not asking for people to become Marxist-Leninists. We are only saying to our composers and to our arrangers and to our lyricists: "our sons and daughters are listening to this music; can we say something about the kind of life that they are leading. About what the options or the lack of options are. Can you do that?"

—Felipe Luciano from *Salsa: Latin Pop Music in the Cities* (1979 DVD)

The rise of Salsa and the development of Latino social consciousness in the early 1970s was fueled in part by the social revolutions of the 1960s and the general situations of Latinos and Latin Americans, and reflected their increasing awareness of class consciousness. At this time, however, many Salsa musicians were still approaching the music as a mainly Cuban-centered endeavor, either by holding on to the true and tried musical structures of *son, mambo,* and *guaracha,* or by literally performing music of 1950s Cuban composers (e.g., Johnny Pacheco and Celia Cruz). Developing social movements made it imperative for the music to be original and express political concerns.

Following suit, musicians such as Eddie Palmieri, Pete El Conde Rodriguez, and Ray Barretto composed and/or performed socially engaged music, expressing the contemporary Latino realities. The approach of these musicians was however, largely grounded upon the idea of Salsa as a medium of a primarily orally based Latino/Latin American culture, dependent on the lead singer's ability to "compose in performance." Parallel to this, by the turn of the 1960s, written forms of Spanish were only beginning to reflect Latinidad as a conscious pathos, and to enrich the language of the colonizer, that is, formal Castilian Spanish, with the linguistic variations of Latin America. Understanding language as one of the main symbols and transmitters of Latino/Latin American culture, I argue that Salsa initially employed a performance-centered and orally transmitted literary form of a Latino-centered/Caribbean Spanish, present not in writing but in song and "street" (i.e., illiterate, inelegant, nonstandard, slangy) speech.

This concept explains why Salsa was centered around performing artists distinguished by their "street credibility" as carriers of the "true Latino language," rather than the literate intellectuals representing a formal writing tradition associated with Spain. The perfect example of an orally based and "street" centered performer is Héctor Lavoe, the Salsa street hero and master improviser of pregones, who to this day remains arguably the most popular and charismatic Salsa singer and performer, and the performer against whom every other Salsa singer is judged. In fact, Lavoe, as a carrier of the oral tradition, predominantly sang music that he had not composed, yet the songs are to this day still associated with his name. Expanding the framework of language and the association of the performer with a song, rather than the composer of the song, the obscurity of such a remarkable composer as C. Curet Alonso, who wrote many of the Salsa hits of the 1970s including Lavoe's, becomes clear, for in such a context of oracy the role of a literate Salsa composer is overshadowed by that of the performer.

Although popular and entertaining, Salsa's message up to this point had mainly revolved around escapism rather than a discussion of issues. But Latino urban folklore, as an expression of the Latino social context, increasingly required composers to develop a more cohesive discourse of current realities. The emergence of, first, Catalino "Tite" Curet Alonso, and later, Rubén Blades as the two most important composers, intellectuals, and theorists of Salsa propelled a critical evolution, from Salsa as a mainly Latino oral art form to Salsa consciente as a Latino literary form. In this sense, and understanding Salsa as popular culture, Salsa consciente fulfills the role that print did in the spread of nationalism, first by standardizing a "Latino language," and second by spreading the concept of a Latino/Latin

American nation "united by class" where vinyl records, as opposed
served as the newly formed sung literature of El Pueblo.

This idea stems from the fact that the arrival of Latinos in New York in
large numbers coincided with the postwar insurrection and general revolutionary feeling of the 1960s and the rise of massive culture distribution
via radio broadcast and long-playing records sold at an affordable price.
Furthermore, the convergence of cultural context and content with tech-
nical form gave birth not only to the Salsa industry but also to the political
tendency that I have called *consciente*. Salsa then, as a cultural product of
the age of mechanical reproduction, became not the literary but the aural
motor of the development of the "Latino nation" as it quickly turned into a
new form of easily distributed social text of Latino nationalism. (TRANSNATION?)

This phenomenon can be linked to the formation of class consciousness as a Latino/Latin American endeavor, where the concepts of the meta-barrio and the Latino meta-homeland, created by an association through
Salsa as the transnational medium of Latinidad, play an intrinsic role. It is
in these symbolically laden spaces that Salsa's newly standardized Latino
language described and, in the meta-barrio of the urban folkloric imagination, eventually shaped the views Latin Americans have of their own communities in terms of what were originally Nuyolatino realities. As opposed
to the nationalistically centered understandings of Salsa, the concept of the
Latino/Latin American meta-barrio became a symbolic space where Salsa
functions as a transnational mediator of a non-nationalistic Latino ethnic
consciousness. DOES THY D THE YORK?

In Salsa's evolution from oral to literate, "Salsa with a message" became NEED
a Latin American endeavor where Caribbean Spanish became the main —?
linguistic medium of Latinidad. In this sense the standardization of a / ?
Latino language via Salsa is a framework that aids in explaining the role of
Puerto Rico as a representative of Latinidad. Given that Salsa was to a large
degree created by the Puerto Rican population of New York absorbing and
reimagining Cuban music without losing its Puerto Ricanness, the standardization of the language of Salsa consequently followed from a Puerto
Rican/Nuyorican perspective. The recording industry's distribution systems of Salsa in Latin America transmitted the descriptions and linguistic

— PROBLEM of NATIONAL / TRANSNATIONAL
— GOMEZ'S CRITIQUE OF NORTON...

developments of the situational realities of Puerto Ricans in New York, and these were eventually reflected and appropriated as Latin America was experiencing a similar set of social situations.

As Salsa began moving away from a performance-centered music, the now standardized language was not equated exclusively with the performer, but became more dependent on the composer as the creator of such language. Thus the second part of this book focuses on the composition and the lyrical outputs of Salsa as the new basis upon which Salsa consciente develops a cohesive discourse. Analyzing the production of both Catalino "Tite" Curet Alonso, as the most important composer of Salsa, and Rubén Blades, not as a performer but as a composer, becomes a critical endeavor to help develop a more thorough understanding of Salsa consciente.

In a Gramscian reading of the role of the composer as the intellectual of Salsa, the roles of Curet Alonso and Blades can be understood as those of intellectuals born from the people and articulating the feelings, concerns, and experiences of El Pueblo. As such, Curet Alonso and Blades as the intellectuals and theorists behind Salsa consciente function as agents against the status quo of the cultural hegemonic precepts of either Spain or the United States. Salsa consciente develops the idea of sung literature as a means of educating and telling the "other history," that of racism, negritude, classism, and Native genocide, coupled with the everyday class-based realities of El Pueblo as a crucial agent in the development of Latino/Latin American consciousness.

I present here an alternative narrative to the tacitly acknowledged role of Salsa performers as exclusive carriers of the lyrical tradition. By exploring this alternate account, I argue that Salsa's language and stylistic approaches have experienced an enormous degree of expansion and innovation through the work of composers operating despite their obscurity vis-à-vis Salsa performers as the stage stars. This methodology, specifically in the case of Curet Alonso as the "obscure" and underpaid composer who wrote many, if not most, of the greatest hits of Salsa, challenges the perceived linear history of Salsa performers as the main informants and developers of Salsa's poetico-stylistic traditions upon which the younger generations of *salseros* base their own knowledge. This, for example, is the case with Cheo Feliciano, who developed a large part of his illustrious career based on Curet Alonso's music, yet most of the poetic advances are still popularly credited to Feliciano as the singer, not Curet Alonso as the one who actually developed the themes and wrote the words. It is necessary to mention that, although outside of the scope of this book, this alternative narrative could be expanded upon to include the work of Salsa arrangers as the unrecognized developers of the aesthetic aspects of Salsa.

In the following chapters I develop case studies based on Curet Alonso's compositions and those of Rubén Blades. Curet Alonso's appearance is chronologically earlier than that of Rubén Blades, but is a critical transitional step in the evolution of Salsa consciente, whereas Blades represents, in a Hegelian sense, a further development of the dialectic.

Much of the output of both composers is related to the lyrics. Curet Alonso worked as a journalist for much of his adult life, and Blades is, aside from a Salsa singer and composer, a lawyer. The working concepts of these composers are thus rooted more, at least initially, in written rather than in musical markers, and while this is not to say that the music has taken a side role, the verbally oriented analyses contained in the following pages are designed to reflect this heritage.

The Works of Catalino "Tite" Curet Alonso

Para mi el guaguancó es una alborada
Es la tristeza que me hace sonreir cada mañana
Es lo que llega desde el barrio al alma adentro
—From "Este es el Guaguancó" by Tite
Curet Alonso, sung by Cheo Feliciano

Despite the large impact of popular music in and from Puerto Rico, the phenomenon has until recently been largely ignored and considered "low culture." This is clearly exemplified by the 1990 documentary *Cocolos y Rockeros*, which explores the musical tastes of late 1980s Puerto Rican youths, and places Salsa as the music of the working class versus the Europhilic- and U.S.-centered taste for rock music. Duany (1984, 199) pointed out that "Salsa music . . . is deeply rooted in Puerto Rico's popular sectors, despite the recent disco and rock fever and the proverbial upper-class disdain for 'native' music." Against this popular and provincial categorization, the works of Catalino "Tite" Curet Alonso had a cosmopolitan impact on Latino and Latin American music, especially Salsa. This chapter can only serve as a mere approximation to the work of Curet Alonso, as the sheer magnitude of his musical output makes it impossible for me to pay proper tribute to the composer within the scope of this book.

Examining Curet Alonso's work and the relationship of his efforts to the conceptualizations of Salsa consciente and Latinidad, I consider him to be the most important Salsa composer of all time. His role in the development of and his impact on the music is enormous. Even though some Latino musicians might not recognize his name, they know his songs, many by heart. Not only is this fact related to the lack of cultural consciousness in a sector of the Latino community, but at the same time Curet Alonso's relative obscurity is strongly related to a matter of class. His catalog of compositions contains over two thousand songs, and to this day, only part of it has been performed. On the Fania Records website, Aurora Flores notes that "Curet's name was ubiquitous, gracing hundreds of album credits by many of the top Latin music artists of the '60s, '70s, '80s and '90s. He penned more than 2,000 songs . . . He was the most sought-after composer in tropical music—Curet's songs were guaranteed hits, revered as classics today." Journalist Jaime Torres Torres added, in a Globovision television special, that "Tite Curet Alonso is the father of Salsa."[1] The list of people that have performed his music reads like a list of Puerto Rico and New York-based Salsa stars: Héctor Lavoe, Rubén Blades, Ray Barretto, Cheo Feliciano, Celia Cruz, Ismael Rivera, Roberto Roena, La Lupe, Pete "El Conde" Rodriguez, Spanish Harlem Orchestra, Fania All Stars, Rafael Cortijo, etc. He literally made the career of several artists by providing them with enormously popular hits. His figure thus looms ever present over the world of Salsa and even begs the question: would Salsa as it is known today even exist without him?

There is, however, in the case of Curet Alonso a dialectical relationship between composer and performer. Curet Alonso has, despite his incredibly numerous and significant contributions to Salsa, remained a relatively obscure figure when compared to the level of stardom the performers of his music have received. His obscurity is possibly related to the fact that he remained in Puerto Rico most of his life and did not physically participate in the New York Salsa scene. Additionally, his social perspective of African pride and class consciousness may have played a role, as it was not one that the record industry, reaping massive profits from his creativity without acknowledging him monetarily, wanted to showcase. Thirdly, there is the fact that Salsa is traditionally "composed-in-performance," thus showcasing the stage star, as opposed to the composer, as the owner of the song. These

WHY OBSCURE?

theories are a heuristic exercise rather than providing a complete answer to the question of his obscurity, yet this is certainly a recurring issue in Curet Alonso's participation in the Salsa movement.

Besides an analysis of Curet Alonso's music, throughout the chapter there are two recurring leitmotifs. The first one plays on the idea of the already mentioned dialectic relationship between performer as the new owner of the song, and composer as creator of the song. I address this issue throughout the chapter by discussing possible additions the singers might have developed in performance and added to Curet Alonso's original compositions, and I also explore the issue by including lyrical analyses of remakes of selected Curet Alonso songs by contemporary artists. As such, I showcase the flexibility of performance and the alternative readings some artists can be seen to have developed on the basis of the original compositions.

The second leitmotif is tied to the idea of poetic indirection, a device often utilized by Curet Alonso to elevate the main concept of the song from what would generally be considered a negative to a positive. In this manner, Curet Alonso's work addresses issues that are often discussed as adverse—social issues, racism, disenfranchisement, poverty, etc.—in such a way that these topics are raised to a position where their qualities are presented in a hopeful rather than adverse manner. As such, this concept helps us understand Curet as a poet of The People who developed his lyrical forms based not only on sonority, versatility, and finesse, but also on a socially aware poetry that aimed to lift up his people.

As I have suggested, the importance of Curet Alonso's work not only to Salsa in general but specifically within Salsa consciente is something that cannot be overestimated. Curet Alonso began participating very early in the New York-based Salsa boom. Even at that stage he helped in developing the consciousness of the *salseros* by including lyrical references that dealt with themes that were not included in the usual trend of escapism and sentiments such as "come on baby let's dance" that were and still are so prevalent in popular Latino music. On the Fania Records website, Aurora Flores's review of Curet Alonso's compilation CD entitled *Alma de Poeta* indicates that "Curet helped father the nascent Salsa movement that was marking time in clave through the streets of Puerto Rico and Latin New

York. His words inspired hope and faith, solace and joy during a time of social upheaval . . . He reflected the face of a community that was in dire need of answers." Regarding Curet Alonso's social conscience/consciousness, Rubén Blades points out that

> He [Curet Alonso] was a conscious person and that consciousness was manifested in many ways . . . Tite saw things clearly and because of that he expressed them: The Puerto Rican sensibility, condemning racism, the need for an expression of a much more fair reality than the one we are living in . . . that was always very present in his music without Tite being a political ideologist, he was not an ideologist. (In Coss 2011 DVD)

Blades (in Shaw 2013, 191) to a certain extent actually credits Curet Alonso as being the original architect of the music when in response to the question "Is it true that you and Willie [Colón] in Siembra were the first to bring social consciousness to lyrics in Salsa?" he states the following:

> No. Before that was "Pablo Pueblo," and Tite Catalino (Curet Alonso), Puerto Rican, was a very important man. He sent me some songs and one was called "Plantación Adentro." It talked about what I consider to be an indigenous guy who was beaten to death by an overseer. I think the Willie Colón/Rubén Blades Album *Metiendo Mano*, as far as the Fania boom was considered, was the first one that made an emphasis with "Pablo Pueblo" and "Plantación Adentro" by Tite.

The historical context upon which Curet Alonso began to develop his discourse was that of the civil rights movements, Pan-Africanism, and Black Power, on the heels of the great Puerto Rican migration to New York, and of Latin American revolutions and dictatorships. Thus his music reflects his views of the world as a place where social justice, awareness of social issues, and consciousness are necessary. In the aforementioned Fania website CD review, Flores (n.d.) points out that "[a] seasoned man in a time of resistance to societal norms, Curet later witnessed the worldwide rage against Vietnam and the tsunami of civil and social change heralded by the

'60s and '70s. This intense, historical climate shaped Curet's life and work." At the same time, Salazar (2007, 32) speaks of the social climate where Curet Alonso began to develop his work:

> During the decade of the 1960s, when Curet Alonso initiated his musical discourse, the intellectual and artistic participants of the Nationalist Thirties Generation and the Populist Generation of the Forties had to face the Materialist Fifties Generation. In that ideological and cultural scenario the prevailing enormous reality of the social decomposition that resulted from the political and economic struggle that attempted to crystalize an exogenous hegemony to the Puerto Rican national reality became completely evident.

Salsa scholar Quintero Rivera (in Coss 2011 DVD) adds to this view of the times, stating that

> something being lived very dramatically in those times is the moment of struggle in favor of civil rights in the United States, the student struggles on a world level, in Paris, in San Francisco, in Mexico. It is a moment where many things are being questioned, many ideas that until that moment were deemed immovable. There are important political movements at the level that [for example] Allende wins in Chile; there are guerrillas in many places of Latin America that were inspired by the Cuban example. So much of Tite Curet's song reflects that entire social world which is in a boiling state, in a challenging state. Now, something special that this expression has, in the case of Tite Curet, is that that is not seen as something different from everyday life, but many times reflects through the closest moments that are found in daily life.

Academic analysis of the musical and poetical breadth of Curet Alonso's work and its impact on Salsa, as well as its impact on Puerto Ricans and Latinos, is something that is lacking, especially from scholars writing in English. His name is often mentioned, but his endeavors as connected to the times rarely receive sufficient attention. Subsequently, arguably the best and perhaps only book thus far to deal with Curet Alonso's work is Norma Salazar's 2007 *Tite Curet Alonso: Lírica y canción,* where aside from a methodical poetic and historical analysis of many of Curet Alonso's songs and poems, Salazar introduces a thematic classification system for Curet Alonso's music, which helps enormously in navigating his impressive musical legacy. Salazar divided Curet Alonso's musical themes into the following categories:

- Indigenous
- Patriotic
- Social
- Romantic
- Blackness (negritude) in festive Salsa
- *Jíbaro*[2]
- Santería
- Movies
- Curet and the children
- Religious anthems in *bomba* rhythm
- Political
- Sport

I have used this system to help build my classification of subjects to aid analysis of Curet Alonso's music within the Salsa consciente model. I do not find it necessary to delve into all of the themes analyzed by Salazar, such as romance, sports, or Santería, as these do not really aid the expression of ideas of Latino ethnic consciousness that I am concerned with here. Salazar's system, however, does identify a series of subjects that are crucial for a thorough understanding of Latino consciousness in Curet Alonso's discourse. Therefore, in building upon Salazar's system, I have divided the selected songs into categories that function mainly as guidelines to understand his work in an abstract manner. In this sense, these categorizations are not closed classifications of Curet Alonso's work or Salsa consciente as these topics often overlap. The categories are as follows:

- African identity
- Social Issues
- Indigenous identity
- Latino identity[3]

Curet Alonso did not exploit the route of Latino identity to the extent that Blades ended up doing. His work, however, does reverberate clearly with concerns for social justice and Latinidad, albeit in a different manner than Blades. Being a proud Puerto Rican, Curet Alonso's points of reference came mainly from his homeland, and since his work was primarily interpreted by Puerto Ricans and New York-based Puerto Ricans, the references quickly connected with this segment of the Latino population. Eventually, with Salsa becoming a Latino and Latin American phenomenon, Curet Alonso's lyrics began to literally and figuratively resonate beyond Puerto Rico and its sister population of El Barrio.

It is unclear whether or not Curet Alonso intentionally aimed at exploring and exploiting the commonalities of Latinos the way Blades did, but it is clear that he was aware of the situations affecting Latinos in New York, as he actively participated in the New York Fania-based Salsa boom of the 1970s. Tied to Curet's awareness of Latino and Latin American social issues, Curet and Blades maintained a good relationship for many years and discussed these topics, with Curet Alonso (cited in Waxer 2002b, 199) indicating that "Salsa music and its many followers have come to accept the singer Rubén Blades without limits. Salsa with a social message has produced a string of hits, and also smoothed out the genre a little, making young people think about the issues of the moment, of the everyday path."

Curet Alonso's work, although based in Puerto Rico, demonstrates the idea of utilizing Puerto Rico as a totem of Latinidad. The Puerto Rican aspect of Curet Alonso's work shines through, especially when interpreted by icons of the Island such as Héctor Lavoe and Ismael "Maelo" Rivera. The totemic phenomenon can be seen clearly in many of the lyrics to Curet Alonso's music even where there is no specific mention of Puerto Rico, as the commonalities and quotidian aspects of the situations and characters included easily expand and apply to the rest of Latin America and the Latino population of New York. This is not to say that Curet Alonso did not explore specific Puerto Rican subjects; on the contrary, he specifically explored and proudly displayed Puerto Ricanness in many songs, as the Venezuelan singer Trina Medina (cited in Coss 2011 DVD) elaborates:

> Tite Curet's songs are successful and stay in the memory of the people because they speak of their own stories. I mean, there are poor people and spiteful women all over the world. John Laborers[4] are everywhere or there would be no houses. So, when people hear one of these songs . . . that touches your fiber, you begin to feel "Hey, that is not the life of La Tirana;[5] that is the life of Trina Medina." Mister John Laborer when [he says] "it's true look at all the houses I built" and walks around there and maybe goes in and says to his son with that pride: "You know, this shopping mall, I laid the bricks there." That is why, because if it gets to your soul and you identify with it, of course you make it yours. So Tite's songs stopped being his when people appropriated them saying: "this is my story, my own."

All of the aforementioned topics are often presented in Curet Alonso's work; however, and despite Spanish heritage being a basic component in the ethnic makeup of any Latino/Latin American, in Curet Alonso's musical exploration of the Latino identity, the African component takes a leading role. He was a proud Black man and was not afraid to show it. Curet's denunciations of racism though are not as prevalent as they are in the work of Blades, but Curet Alonso takes pride in his negritude and celebrates being Black. As a counterpoint, the exploration of the Indigenous component, as part of the ethnic makeup of any Latino/Latin American, is less prominent in Blades's work than it is in Curet Alonso's. Interestingly enough, one of Rubén Blades's few dealings with the Indigenous side of Latinos/Latin Americans came from one of his earlier recordings (Willie Colon Presents Rubén Blades *Metiendo Mano*, Fania Records 1977) where he interpreted Curet Alonso's song "Plantación Adentro," a song (analyzed later) that deals with Indigenous slavery and abuse in colonial Latin America. As we shall see, the combination of the Indigenous and African components of being Latino/Latin American shows Curet Alonso to be a very informed man with a deep interest in understanding and embracing the identity of Latinos/ Latin Americans as a mixed ethnic group.

The other component to Curet Alonso's readings of Latinidad stems initially from a mostly Puerto Rican perspective, although, it shows a remarkable level of sociological awareness as it not only includes ethnicity and race among its main factors but also speaks of social class. Tying the idea of social issues to Salsa, I argue in what follows that a majority of these issues stem from what can be termed an urban perception of society and, in the case of Salsa, from an urban Latino perception. It is no coincidence that Cesar Rondón's now famous work *The Book of Salsa* (1980/2008) is subtitled a "Chronicle of the Music of the Urban Caribbean." There is a clear understanding in the title that Salsa is primarily an urban phenomenon, and it is from this context that the concern with social issues emerges. Much of what Salsa consciente chronicles stems largely from a set of social issues derived from the shared experiences of poverty, oppression, politics/political unrest, and discrimination. Blades himself often referred to his music as *Folklore de ciudad Latina* or Latin American Urban Folklore (*Focila*).[6] Thus it is this idea of discussing the social urban quotidian, present in both Curet Alonso's and Blades's work, that categorizes the marker of Pueblo identity (to use Santos Febres's term [1997]) and that stands as one of the main issues within Salsa consciente.

Regarding the urban positioning of Latinos and Latin Americans, the migration of rural Puerto Ricans first into the capital of San Juan and the later migration of Puerto Ricans into New York following World War II is a great example of the contemporary urban Latino. At the same time, within Latin America there was a shift in the social landscape when the rural populations migrated to the cities in search of work. Quintero Rivera (in Coss 2011 DVD) remarks on the urban parallel between the move from the rural communities in Puerto Rico to the San Juan suburban neighborhood of Santurce and notes the same type of migration that developed in Latin America, as well as eventually the Latin American migration into New York City spearheaded by the postwar generation of Puerto Ricans:

Santurce then becomes that melting pot of a populous world that has had to leave its rural surroundings to form a new urban life, and in that sense Santurce exemplifies that urban migration that will later represent the Puerto Rican Migration to New York, or the migration of so many other rural places to the capitals of Latin America. In that sense what Tite says about Santurce is understood by the people of Cali that have migrated from areas like Chocó or the people of so many countries, or the people that have come to New York from so many countries.

Rapid urbanization accounts for many of the social issues now present in some of the great urban Latino/Latin American enclaves, be it El Barrio in New York City, or the barrios of Cali, Bogotá, San Juan, Lima, or Caracas, for example. It is in this urban factor that Blades's and Curet Alonso's works cross paths significantly, as both aimed to chronicle the social happenings experienced in these urban centers. In the case of Blades, he created a fictional meta-barrio that included the characters, places, and smells of "any town Latin America," and certainly included El Barrio in New York within that concept. Similarly, Curet Alonso often did not specify the location of an urban center, but whereas Blades's discourse became intrinsically Pan-Latino and highly political, Curet Alonso remained distanced from heavy political involvement and continued to pursue nationalistic (i.e., Puerto Rican) discourses while at the same time exploring issues regarding social justice that pertained specifically to El Pueblo, and The People in a larger context. As such, he demonstrated an understanding that pertained not only to specific places but to a trans-local approach to the everyday problems of the people. Salazar (2007, 18-19) explains that

> As an underlying and constant line in his compositions and in his poetry, his hyper sensibility can be seen when faced with the social, political and economic events lived daily by "his people." And "his people" was understood in a larger sense: his Puerto Rican People wherever they were, his Latin American people, his world people, wherever the ones hurting, oppressed and suffering were.

My analysis of the songs of Curet Alonso follows the thematic development of his work. This is in contrast to my focus on the development
of Blades's work over time, as he was almost always the lead singer and
composer of his pieces, and thus a chronological approach proved fruitful
in determining issues such as concept albums, with specific issues laid out
in a whole release. In the case of Curet Alonso, the same methodology is
less fruitful as his music was performed by myriad artists, including Blades
himself, in records that also often included compositions by other artists.
Therefore, I approach Curet Alonso's work from a thematic point of view
and group the songs by the aforementioned categories.

Within the following analysis I present lyrics and *pregones* (lead singer
ad-libs in the call-and-response sections) as performed in the original
recording of the songs. When they are available, I compare these performances with revisited versions of the same songs. Some of these were presented in the 2011 Banco Popular-produced DVD *¡sonó sonó . . . TITE CURET!*,
which was released as a posthumous homage to Curet Alonso's oeuvre. The
DVD features rearranged, and at times partially re-lyricized, performances
of Curet Alonso's works by several artists other than those that were in the
original recording of the songs.

Africanizing Latinidad, Africanizing Salsa: The Africanist
Approach of Curet Alonso

Within Curet Alonso's discourse, the idea of being a Black man and African
are two paradigms of the utmost importance. Rondón (2008, 198) actually
begins his description of Curet Alonso by indicating that "Catalino Curet
Alonso, 'El Tite,' was a very Black Puerto Rican." Curet Alonso was not only
Black but he was proud of it. It is no coincidence that his writing, having begun in the 1960s, reflects to a great extent the concerns of the civil
rights movement, African political independence, and the growing general
Pan-African consciousness of the time. Dr. Juan Otero Garabís (in Coss 2011
DVD) characterizes the feeling upon which Curet Alonso began to develop
the racial concepts of his music:

During the '50s, part of this rebirth of the identity and African pride has a lot to do with the visibility reached by the people of the Black communities in sports and music. In the times of Cortijo[7] as a central figure in television and his combo and his bunch[8] of Blacks and mulattos, and also in the years in which Black Puerto Ricans enter the big [baseball] leagues, and figures like Victor Pellot [Vic Power], Orlando Peruchín Cepeda, Roberto Clemente become figures loved by everybody. So, to that visibility of the pride of being Black, Tite gives a voice to that image in a very particular way because he links it with a very poetic, lyrical quality.

Curet Alonso, once again, reflects and exalts rather than straight-out denouncing racism or racial injustice. His approach is one of pride and equality. In his lyrics, the internal Puerto Rican racism inherited from years of colonialism is indirectly contested by elevating the qualities of his African heritage. Curet Alonso (in Fritz 2002 DVD) remarked that

> Right now in Puerto Rico there is a wave of putting the things of the Black race at the level that they should be, and it is a race that has given so much in music, in literature that it is not taken to its proper level. So, I belong to that kind of informal social club, and I join them in many things because I think there are too many injustices against the Black race; I do not understand because it is a race like any other. If you make a cut in the arm of a White man or a Black man, the blood that flows is the same.

LAS CARAS LINDAS

This song is one of Curet Alonso's biggest hits. Written specifically for the Puerto Rican singer Ismael "Maelo" Rivera, Curet Alonso penned the composition purposely for Rivera's delivery. Curet Alonso (in Fritz 2002 DVD) declared that "so when I met with Ismael Rivera upon my return to Santurce, I told him: 'Look I have this for you.' He went half-crazy because he was looking for something, and since Ismael is very dramatic when he sings, well, it fit him perfectly." Regarding the original composition, Curet Alonso (in Fritz 2002 DVD) recalls that "In the town of Loíza were the Black women with the most beautiful faces in Puerto Rico, those were in Loíza Aldea, I wrote the song there." The town of Loíza is historically one of the largest enclaves of African heritage in Puerto Rico, as Alegría (1956, 124) confirms when he states that "By the middle of the seventeenth century, the concentration of Negro slaves in the sugar plantations was so great that Loíza ranked at the top of the island in percentage of Negro population." Flores (2001) indicates that Curet Alonso's inspiration probably stems from his observation of the negative attitude Afro-Latinos have created about themselves, as well as the state of mind created as a result of centuries of enslavement and colonialism. Indeed, Curet Alonso himself (in Flores 2001, 5) speaks of this nonacceptance of one's own African heritage as one of the main themes of the song:

> Black people still carry along sorrow with them from the era of colonialism, "invisible chains." I look at these faces of dark-skinned people and they're all so different from one another. There is a certain beauty in them, in the attitude they carry through life. That is what I was thinking, the lovely faces of my Black people.

"Las Caras Lindas" is a song that speaks directly to notions of African pride, while it is one that also aims at dismantling internal racism by humanizing its representation of Blackness. The song became a major hit, and is today an anthem of Afro-Latino pride. Carlos Flores presents a potential parallel between Curet Alonso's song and James Brown's own anthem "Say It Loud, I Am Black and I Am Proud" (King Records, K1015, 1969). Flores (2001, 4) further indicated that

> [Brown's song] had a personal impact on millions of African Americans, particularly during a crucial point in the history of the civil rights movement in the United States. The voice provided a voice of self-acceptance, pride, hope, and dignity to those individuals who for centuries felt excluded and disenfranchised from the rest of the American society. This song fueled and celebrated a new identity for Black Americans, which included a new greeting toward one another (brothers and sisters) . . . I

believe that the James Brown tune had a profound impact on many more people because of its timeliness with the civil rights movement. *Las Caras Lindas* caught the attention of many and has become significant because it raises awareness about the beauty of Afro-Latinos. For so long Afro-Latinos continued to be bombarded by Eurocentric images that became the standard of beauty communicated by print and other media within their societies.

Peruvian singer Susana Baca famously covered the song in the style of the Afro-Peruvian *Landó*, and remarked (in Flores 2001) that "the words of this song pertained to all Black people throughout the Americas."

In connecting the idea of Susana Baca's version of the song in an Afro-Peruvian style, it should be noted that while *Las Caras Lindas* could easily lend itself to developing a musical aesthetic constructed on *bomba sicá*, as a signifier of Puerto Rican Black pride, and specifically centered on the fact that the song as introduced by Curet Alonso was based on the town of Loíza, the cradle of *bomba*, and on Ismael Rivera's past as a *bomba* singer, the song develops exclusively, albeit creatively, over the Cuban *son* structure. This can be explained by the fact that the musical arranger and musical director of Ismael Rivera's band at the point of this recording was the Cuban-born pianist Javier Vazquez.

This song also presents another example of the relationship between composer, song, and performer. The song has been associated with the figure of Ismael "Maelo" Rivera, as it was Rivera's presence and interpretation in general that pushed this track into stardom. While the lyrics were of the utmost importance, Rivera's presence as a proud Black male in Puerto Rican society delivering such poignant lyrics was an inspiration. Not only his presence, but Rivera's masterful performance style is so unique that it presents a challenge for anyone trying to reinterpret this song. Regarding Rivera's unique phrasing, Rondón (2008, 210–211) indicated that

Ismael brashly elided the traditional structure of the four lines and instead improvised numerous phrases and melodies between the refrains. These four lines were one of the most profound legacies of the Cuban son.

Traditionally, once the montuno arrived, the singer would limit himself to inspiring phrases that complemented the idea exposed in the son. Thus, between one refrain and the next, there was a free space of about four measures that could be filled with the inspired riffs of the improviser. Generally, they used four verses or phrases that corresponded to each of the four measures . . . Ismael not only committed himself to inventing melodies over the montuno, but he also was irreverent enough to break with the particular demands of each song. He would reduce to two lines all of the measures intended for him, or he would extend them to eight or ten verses that he would spew out, breathlessly, like a machine gun. For these reasons, in his early years, Ismael was ignored, often purposefully, by the experts and the musically orthodox. To them, Ismael sung so many things that he ended up saying nothing, and he played with so many melodic possibilities that, to them, the result sounded jumbled. It did not take Rivera long, however, to demonstrate the validity of his style. Just as [Benny] Moré's innovations both shaped and represented the characteristic spirit of the son in the 1950s, so Ismael's improvisational style represented the texture of Salsa that would take over the region from the 1960s on. From this perspective, Salsa improvisation cannot define itself without acknowledging its relation to Ismael, since it was he who gave it a face and anticipated its greatest possibilities.

The effectiveness of the verse of the song is achieved by developing a form of poetic indirection as a means of showcasing the main concept of the song of being Black, which here is elevated to a position where the qualities described are presented in a positive rather than a negative light. In this case, Curet Alonso tackles the almost endemic internal racism of Latin America and develops the idea of African pride by singing about the "beautiful faces of my Black people." In the construction of "my people" it can be seen that Curet Alonso as the composer, and by extension Ismael Rivera as the medium of delivery recognize themselves as being one of the people and, thus, with El Pueblo. They therefore also tie every listener into a concept beyond color where they are also seen to be part of "my" people and part of Latino African heritage.

The descriptions used by Curet Alonso speak to the idea of the faces being characterized by weeping, suffering, and pain, while still carrying much love. In this way, Curet Alonso humanizes the subjects of his song beyond being signified merely by their color. Through Ismael Rivera's delivery, the listener is emotionally engaged and invited to help in the dismantling of internally acquired racist preconceptions associating beauty with Whiteness only. Instead the song invokes the beauty of Blackness through its details, which counter forms of racial denial of Latinos inherited from the colonialist bombardment of Eurocentric images emphasizing the beauty of Whiteness, by invoking the incredibly varied color of molasses.

"LAS CARAS LINDAS" AS PERFORMED BY ISMAEL RIVERA

Las caras lindas de mi gente Negra,	The beautiful faces of my Black people,
Son un desfile de melaza en flor,	Are a parade of molasses in bloom,
Que cuando pasan frente a mí se alegra,	And when they pass before me,
De su Negrura todo el corazón.	Their Blackness cheers my heart.
Las caras lindas de mi raza prieta,	The beautiful faces of my dark race,
Tienen de llanto, de pena y dolor,	Are made of weeping pain and suffering,
Son las verdades que la vida reta,	They are the truths that life challenges,
Pero que llevan dentro mucho amor.	But they carry within so much love.[9]

The second part of the verse continues Curet Alonso's poetic descriptions and advances the idea of humanizing representations of Black people through invocations of emotion, of the "beautiful faces" as ones that cry and laugh. The second section of this verse paints a picture of pride and softness, alongside one that exemplifies the often alluded-to "African rhythm." Otero Garabís (in Coss 2011 DVD) analyzed a section of the verse that includes the lyric "We are friendly shoe polish of clear poetry," showing how "that beautiful face is linked to the spiritual, the face, the visage is the mirror of the soul and in that manner gave some elements that were not acknowledged in the African heritage."

Somos la melaza que ríe,	We are the molasses that laughs,
La melaza que llora,	The molasses that cries,

Somos la melaza que ama,	The molasses that loves,
Y en cada beso es conmovedora.	And moves us with each kiss.
Por eso vivo orgulloso de su colorido,	That's why I live proud of their coloration,
Somos betún amable, de clara poesía,	We are friendly shoe polish of clear poetry,
Tienen su ritmo, tienen melodía,	They have their rhythm, they have their melody,
Las caras lindas de mi gente Negra.	The beautiful faces of my Black people.

The song ties into an emergent Latino ethnic consciousness by including mentions of Portobello, Panama, and an explicit dedication "To all the beautiful faces of Latin America." Despite the theme of the song, Rivera in his dedication to Latin America does not follow the subject with some kind of negritude epithet, but leaves it open. The negritude component, and therefore the connection of a shared Latino ethnic (African in this case) consciousness with Latin America, is implied in the dedication:

Coro: Las caras lindas, las caras lindas,	**Chorus:** The beautiful faces, the beautiful faces,
Las caras lindas de mi gente Negra.	The beautiful faces of my Black people
Te digo que, en Portobello Panamá,	I tell you that in Portobello, Panama,
Yo vi la cara más bella y pura,	I saw the most beautiful and pure face,
Y es por eso que mi corazón,	And because of that my heart,
Se alegra de su Negrura.	Rejoices with its Blackness.
Interludio instrumental	**Instrumental interlude**
Hablado: Para todas las caras lindas de Latinoamérica.	**Spoken:** To all the beautiful faces of Latin America.

The spoken section of the song contains a very innovative musical part that sees Rivera singing in unison with Mario Hernandez's *tres* solo.[10] Curet Alonso's composition aside, this type of phrasing and innovation is truly what marks Rivera as one of the greatest Salsa singers of all time. In her review of the record for the Fania website, Aurora Flores (n.d.) recounted the development of the section:

As the music would start up again, he'd lean into the recording as if caressing it with his face, listening and snapping his fingers in clave before suddenly picking his head up sheepishly and saying, "Oyeme," and then humming the notes from the tres in a semi-scat form before coming up with the words that would syllabically conform to the rhythmic melody of instrument and voice.

Aside from the already mentioned construction of "my people," there are several other Pueblo markers in this song. During the pregones, Ismael Rivera references Calle Calma, a street located in the suburban district of Santurce and actually the street where Rivera grew up. In this way, Rivera reinforces his humble beginnings and reaffirms that he is one with the people of his street. The following marker is one where Rivera indicates "a parade of pure Blackness that comes from down there," thus including "down there" as a place where social issues such as displacement and poverty live alongside racial implications. The last Pueblo marker makes reference to the public housing projects in the outskirts of San Juan officially called Residencial Luis Llorens Torres, which actually constitute the largest public housing project in the Caribbean. Thus Rivera once again recognizes El Pueblo, The People, as the residents of the housing project, as intrinsically tied to the understanding of the beauty of the Black faces proposed by Curet Alonso. Just like in the case of the aforementioned dedication to Latin America, Rivera does not include an epithet of negritude in the Llorens Torres dedication, once again implying the African heritage to be found in places such as Llorens Torres:

Caritas lindas de gente Negra,	Beautiful little faces of Black people
Que en la Calma tengo un montón.	Those that in Calma street I have a ton.[11]
Hablado: Pa' las caritas lindas de Llorens Torres.	**Spoken:** To the beautiful faces of Llorens Torres.
Desfile de Negrura de la pura,	A parade of pure Blackness
Que viene de allá abajo.	That comes from down there.

Given the intersection between race/ethnicity and class, the song bridges racial and class concerns. I choose to place it in the category of

African identity, as the context of the song's performance and reception has historically been understood as related to African pride, but the song could potentially be put in either category depending on the point of view of the analysis because, as I mentioned, the categorizations of Curet Alonso's work that I advance here are not closed, and the concept of class in Latin America, and so often in the United States, is intertwined with racial issues.

SORONGO

"Sorongo" is a song originally performed by the famous Puerto Rican artist Rafael Cortijo. It is fairly short, as was common of a release in that time period, and it seems at times to be almost comedic. In analyzing the title of the song, a native/fluent Spanish speaker would note that the word *sorongo* is actually not one used in standard conversational language, or for that matter used much at all. In fact, the word *sorongo* potentially refers to three different concepts. First, the word can be construed as an insult as indicated by its urban usage.[12] The second usage, often written as *zorongo*,[13] can also be understood as a hair accessory or bow in the hair, or as an Andalusian form of dance and music. Finally, the third definition is confirmed by the *Almanac of African Peoples and Nations*: "The Sorongo are a Central and southwest African People. They are concentrated in Angola and the democratic Republic of Congo (Zaire)" (Yakan 1999, 639). As the following analysis makes clear, this combination of references sees Curet Alonso play with ways to acknowledge that no matter how white the skin of a Puerto Rican person might be, there is always an African component to their heritage.

The chorus of the song poses the following question: "Tell me sorongo: What does the Black man have of white and what does the white man have of Congo?"[14] Before answering the actual question, we are invited to ponder what or who sorongo is. The answer might be as a form of mockery or insult to somebody, as in potentially asking: "Tell me fool: What does the Black man have of White and what does the White man have of Congo?" This could actually be a question posed to any Puerto Rican who has never questioned his/her ethnic heritage, and has simply aligned themselves with being of Spanish descent, that is, White. The second possibility ties it to the idea of the Andalusian dance, and in this case the question posed would be:

"Tell me Spaniard: What does the Black man have of White and what does the White man have of Congo?" This helps pose the question to the people who unquestioningly tie their heritage to that of Spain and not Africa, the inference being that you are a fool in thinking you come only from Spain. The final possibility foregrounds the idea of a full association with the Congo so that the question posed would read: "What does the Black man have of White and what does the White man have of Congo?" In this case, it can be seen to be addressed to a Puerto Rican denying his/her heritage and so directly confronting them with their African legacy and asking them to answer the question specifically.

Ultimately the right answer is not made clear, as Curet Alonso sustains ambiguity in order to keep all these possibilities alive. Upon analysis of this etymological uncertainty, the lyrical analysis makes it clear that sorongo in this song is used as a synonym of Black, or as a euphemism for Blackness. As such, there is a play on forms of Latin American racism as it was not always deemed polite to directly call someone Black. This argument, however, ties clearly into the questioning of the racial heritage of Puerto Rico and perhaps finds a parallel in the popular Cuban saying "Aquí el que no tiene de Congo Tiene de Carabalí" (Here, the one that does not have roots from the Congo, has them from Calabar [Nigeria])

The song's introduction presents a very unusual musical example for the Salsa of the time, where the actual rhythm utilized was specifically devised to accompany the song. This fact is confirmed by the original LP release where it is indicated that the style utilized is called *Ritmo Sorongo*.

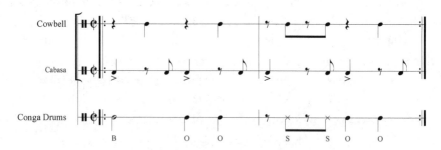

Figure 1. *Ritmo sorongo* as performed by Cortijo y su Bonche in "Sorongo."

This is perhaps an attempt by percussionist Rafael Cortijo to tie the music into the idea of the Africanism where the case of having specific rhythms for specific songs is actually fairly common.

The song starts with a rare appearance by Curet Alonso himself asking what kind of a "bunch" is this, an introductory reference to Cortijo's newly formed band following the separation from his own combo. The song basically has no verse as it starts directly with the chorus, which asks Sorongo: "What does the Black man have of White and what does the White man have of Congo?"

"SORONGO" AS PERFORMED BY RAFAEL CORTIJO

Hablado: ¿Qué bonche es este?	**Spoken:** What bunch is this?
El de Cortijo	Cortijo's
¿Como lo sabes?	How do you know it?
Él te lo dijo	He told you so
Coro: Dime Sorongo, dime Sorongo	**Chorus:** Tell me Sorongo, tell me Sorongo
¿Qué es lo que el Negro tiene de Blanco?	What does the Black man have of White
Y ¿qué es lo que el Blanco tiene de Congo?	And what does the White man have of Congo?[15]

The call-and-response section has lead vocals sung by Cortijo himself, and not the usual singer. During his pregones, Cortijo does not answer the originally posed question. Instead, he poses another set of questions with the general concept of trying to find the actual differences or similarities between "the White" and "the Congo."

Coro: Eh Sorongo	**Chorus:** Hey Sorongo
¿Serán las manos?	Might it be the hands?
Sorongo, Sorongo	Sorongo, Sorongo
¿Serán los ojos?	Might it be the eyes?
¿Los pies y la boca?	The feet and the mouth?
...	...

| ¿Serán los pies? | Might it be the feet? |
| ¿Serán los dientes? | Might it be the teeth? |

The end of the song truncates the original question and leaves out the first part only to ask: "So, what is it that the White man has of Congo?" The answer is finally "revealed," yet it is equally cryptic as the question: "Parap parap pa." Cortijo's work here hits a very fine point as in declaring such ambiguity, and leaving the answer open-ended, he, in many ways, declares his discontent with the current state of racial affairs by giving an answer that is truly devoid of content. By imposing this ambiguity, Cortijo also opens up the floor for questions from the audience, but as he is not available to respond, the audience members must now reflect and work on their own critical answers. Related to the ambiguity presented by Cortijo's "answer," it should be noted that there is in this song a very minimalistic approach on the part of Curet Alonso where, perhaps, all he wrote was the chorus of the song, only to later work the rest out with Cortijo. There is, however, much as in Cortijo's "answer," a significant force to the original question. Comedic as Cortijo's performance might sound, the racial implications are decidedly present.

The song was re-recorded in the posthumous DVD homage to Curet Alonso by the fairly well-known hip-hop/contemporary urban fusion/reggaeton group Calle 13. It is interesting to compare and contrast these two versions as they have significant similarities and differences. The later version also includes a large addition of politically charged lyrics devised by Residente/Calle 13 that were inspired by the original version. The fact that this song was covered, and expanded upon, shows the dialectic relationship between composer and performer. In this version, the fertility of the composer's concept is juxtaposed to the flexibility of performance. Moreover, the renewed version also shows the effect of the passage of time, as the "same" message changes meaning depending on the context. In this sense, Residente/Calle 13's readings of Blackness are not the same in 2011 as when the track first appeared in 1968. Furthermore, Cortijo's minimalistic version, unlike Calle 13's rendition, plays with the idea of "less is more" insofar as it allows listeners to draw their own conclusions. This fact perhaps plays to the advantage of Cortijo, as Calle 13's version ultimately produces a sensory excess of loaded words and leaves the listener with no possibility other than to accept the new answers.

The lead singer of Calle 13, René Lopez aka "Residente" (in Coss 2011 DVD) offered this explanation of his approach to the song:

> Sorongo is one of his known songs but it did not have many lyrics and I really liked that because it gave me space to write. So when I heard it I thought that Tite was posing a question: What does the Black man have of white and what does the white man have of Congo? He was not making a joke. Cortijo posed another question: Might it be the teeth? Might it be the hands? So, I said there are many questions, let's put some direct answers and that is what I did, put some answers of what I thought that the white man has of Congo and the Black of white. I then went to history of when Belgium entered the Congo and when Leopold, a macabre king killed almost everyone there, cut people's hands off so they would only function as carrier as if they were mules. He enslaved them to mine gold, diamonds and rubber.

The arrangement includes a musical identity marker similar to the earlier version. In this case the rhythm utilized is that of a *bomba yubá*. It should be noted that the musical complex of the *bomba* is quite large and contains several styles within it. *Bomba* is the style most often associated with people of African descent in Puerto Rico, and is quite popular in the aforementioned village of Loíza. Thus, the inclusion of a particular style of *bomba* not only plays on the African connotation of the song but offers homage to Cortijo, as in the 1950s he popularized another variation of the *bomba* called *sicá*. By comparison, in the original version of "Sorongo," Cortijo can be seen to have attempted to Africanize and "de-salsify" the song by inventing a new rhythm to enhance the composition. By the same token Calle 13's version utilized the *bomba yubá* as a signifier of Afro-Puerto Rican heritage and in this way paid homage to the influence of the African continent as well as the African diaspora. While Cortijo attempts to replicate and make references to these roots, Calle 13 recognizes and pays homage to this precursor by performing the branches of the same tree.

Figure 2. *Bomba yubá* as performed by Calle 13.

In the case of this arrangement, the style utilized is a ternary variation of *bomba* as opposed to the originally devised binary *Ritmo Sorongo*. The style of *yubá* is the one performed specifically in the Santurce region. The choice of region, as opposed to the Loíza style of *bomba yubá*, is significant as it pays homage to Curet Alonso by playing the *yubá* style of his neighborhood.

"SORONGO (CONGO)" AS PERFORMED BY CALLE 13

As in the original version, the song is introduced by the chorus asking the same question: What does the Black man have of White and what does the White man have of Congo?[16]

Coro: Dime Sorongo, dime Sorongo	**Chorus:** Tell me Sorongo, tell me Sorongo
¿Qué es lo que el Negro tiene de Blanco?	What does the Black man have of White
Y ¿qué es lo que el Blanco tiene de Congo?	And what does the White man have of Congo?

Despite having the original version as a point of reference, it comes as a surprise to find some kind of answer offered to the question other than Cortijo's cryptic ending. In this case it comes straight from the pen of René Lopez, aka Residente: The Black man has of the White man actually nothing; he had something of his own that was actually stolen from him. The White man now has what he stole from the Congo. In this verse there are a large number of violent acts that, as Residente describes, pertain to the genocide perpetrated by the Belgian king Leopold II on the people of the Congo:

Llegó el diablo Blanco Cristianizando	The White devil came Christianizing
Con veneno de culebra dejando el alma en quiebra	With snake poison breaking the soul
Se bajaron la ostia con un poco de ginebra	They gulped the host with some gin
Y los mataron, de un palo los ahorcaron	And they killed them, hung them from a branch
El diablo Blanco	The White devil
A to's en la aldea los dejaron mancos	Made everyone in the village a cripple
Qué es lo que tiene el manco de Blanco?	What does the amputee have of White?
Y qué es lo que tiene el Negro de manco?	And what does the amputee have of Black?
El Negro tiene lo que se le quitó	The Black man has what was taken from him
Y el Blanco tiene lo que se robó	And the White man has what he stole
...	...
Las memorias son muerte vivida	Memories are lived death
Lo que duele nunca se olvida	What hurts is never forgotten

The inclusion of Seun Kuti, the son of afrobeat creator Fela Kuti, reaffirms the African theme as well as the earlier message delivered by Calle 13 by reinstating the idea of greed versus the assassination of Black people in Africa.

Coro: Dime Sorongo, dime Sorongo	**Chorus:** Tell me Sorongo, tell me Sorongo
¿Qué es lo que el Negro tiene de Blanco?	What does the Black man have of White?
Y ¿qué es lo que el Blanco tiene de Congo?	And what does the White man have of Congo?
Verso de Seun Kuti (original en inglés)	**Seun Kuti's verse (original in English)**
I saw you kill my people, for some shiny blood	I saw you kill my people, for some shiny blood
Africans must die to make the world bright (shiny blood)	Africans must die to make the world bright (shiny blood)

My people are dying, I tell you (shiny blood)

For the oil and gas to flow (shiny blood)

And you wear it all over your body (shiny blood)

Shiny African blood representing your love

You cannot get enough

Kill us; take it, just what I know, wear it

Blood can't shine on me

Following Seun Kuti's verse, Puerto Rican musician Sammy Tanco delivers a verse written by René Lopez for Tanco to convey. Lopez (in Coss 2011 DVD) explains the verse as follows:

> Part of the design was also that since there are many people that talk about negritude and were the first to wear a gold necklace, and they don't know that to get that gold chain a bunch of young kids had to go and die to find a little golden rock. You know? [All of that] so he can wear a gold necklace and those diamonds in his teeth.

There is a fair amount of symbolism in this verse in which the images of chicken blood and tobacco smoke evoke traditional African religions that are present in the Caribbean basin such as *Santería* or *Palo Congo*. There is also a reference to the original version of the song in which Cortijo asked what the teeth might be? In this case, Sammy Tanco (a Black man) compares his white teeth to those of Residente (a White man) and asks, "what does that have of black?"

Verso de Sammy Tanco	**Sammy Tanco's verse**
Sangre de gallina, humo de tabaco	Chicken blood, tobacco smoke
Con un poco de piña pa' protegerte de los demonios,	With some pineapple to protect you from the demons,
...	...
Un Negro buscando oro, entre el lodo un destello	A Black man looking for gold, in the mud a sparkle

Para que venga un idiota y se lo cuelgue en el cuello	So an idiot comes and hangs it on his neck
Si veo a un Negro con diamantes le corono su dentadura	If I see a Black man with diamonds, I crown his teeth
¿Dónde quedó la negrura? ¿Dónde quedó la negrura?	Where is the negritude? Where is the negritude?
Yo tengo los dientes blancos y también el Residente	I have white teeth and so does Residente
¿Qué es lo que tiene de Negro?	What does that have of Black?
Quiero que el Blanco me cuente	I want the White man to tell me

The last part of the verse sees Residente return as a lead vocalist where he develops a poetic scheme based on the words black and white. He states that "in the end I started to play a little with the colors and the words black and white . . . I also play a little at the social level as the middle class also lives it black" (in Coss 2011 DVD). Residente also indicates the idea of two colors as zebras, which is directly related to the denial of African heritage by many light-skinned Puerto Ricans. Finally, Residente also asks, "what does the Puerto Rican have of Congo?," and closes his verse by referring to the colonial status of Puerto Rico vis-à-vis the United States.

Verso de Residente	**Residente's verse**
Creo en el sol y en la magia negra	I believe in the sun, and in black magic
Tengo a dos o tres en la lista negra	I have two or three in the blacklist
La clase media también la pasa negra	The middle class also sees it black
Mi mai es blanca y baila como Negra	My mom is White and dances like a Black woman
...	...
Dos colores como las cebras	Two colors like zebras
Dime Sorongo, dime Sorongo	Tell me Sorongo, tell me Sorongo
Que es lo que tiene el Boricua de Congo	What does the Puerto Rican have of Congo
...	...
Misma fragancia de Babilonia	Same fragrance of Babylon
Mismo perfume, misma colonia	Same perfume, same colony

The ending of the song reintroduces Curet Alonso's original wording of the chorus. In a reference to Cortijo's version where the song ended by the question "So, what is that the White man has of Congo?" Residente in this case inverts the question: "What does the Black man have of White?"

Sorongo, Sorongo, Sorongo	Sorongo, Sorongo, Sorongo
Dime Sorongo	Tell me Sorongo,
Dime Sorongo	Tell me Sorongo
¿Qué es lo que el Negro tiene de Blanco?	What does the Black man have of White?
Y ¿qué es lo que el Blanco tiene de Congo?	And what does the White man have of Congo?
Dime Sorongo	Tell me Sorongo,
Dime Sorongo	Tell me Sorongo
¿Qué es lo que el Negro tiene de blanco?	What does the Black man have of White?

As I have shown, Calle 13's version of "Sorongo" expands significantly on the subjects implied in Cortijo's version, as well as tying Curet Alonso's words to a great deal of historic facts. This is not far off from Curet Alonso's own endeavors, where history is explored in relation to contemporary events, such as in his songs "Anacaona" or "Plantación Adentro." Residente/Calle 13's version is obviously more racially charged but maintains the spirit of Curet Alonso. Though the delivery is much more direct in Residente/Calle 13's version, perhaps more akin to a Rubén Blades song, the new version still ties in clearly to the message of the original song, and to Curet Alonso's overall racial discourse.

Salsifying Social Issues: Social Critique in the Music of Catalino "Tite" Curet Alonso

Social criticism is one of the main characteristics of Salsa consciente. In Curet Alonso's work, the expression of social issues in song is presented in the form of despair at unemployment, poverty, and lack of social mobility. A crucial signifier of these issues in this section is the idea of El Pueblo, The People. As we will see, being part and developing an identity of being Pueblo plays a crucial role in determining the "true value" of somebody. Within the following songs, Curet Alonso exalts the idea of "coming from below" or "belonging to the slums," or even the beauty found within poverty. This idea certainly ties into the second leitmotif of the chapter, as related to the exaltation of what could easily be a negative discussion towards beauty and pride via poetic indirection.

LAMENTO DE CONCEPCIÓN

"Lamento de Concepción" is a song that speaks of the despair of the unemployed. Salazar (2007, 90-91) indicated that the song was originally written for singer Billy Concepción when he was unable to find work as a musician. The context surrounding this shows Fania Records executives to have been absolutely intransigent, as after hiring singer Concepción for a new record, they asked Concepción not to use the original musicians from his band for the recording and instead use musicians hired by Fania. Concepción's refusal resulted in a dissolution of the contract and his being virtually shut out of the live music circuit. Concepción thus suffered a long bout of unemployment, eventually leaving Puerto Rico for New York in search of new opportunities. Curet Alonso heard about Concepción's troubles in a restaurant and wrote the song for him. Aurora Flores, in her online review of the compilation CD of Curet Alonso titled *Alma de Poeta* (Fania 2010), confirmed the story:

> Curet combats the social issues of his time with lyrical laments within a dance format. Once, his friends Rafael Viera and Franklin Hernández introduced singer and musician Billy Concepción to Curet in a restaurant. Concepción was blacklisted by the music industry and couldn't find work. A father of six, he recounts the overwhelming feeling of having the world on his shoulders. Curet immediately took his pen and wrote "Lamento de Concepción" on a napkin. "Concepción eleva la vista al cielo / Va gritando, hay niños que mantener"—expressing the universal feeling of impotence at not being able to support his family.

"Lamento de Concepción" is a song constructed around the character of Concepción, a man telling the story of his sorrows. The lyrics show Concepción's despair as a clear example of the stories of many people who on a daily basis find themselves unemployed and at the same time as the head of a household and main provider for their families. While Concepción tells the skies that he has children to feed, he notes that his identity is as "one that comes from below," and questions the unfairness of a system that has alienated him. By the same token, Concepción speaks of the difficulties of being unemployed and trying to find work.

"LAMENTO DE CONCEPCIÓN" AS PERFORMED BY ROBERTO ROENA Y SU APOLLO SOUND

Y decía: hay niños que mantener	And said: there are children to support
...	...
Y decía: hay niños que mantener	And said: there are children to support
Si yo soy de los de abajo	If I am one that comes from below
¿Qué tiene que ver?	What is the difference
Yo tengo el mismo derecho de vivir.	I have the same right to live.
Que mucho trabajo da,	It is so much work,
Hallar en que trabajar	To find in what to work
Que trabajo da, el no trabajar.	Not working, it's so much work.[17]

The chorus and the responses sung by Carlos Santos eventually reaffirm Concepción's position and his agony over not being able to support his family. In this section, the lead vocals tell Concepción's story in the third person, thus speaking to the listener and placing the situation in a realm where the listener can connect to Concepción:

Coro: Concepción eleva la vista al cielo	**Chorus:** Concepción looks up to the sky
Va gritando, hay niños que mantener	And yells: there are kids to feed
Concepción en su lamento	Concepcion in his lament
Y en su terrible agonía	And his terrible agony
Va pidiendo al Señor	Asks the Lord
Que le ayude a buscarse el pan de cada día.	To help him find his daily bread

...   ...

Oiga, el que yo sea de abajo,	Listen, the fact that I come from below,
Nadita tiene que ver	Has nothing to do
Yo también tengo derecho	I also have the right
De mis hijos mantener y comer.	To support my children and to eat.
Interludio instrumental	**Instrumental interlude**

Following the interlude, the chorus is introduced again, but this time during the pregones, Carlos Santos speaks to Concepción directly. In this set of pregones, there is a reference to "los de arriba," the ones up top, pointing to a problem that at the time was unquestionably endemic in Latin America, where in order to succeed professionally, a favor to "the ones up top" must be made. Without this it was basically impossible, in this case for Concepción, and by extension people from "down below," to achieve success as long as the alignment with "the ones up top" did not exist. Eventually Concepción blames himself and considers himself "jinxed."

Coro: Concepción eleva la vista al cielo	**Chorus:** Concepción looks up to the sky
Va gritando, hay niños que mantener	And screams, there are kids to feed
No importa que los de arriba	It does not matter if the ones up top
No te quieran ayudar	Don't want to help you
...	...
Concepción me dice a mí	Concepcion tells me
Que anda muy desesperao	That he is very desperate
Y se la pasa diciendo	And keeps saying
Que todo su ser esta salao.	That all his being is jinxed.

"Lamento de Concepción" was once again performed in the above-mentioned 2011 DVD *SONÓ SONÓ . . . TITE CURET* by Venezuelan singer Trina Medina.[18] In comparing the verses of both versions, no difference is found. Trina Medina's 2011 version, however, presents a specific spoken opening to the song tying her native Venezuela and arguably all of Latin America by including "our people" to the originally Puerto Rican character of Concepción. This is certainly the case of a very clear Pueblo marker directly following, yet expanding, the main message of Curet Alonso's original verses.

"LAMENTO DE CONCEPCIÓN" AS PERFORMED BY TRINA MEDINA

Este es el lamento de nuestros Pueblos,   This is the Lament of our people in the
en la voz de un hombre: Concepción   voice of one man: Concepción

While the verse of the song was kept intact, the call-and-response section presents several changes in comparison to the original version:

Original pregones (Roberto Roena)	Translation	New pregones (Trina Medina)	Translation
Concepción en su lamento	Concepción in his lament	Han pasado 30 años del lamento de Concepción.	It has been 30 years since the Lament of Concepción
Y en su terrible agonía	And in his terrible agony	Cambian gobiernos, cambia la moda,	The governments change, the fashion changes,
Va pidiendo al señor	Asks the Lord	Pero es la misma situación.	But it is the same situation.
Que le ayude a buscarse el pan de cada día.	To help him find his daily bread.		
Oiga, el que yo sea de abajo	Listen, the fact that I come from below	Se refugia en falsos profetas, en la bebida y en el juego con sus panitas Pedro Fango, Juan Albañil y el solidario Pablo Pueblo	He finds refuge in false prophets, drinks and gambles with his buddies, Peter Mud, John Laborer, and the caring Paul People
Nadita tiene que ver	Has nothing to do		
Yo también tengo derecho	I also have the right		
De mis hijos mantener y comer.	To support my children and to eat.		

Ta bueno ya, ta bueno ya, y es que yo no aguanto más.	That's enough, That's enough, I can't take it anymore.
Ay ayúdame dios mío, mis hijos lloran por hambre, dame la luz pa' salvarlos te lo pido	Help me my Lord, my children cry of hunger. Give me the light to save them I ask you
Que mi hijo me salga vagabundo no quiero señor.	I do not want my son to be a vagrant my Lord
A pesar de mis errores,	Despite my mistakes,
Que supere los rencores, para que viva mejor que yo.	I want him to overcome the resentment so he can live better than me

Not only is the version longer but the emphasis is quite different. Trina Medina initially shows how the situation has not changed since the release of the original version. While not directly blaming politicians, she does mention the fact that governments ultimately have not helped improve the poor man's situation. During her second ad-lib, Medina, much like in the original version, expresses a belief in God as the means to salvation as she sees Concepción looking for evasive tactics or what she calls "false prophets." This particular *pregón* is especially significant as it actually places a real person (the singer Billy Concepción to whom the song was originally dedicated) within the realm of what I have previously dubbed urban characters. In this section she calls Peter "mud" as an analogy to the people walking the dirt-covered roads so often found in the slums. And in a nod to both Curet Alonso and Rubén Blades she includes two of the urban characters created by those composers. First she mentions Curet Alonso's "Juan Albañil" (John Laborer) and second Blades's "Pablo Pueblo" (Paul People). All of these characters are archetypes of the common man.

Trina Medina continues the section with two pregones that actually take the original version's idea of looking up to the sky and asking God for help. In closing the section, there is an admission of mistakes made as Concepción places the blame on himself and asks the heavens that his son do well in life.

Following the section, Trina Medina speaks directly to Concepción and pushes him to continue the fight, and tells him that he will accomplish his goals. In speaking to Concepción, Medina is ultimately speaking to the common man who has been brought down by circumstances and urges him to move forward.

Hablado: Concepción: Lo difícil no es caerse, es levantarse con rapidez. Yo sé que tú lo lograrás, amigo mío. Pa'lante	**Spoken:** Concepción: The difficulty is not in falling down but in getting up. I know you will do it my friend. Forward

The last set of pregones show Concepción as a victim who has been deceived by the populist slogans of governments. The case here shows Medina taking the argument beyond the original concept and equating Concepción to the common man deceived by "the people up top." Originally "the people up top" were the record executives closing the doors on Concepción, but now the signification of the character has been expanded to include the despair of all unemployed people and to highlight the deceit of those in power.

Coro: Concepción eleva la vista al cielo	**Chorus:** Concepción looks up to the sky
Va gritando, hay niños que mantener	And yells: there are kids to feed
Víctima de la ignorancia y del populismo gobiernero.	Victim of ignorance and the government's populism.
Va Concepción con su faz desnuda esperando que llueva café del cielo.	Concepción walk with his nude face waiting for coffee to rain out of the sky.
Homenaje a Tite Curet, escritor de pluma infinita	A tribute to Tite Curet, writer of infinite pen
Pa' que lo goces allá en el cielo con los salseros	For you to enjoy there in heaven with the salseros

Te lo dedica Trina Medina, de   Dedicated to you from Trina Medina
Venezuela.   from Venezuela.

Even though the song is dedicated specifically to Billy Concepción, it ultimately speaks of the realities of poverty and unemployment. The song makes reference not only to unemployment and the despair that comes with it, but to the inner workings of a system where despite talent and dedication, success is not attained unless one is aligned with the right people. The song is thus a clear example of a Pueblo identity marker constructed on the quotidian realities of an urban character. There is, however, an internal contradiction that comes through the fact that Billy Concepción was actually deceived by the music industry. As such, he is not merely one among many representatives of The People; he is the archetypical Latino, the bearer of Latino popular identity. This latter analysis is based on the circumstances of the creation of the song rather the song itself and stems from an element of artistic self-consciousness. Even though the circumstances are generally unknown to the listener, the secondary analysis is important as it connects real life to song, rather than the song being based on abstract ideals.

The song additionally elaborates upon the idea of a lament; in this case the one lamenting is Concepción. There is a connection here to Latin American song in general, where there are several instances when the form of a lament is utilized and could arguably be referred to as a traditional form. Some of these songs, for example, include "Lamento de un Guajiro" (The Lament of a Peasant)—originally "Al Vaiven de mi Carreta")—made popular in the United States by Ismael Miranda and the Fania All Stars; the "Lamento Esclavo" (A Slave's Lament), made popular originally by the Sexteto Habanero; and "Lamento Negro" (Black Man's Lament), made popular by Rita Montaner. The most direct link in this case is probably Puerto Rican composer Rafael Hernandez's song "Lamento Borincano" (Puerto Rican Lament) written in 1929, where the song tells the story of a peasant who happily heads to the market to sell his products only to find that he is not able to do so, and sadly returns home empty-handed. Links beyond the form can be found in the idea of suffering through poverty and not being able to provide for one's family. Within the form of the lament, the Curet Alonso song, however, marks a clear difference by bringing Concepción's sorrows into contemporary life, where the lament is actually based on urban realities brought on by poverty and unemployment as opposed to the rural realities and agricultural context of "Lamento Borincano."

JUAN ALBAÑIL

"Juan Albañil is a song that speaks of class inequality.[19] The main argument of the song is constructed around a fictitious urban character, another representative of the common man, who in this case is a construction worker. Curet Alonso plays with the idea of the character's last name describing his profession, a type of characterization akin to Blades's hit "Pedro Navaja" (Peter Knife) telling the story of a street thug. The idea of creating an archetype for the common man is neither new nor exclusive to "Juan Albañil," as Blades developed and emphasized this archetype.

In the first part of the verse, the class discrimination issue is quickly underlined as construction workers are not allowed to enter the buildings they have erected. It is worth noting that the location of these buildings is on "the avenue." The construction of the concept of "the avenue" quickly denotes not only the building's location as the part of the high-class city that contains avenues, but also Juan Albañil's home location as a part of town, namely, the outskirts of the city, where such an avenue does not exist, as it is characterized instead by poorer streets and lanes.

"JUAN ALBAÑIL" AS PERFORMED BY CHEO FELICIANO

Juan Albañil, el edificio que levantaste,	John Laborer, the building you put up
Con lo mucho que trabajaste,	As much as you worked
Está cerrado, está sellado,	It is closed, it is sealed
Es prohibido para ti, Juan Albañil.	It is forbidden for you John Laborer
Como es domingo Juan Albañil por la avenida,	Since it is Sunday, John Laborer walks the avenue
Va de paseo mirando cuanto construyó,	Looking at all he built
Hoteles, condominios, cuanto lujo,	Hotels, condominiums, so much luxury
Y ahora como no es socio no puede entrar,	And now since he is not a member, he cannot go in.[20]

In the second part of the verse, Juan Albañil is positioned as "neighbor man," thus my neighbor or your neighbor. In speaking to Juan Albañil, Curet Alonso tells him and by extension the listener that there is no future in cement. This fact points towards the idea of pursuing education over manual labor, a thought that can then be tied to Blades's "Plástico," where he proclaims "study, work, and be people first."[21] There is also the component of a lament where Juan Albañil cries over the insignificance of his work after his labor is finished:

Juan Albañil, hombre vecino,	John Laborer, neighbor man
Cuanto ha soñado con la llamada igualdad,	How much he has dreamed of the so-called equality,
Juan Albañil pero dile a tus hijos	John Laborer tell your children
Que en el cemento no hay porvenir.	That in cement there is no future
Como es domingo Juan Albañil por la avenida,	Since it is Sunday, John Laborer walks the avenue
Pasa llorando, mirando cuanto construyo,	Passes crying, seeing how much he built
Va lamentando la importancia insignificante,	Lamenting the insignificant importance
Que el que trabaja tiene después que trabajó.	That the one that works has after the work is done

With the introduction of the chorus, Juan Albañil realizes the levels of inequality in which he lives. During the pregones, Cheo Feliciano plays with the idea of a house of equality where he includes the idealistic image of "trowels of brotherhood" helping create an idyllic state of equality. It is interesting to consider that in this song, Juan Albañil is presented as a hardworking man who is not afraid to meet his destiny. Despite the fact that the song makes no mention of other possible destinies or courses of action on the part of the main character, Albañil is not blind to the realities of inequality around him. He does not hide from them but rather expresses them. This is all he can do as he is powerless, but at least he does not hide or escape from facing the facts of his situation:

Coro: En los andamios, sueña que sueña,	**Chorus:** In the scaffolding, dreams and dreams,
Juan Albañil, con el día de la igualdad.	John Laborer, of the day equality arrives.
Pero cuantos condominios ese hombre va construyendo,	But how many condominiums has that man built,
y mañana en la misma puerta,	And tomorrow morning at the very door,
De ahí mismo lo van huyendo, que sí, que sí.	from right there they shoo him away, yes, yes.
Y en los andamios de la vida,	And in the scaffolding of life,
Con palustres de hermandad,	With trowels of brotherhood,
Fabricaremos algún día la casa de la igualdad, y digo yo,	We will build someday the house of equality, and I say,
Y en esa casa señoras y señores,	In that house, ladies and gentlemen,
No habrá distinción jamás, gente de toditos los colores,	There will never be distinctions, people of all colors,
Con Juan Albañil toditos podrán entrar.	With John Laborer all will be able to enter.
Interludio instrumental	**Instrumental interlude**

The second iteration of the chorus has Feliciano's pregones describe Juan Albañil walking the city and talking to his children, who are already wondering about the inequality of their society. An interesting and contrasting analysis to the literal thoughts of Feliciano's pregones is Venezuelan singer Trina Medina's thought regarding Juan Albañil's pride, which is a thought that is not actually mentioned in Feliciano's version. Trina Medina, speaking for Albañil, says, "it is true, look at all the houses I made," and walks around there and maybe goes in and says to his son with that pride: "You know, this shopping mall, I laid the bricks there." (In Coss 2011 DVD):

Coro: En los andamios, sueña que sueña,	**Chorus:** In the scaffolding, dreams and dreams,
Juan Albañil, con el día de la igualdad.	John Laborer, of the day equality arrives.

Como es Domingo Juan Albañil pasea por todita la ciudad, y sus nenes le preguntan: ¿Papi a ese edificio tan grande, por qué yo no puedo entrar?	Since it is Sunday, John Laborer walks all over the city, and his children ask him: Daddy why can't I go into that big building?
...	...
Como Juan Albañil, esta es la desigualdad.	Like John Laborer, this is inequality

There is also in this song an appearance of the composer/performer dialectic tension leitmotif in the form of the spoken sections of the song. While it is unclear if the spoken sections were devised originally by Curet Alonso or added by Cheo Feliciano, they clearly play an important role in understanding the character of Juan Albañil. Cheo Feliciano opens the song not by singing but speaking to the audience and stating that the song is based on a true story. In his usual manner of addressing the audience, he involves every listener by making them part of a family. In the second spoken section, Feliciano speaks directly to the Puerto Rican people, exhorting them to join in the hard work that Juan Albañil as a member of the proletariat has displayed. Once again exalting Juan Albañil as the hero of the common man, the next spoken section sees Albañil praised as one who confronts his fate, which means the inequality to which he has been subjected. The closing of the song sees Cheo Feliciano once again speaking, but this time directly to Juan Albañil. Here Feliciano honors Albañil, and by extension the working man, and places him in the category of a "sir."

In analyzing these sections, it is evident that the character is based on a true, everyday story of a hardworking man who resonates closely with many Puerto Ricans, and by extension with working people all over Latin America. Expanding upon the idea of poetic indirection, this man is painted as a brave person who meets his fate head-on and is not afraid to do what he has to do to survive. Finally, in the last spoken section Cheo Feliciano, speaking directly to Juan Albañil, shows much respect for his work ethic.

Hablado: Bueno familia esto es una historia verdadera, y viene sucediendo hace rato, y el hombre ahí.	**Spoken:** Well, family this is a true story and it has been happening for a long time, and the man is still there.

Hablado: Recoge esa pala, tira mezcla, pásame ese balde, rómpete la espalda Boricua que esto es así.	**Spoken:** Pick up that shovel, throw the mix, give me that bucket, break your back Puerto Rican this is how it is.
Hablado: ¡Bendito! Obrero, valiente Juan Albañil,	**Spoken:** Good lord! Workman, brave John Laborer.
Oye, hombre que le mete frente al destino.	Listen, a man that meets fate head on.
Hablado: Definitivamente Juan Albañil,	**Spoken:** Definitely John Laborer,
Por lo menos para mí, tú eres un señor.	At least to me, you are a sir.

CON LOS POBRES ESTOY

"Con los Pobres Estoy," meaning "with the poor people I am," or "with the poor people I stand," is a song interpreted by Roberto Roena and his Apollo Sound. The song deals with being true to El Pueblo, and being a person proud of his humble origins no matter how much success and wealth is achieved.

There are many references in this song to *arrabal*, which I have translated as "slum" for lack of a better word. The ultimate meaning of the word does not carry the many negative connotations of slum, but it does include the concept of poverty to a great extent. As such, slum parallels the concept of *arrabal*, yet the Spanish concept includes a suburban factor peripheral to the possible location of the *arrabal*. *Arrabal* thus is probably better understood as a peripheral and impoverished section of a city, similar to a *favela* in Brazil.

The verse of the song is spoken in first person, and presents the main character as someone who is described as being "sesame milk" to the poor people. This metaphor has a distinctly Caribbean flavor where sesame milk is a popular drink. In the case of the song, the analogy points to the idea of someone being with poor people everywhere (e.g., in the slums) the same way that the easily and cheaply available sesame milk would be. The analogy can also be seen to point to the idea of sesame milk as a form of relief both in terms of cooling one down and assuaging hunger. Sesame milk is often served cold in hot weather and has a high nutritional value. The second part of the verse develops the idea of belonging to The People and not being ashamed, but full of pride in belonging to the poor.

"CON LOS POBRES ESTOY" AS PERFORMED BY ROBERTO ROENA Y SU APOLLO SOUND

Agüita de ajonjolí,	Sesame milk
Para los pobres soy, para los pobres soy.	I am for the poor people; I am for the poor people;
Y no me digan que no,	And don't tell me otherwise
Porque con ellos estoy, donde quiera que voy.	Because I am with them, wherever I go.
Agüita de ajonjolí,	Sesame milk
Para los pobres soy, para los pobres soy.	I am for the poor people; I am for the people;
Búsquenme en los arrabales	Look for me in the slums
Que abundan por la ciudad,	That are all around the city
Para mí en esos lugares, solo hay felicidad.	For me there is only happiness in those places.
Orgullo no va conmigo, por doquiera que yo voy,	Pride does not go with me, wherever I go,
En cada pobre un amigo, a ese la mano le doy.	Each poor person is a friend, to whom I lend my hand.[22]

The chorus section reaffirms this idea of pride and belonging and of being allied to the poor. The second pregón shows the main character as a noble person who potentially has acquired some kind of wealth and is able to offer more than asked. Thus, the analogy of sesame milk as a form of relief is once again established:

Coro: Con los pobres estoy, donde quiera que voy.	**Chorus:** I am with the poor people wherever I go.
Por donde quiera que yo voy,	Wherever I go
Con los pobres siempre estoy, siempre estoy.	I am always with the poor, always am
Si tú me pides quince chavos,	If you ask me for fifteen cents
Una cuara (quarter) yo te doy, noble soy.	A quarter I give you, noble as I am

The spoken section restates the character's placement and his standing until the day he dies. This section paraphrases the 1891 poetry collection *Versos Sencillos (Simple verses)* by the Cuban poet and independence hero Jose Martí. The particular verse was popularized by its inclusion in the popular song "Guantanamera" composed by Joseíto Fernández. The original Martí verse is: "Con los pobres de la tierra quiero yo mi suerte echar" (With the poor people of earth I want to try my luck). In the same vein as many other songs, the idea of flexibility of performance versus the pre-composed becomes evident in the fact that the variation used in the Roena version was likely included by singer Frankie Calderón and not necessarily included in Curet Alonso's original version.

Hablado: Con los pobres hasta la muerte, quiero yo mi suerte echar	**Spoken:** With the poor people until death, I will try my luck
Interludio instrumental	**Instrumental interlude**

The re-introduction of the chorus reinforces the idea of the poor people as real. This time the reinforcement is achieved through use of the first person, where the main character indicates that there is no hypocrisy in him, only heart and humility. The main character has earned sufficient wealth, and/or fame—perhaps as a Salsa singer—to maybe not be considered someone from the slums; yet he is not one to forget who he is, and we should look for him in the slums:

Coro: Con los pobres estoy, donde quiera que voy.	**Chorus:** I am with the poor people wherever I go.
En mí no existe hipocresía,	In me there is no hypocrisy,
Hay corazón nada más, y humildad	There is just heart, and humility
...	...
Búsquenme en los arrabales,	Look for me in the slums
Que allí mismo es donde estoy.	Right there is where I am.

This song was re-recorded by reggaeton/rap artist Tego Calderón and the Salsa group Guasabara in the posthumous homage DVD to Curet Alonso titled ¡SONÓ, SONÓ . . . TITE CURET! For that performance, the verse of the song was kept intact and a series of pregones as well as a rap section developed by Tego Calderón were added. In this section, Tego Calderón reaffirms the message delivered originally by Curet Alonso to stand true with the poor people and no matter how much wealth or fame one may achieve—plenty in the case of Calderón—it is necessary to stay humble and true to one's roots.

Unlike Roena's version, Tego Calderón's adds a rap section that talks directly to the listener, and in the same manner as Blades does in "Plástico," the lyrics celebrate not being carried away by vanity, but being real.[23] The section emphasizes the idea of belonging, in this case placing the idea of inequality arising from the higher class not allowing the working class to become one of them. In the same manner, the idea also questions the concept of social mobility by asking "Belong to what? You are from here," emphasizing once again the importance of the *arrabal* as a place that besides being a slum retains the true essence of El Pueblo.

"CON LOS POBRES ESTOY," RAPPED SECTION BY TEGO CALDERÓN

Rapeado:	Rapped:
Por más que tengas recuerda siempre,	No matter how much you have, always remember
De dónde vienes, quien es tu gente	Where you come from, who your people are
Allá eres uno más, pero acá de verdad	There you are one more, but here you are for real
No te dejes llevar de la vanidad	Don't let yourself be taken by vanity
Porque los pobres son gente probá	Because poor people are proven people
¿Pertenecer a qué? Si usted es de acá	Belong to what? You are from here
Y tú lo sabes ¿Entonces?	And you know it. So?
Si del cielo te llueven plátanos, aprende a hacer tostones	If plantains fall from the sky learn how to fry them
Haga lo que debe brother, no lo que se supone	Do what you must brother, not what you are supposed to
¿Tú oyes? ¿Copiaste?	You hear? Do you copy?

"Con los Pobres Estoy" is a perfect example of Curet Alonso's use of poetic indirection where the potential problem is celebrated rather than denigrated. In this case, the idea of poverty is given dignity and made to mean "being real." In this case, the identity marker is once again based on the concept of Pueblo. It is by using this marker that both versions of the song develop their key points. In Roena's version, the idea of being poor equates to non-hypocrisy, and this sentiment is replicated in the 2011 version by calling poor people transparent. Both versions develop their arguments and place the main character as one that belongs to the "real people," one that stands with the poor.

PURA NOVELA

This song was included in the 1980 Ray Barretto release entitled *Fuerza Gigante/Giant Force*, which had Barretto working steadily with his newly formed band that included lead singer Ray de la Paz. The compositions include another Curet Alonso piece entitled "Tu Propio Dolor," as well as the remarkable Barretto/Lopez compositional collaboration of Fuerza *Gigante/ Giant Force* that lyrically deals with Latino unity and can be classified as within the Salsa consciente tradition. The arrangements throughout the album are based mainly on modernized Cuban musical structures. In the case of "Pura Novela" composed by Curet Alonso, the arranger was Gil Lopez, and the style utilized a basic framework of a modernized Cuban *son*. This is not to say, however, that the arrangement is simple. This piece is highly sophisticated but does not rely on sonic signifiers that identify Latinidad or Pueblo.[24]

"Pura Novela" is a song that stands out from everything else Curet Alonso wrote insofar as the song deals with the feminization of poverty (Pearce 1978). While gender issues are in general avoided by Salsa musicians,[25] this song foregrounds the issue of Latinas "marrying up" as a practice to escape poverty. The song can thus be analyzed as a study in Latina hypergamy whereby the idea of analyzing the reception of the female who has gained material wealth conveys a reflection on the idea of a lack of spiritual wealth. Besides gendering poverty, the song offers an indirect comment on the "market" value of Latina women and the contemporary hyper-erotization of being Latino/a. Despite the loaded insights of the song, the piece fails to comment on the flip side of this social complex, namely, the sadly common and irresponsible behavior of ghetto males, who lack the means to become a head of household.

Hypergamy aside, "Pura Novela" exalts the beauty of poverty. Once again, Curet Alonso utilizes the poetic indirection strategy of using poverty or lower social status, which is ultimately the Pueblo identity marker, as a tool to denote the "real value" of people. In this manner, this song is related to Rubén Blades's "Plástico," where the message is not to let oneself be taken in by the vanity of the "plastic" society. In this case, two years after "Plástico," Curet Alonso deals with a very similar subject.

The title of the song speaks of the ever popular (tele)novelas—soap operas of Latin America—and the images of success portrayed by such series. By this television token, the social mobility and wealth portrayed by the stars of the series equal the success of a person. Curet Alonso, on the other hand, declares that the success and value of a person is actually measured by their commitment and willingness to be real—true to oneself and one's roots—and equating that reality to being part of The People, El Pueblo.

The song begins with spoken advice specifically directed at materialistic women looking to climb up through social mobility. The gender of "ricas" indicates specifically that the song is sung from a male to a female.

"PURA NOVELA" AS PERFORMED BY RAY BARRETTO

Hablado: Para las que ambicionan el ser ricas y viven en fantasía.

Spoken: To the ones that pursue being rich and live in fantasies

The verse places the two main characters, one male and one female, as poor and coming from the same neighborhood. The female character, however, dreams of wealth that the poor man cannot provide

Empezamos la novela	We began the soap opera
Como la empieza cualquiera,	As all of them begin
Yo pobre y tu soñadora,	Me poor and you a dreamer
Los dos en la misma acera	Both of us in the same sidewalk
Pero riquezas yo no te podía dar,	But wealth, I could not give to you,
Ni el lujo que llegaste a ambicionar.	Nor the luxury that you eventually pursued

| Quisiste ser la duquesa | You wanted to be the duchess |
| Ocultada en un castillo | Hidden in a castle[26] |

Once the female character has achieved the desired wealth, she realizes that even though she has achieved her dream, she has turned her back on her roots, fallen prey to the falsehood of luxury, and wishes to return to the simple life of the suburban slums.

Y así perdió tu novela, su detalle de moral,	And just like that, your soap opera lost its moral compass
Hoy darías el castillo	Today you would give away the castle
Y el título de nobleza,	And the nobility title,
Con tal de ser otra vez,	Just to belong again,
Muchacha, de este arrabal	Girl, to this slum

The chorus places an emphasis on the beauty of poverty in which the idea is tied not to the physical surroundings but to the beauty of the people that live in this situation, a group of people praised for their solidarity standing up for themselves. This thought is reinforced by the third pregón, where singer Ray de la Paz declares that a return to "the poor man that [actually] loved you" is desired, thus placing the love of a rich man not as true love but a love likely born out of self-interest.

Coro: Envidias tú la riqueza que se tiene en la pobreza	**Chorus:** You envy the richness that is had in poverty
...	...
Hoy quieres tu volver al pobre que te quería	Today you want to come back to the poor man that loved you

Before the instrumental interlude, Ray de la Paz speaks to the female character and tells her to listen to "what is good for you," and run away. This section anticipates the pregones that follow the instrumental interlude.

| **Hablado:** Óyelo bien que te conviene nena. Huye | **Spoken:** Listen what is good for you baby. Run |
| **Interludio instrumental** | **Instrumental interlude** |

The reintroduction of the chorus changes the tone of the song from a warning to a reflection on consequences as the male character actually rejects the female, as he states, "Don't you come crying to me. What for?" while the band plays an arranged unison stop time accentuating the situation described.

Figure 3. Rhythmic break utilized in "Pura Novela."

Coro: Envidias tú la riqueza que se tiene en la pobreza

¿De qué te vale, de qué te vale pedir perdón mamita?

Si tú a mí no me interesas

Tu no me vengas llorando,

¿Para qué?

Chorus: You envy the richness that is had in poverty

What good is it, what good is it asking for forgiveness baby

If I am no longer interested in you

Don't you come crying to me

What for?

The half chorus is reduced to a single yet incredibly effective noun: poverty. Once again, the consequential tone is continued as Ray de la Paz still rejects the female and tells her to "check your head," thus inviting her to analyze and eventually change her own value system:

Medio coro: La pobreza

Que no, no, no, no, que no, no me interesa

Yo te aconsejo mamita que te examines la cabeza.

Half chorus: Poverty

Oh no, no, no, no, oh no, no I am not interested

I advise you baby to check your head.

The Native Perspective: Indigenous Concepts of Latinidad in the Music of Curet Alonso

PLANTACIÓN ADENTRO

"Plantación Adentro" was a very important release for Blades, and the early collaboration between Blades and Curet Alonso was very significant. The album marked the arrival of Salsa consciente into the mainstream of the Salsa world. While Curet Alonso had been pushing the idea for a while with songs such as "Anacaona," or "Con los Pobres Estoy," the fact that this song was a major hit gave both Blades and Curet Alonso a platform to further develop their ideas on a large scale.

Regarding the song, Blades (in Coss 2011 DVD) indicated that

> Tite's song was the hit from that album *Metiendo Mano*. When I chose "Plantación [adentro]," don't you think that it was a song that right away people at Fania said: "oh, great this is going to be a hit," because it had a political content that I developed further in the soneos . . . and the soneos show the injustice and the hazing that existed. Inside that there was also an anti-colonialist argument that is inside the song, and that refers specifically to a situation in Puerto Rico. So, it was not something that was openly "pacata" but it was there.[27] That was in '76, so also Panama, because we had the canal zone, a colony that the North Americans had disguised as something else.

Included in the first major release of Rubén Blades with Fania's 1977 *Metiendo Mano*, the song performed in the record depicts how the Native Americans were treated by the colonialist foremen. This particularly poignant song fits perfectly within Blades's progressive discourse, as it speaks of the often-ignored Native ethnic makeup of Latinos.

It is interesting to juxtapose the performance and reading of the piece as recorded by Blades with how Curet Alonso (in Fritz 2004 DVD) describes it himself:

> That is a song about rubber. "Plantación Adentro" paints the life that exists between Uruguay and Venezuela with the ones that work in the rubber

farms. The one that works there does not get paid directly, the salary is sent to the family, but he is almost not paid, so there are many that are there and never leave the plantations and die of jungle diseases, many of them in many cases between Brazil and Venezuela. So, I made this story wanting to show that really the criminal is not a criminal, it is the jungle that kills them, and that fight in the jungle between the animals and all that people; well, that is where that song came from.

Blades's reading of the song, and to a great extent almost everybody else's, in contrast points to a colonialist past in which the foremen brutally abused the Natives. This reading is framed very clearly by the introduction as spoken in the recording by Willie Colón.

The initial spoken description places the subject in colonial Latin America. This section was actually devised by Blades himself and not originally written by Curet Alonso. Blades (in Coss 2011 DVD) describes "that first part where Willie Colón speaks 'it is the year 1745 in Latin America . . . ' I wrote that. That way we place the issue in the correct framework."

"PLANTACIÓN ADENTRO" AS PERFORMED BY RUBÉN BLADES

Hablado: Es el año 1745,	**Spoken:** It is the year 1745,
En la América Latina el Indio trabaja	In Latin America the Indian works
En las plantaciones	In the plantations
Bajo el palo implacable del mayoral.	Under the relentless stick of the foreman.[28]

Musically speaking it is interesting to note the appearance of a samba feel at the beginning of the song as well as during the interlude. The arrangement by Willie Colón features an interlude that denotes traveling in the jungle in Latin America as well as its connection to the Caribbean as the interlude moves between three distinct phases: an Andean feel (2:26-2:35) exemplified by the appearance of the hi-hat cymbal on the upbeats, and a rolling snare drum, giving a marching-band feel to the song that is very unusual for Salsa yet very common in musical forms such as the Peruvian *huayno* and Colombian *porro*, two places that have a high concentration of Native peoples. The second feel of the interlude (2:35-2:44) moves to a quasi-*son montuno* as exemplified by the I-IV-V-IV progression utilizing the anticipated bass of the *son* in the following manner:

Figure 4. Quasi-*son montuno* as played in "Plantación Adentro."

I call the section a quasi-*son montuno,* as traditionally the *son montuno* would only utilize the primary diatonic I-IV-V-IV progression (Eb/Ab/Bb/Ab) either in a major or a minor key. In this case this holds true only for two bars, whereas the second part of the section temporarily modulates a step down to Db and repeats the progression with a different tonal center (Db/Gb/Ab/Gb) only to quickly return to the original tonal center. This type of progression is very unusual in Cuban *son,* and by extension Salsa, yet this stepwise type of movement is very common in Brazilian music. In this manner, Colón not only pays tribute to the music of Brazil via Cuba, but places the sonic marker in the Amazon jungle. The sequence is then repeated (2:45-3:03) only to finish on a samba feel, and eventually return to the chorus section.

The first part in which Curet Alonso's authorship is shown opens the song with the poetic concept of people as shadows. In this manner, Curet Alonso makes a reference to the passing spirits of people, the transient state of being where death waits at any time:

Sombras son la gente   Shadows are the people

The verse situates the story deep "inside the plantation," the place where the truth shall be learned. This is not a place known to the owner of the plantation; deep inside where the journey is bitter is where the truth of this story actually lies.

Plantación adentro camará	Deep inside the plantation brother
Es donde se sabe la verdad	Is where the truth is known
Es donde se aprende la verdad.	Is where you learn the truth.
Dentro del follaje y de la espesura	Into the foliage and the thickness
Donde todo el viaje lleva la amargura	Where the whole journey is bitter,
Es donde se sabe camará	That is where you know brother
Es donde se aprende la verdad.	That is where you learn the truth.

The main human character, as opposed to the plantation/jungle concept, is ultimately revealed. His name is Camilo Manríquez and he is dead after having been beaten by the foreman. The contrast in this phrase to what was described as the actual meaning of the song by Curet Alonso (in Fritz 2004 DVD) where Natives were dying from jungle diseases calls attention to the appearance of the foreman. In this case it is possible that Blades's reading of the song is actually more accurate than Curet Alonso's. This part of the verse paints Camilo Manríquez as an unknown man for whom no one cried at his burial and who only received "a cross made of sticks," and not even a name on his tomb.

Camilo Manríquez falleció	Camilo Manríquez died
Por golpes que daba el mayoral	From the blows that the foreman gave
Y fue sepultado sin llorar	And was buried without crying
Una cruz de palo y nada más.	A cross made of sticks and nothing more.

The chorus section highlights the truth of the song hidden in the place where Camilo Manríquez died: deep inside the plantation. The pregones in this section were actually developed by Blades: "the song was written by Tite and I developed the *soneos*."[29] As an example of his pregones, Blades explains: "And the doctor on duty is quoted in the song declaring: 'Death by natural causes.' Of course, since after a beating with a stick it is only natural to die. You know, you are speaking of injustice against indigenous people" (in Coss 2011 DVD).

Coro: Camilo Manríquez falleció,	**Chorus:** Camilo Manríquez died
Plantación adentro camará.	Deep inside the plantation, brother.
...	...
Se murió el Indio Camilo	Camilo the Indian died
Por palos que daba el mayoral.	From the blows that the foreman gave
Y el medico de turno dijo así:	And the doctor on duty said:
Muerte por causa natural.	Death by natural causes.
Claro, si después de una tunda e' palos	Of course, since after a beating with a stick
Que te mueras es normal.	It is normal to die.
...	...
Interludio instrumental	**Instrumental interlude**

There is in the reintroduction of the chorus an important connection in the aforementioned discrepancy regarding the meaning of the song between Curet Alonso and Blades. While the section continues the main argument of the song, that of the foreman versus the Native, the metaphorical character of the jungle shows both a connection and a contrast between Curet Alonso's reading and Blades's reading. As I have already mentioned, this dialectic between performer and composer is a common theme, yet the level of disconnectedness between both readings in this song makes the discrepancy a clear point of controversy in understanding the real meaning of the song. The incongruity between composer and performer once again pointed to the idea of Salsa as mainly being "composed in performance," but in reading the original verse, which was written by Curet Alonso himself, the section that indicates "Camilo Manríquez died from the blows that the foreman gave" actually contradicts Curet Alonso's 2002 reading of the song. It should be noted that according to Blades's reading of the song, Curet Alonso showed a subtle hint of the colonialist case of Puerto Rico and the United States. While this might be a conjecture on the part of Blades, it is a definite possibility, as Curet Alonso's work regarding Salsa consciente comes across as very subtle in comparison to Blades's "in your face" approach.

Coro: Camilo Manríquez falleció,	**Chorus:** Camilo Manríquez died
Plantación adentro camará.	Deep inside the plantation, brother.
…	…
Selva adentro, selva traga	Deep inside the jungle, the jungle swallows
Selva nunca dice na.	The jungle never says anything.
Recoge café y coge pa'lla	Pick coffee and move that way
Si no te pega el mayoral.	Or the foreman hits you.
Eh, Camilo Manríquez falleció	Hey, Camilo Manríquez died

Given this ambiguity of interpretation, it is an open question whether this song actually belongs in this chapter with Curet Alonso as the composer, or along with Blades's work as the performer. Blades's extensive contributions in the pregones and the spoken introduction make this issue even sharper. I place this song in this chapter specifically as the chapter on Rubén Blades not only analyzes music composed fully and exclusively by Blades, but the focus of these two case studies is ultimately on the composition and not performance of Salsa.

ANACAONA

"Anacaona" is a song written specifically for Cheo Feliciano as part of an album devised especially for him by Curet Alonso. Feliciano had been dealing with drug addiction and this recording marked his return to the stage. The album—and according to Salsa folklore, Cheo Feliciano as well—was produced by Curet Alonso. In that manner, the album marks Cheo Feliciano's return as much as it marks Curet Alonso's appearance among the Salsa elite. "Anacaona" was a major hit and became a true Salsa standard. Moreno Velázquez in his Fania website review of the album indicated that "With the mythic 'Anacaona,' also written by Curet Alonso, Feliciano made the top play lists at radio stations in New York as well as Puerto Rico." Rondón (2008, 202) mentioned that "Cheo also recorded a song that became the first great hit or success of the Salsa explosion, 'Anacaona.'" The song was originally recorded using the sextet sound that included the vibraphone as a link to the distinctive sound that Cheo Feliciano made originally in his early days with the Joe Cuba Sextet.

The lyrics of the song deal specifically with the female *Taíno* (native Caribbean) chief Anacaona. Cadilla de Martinez (in Salazar 2007, 40) indicated that "Anacaona, was a celebrated Dominican poet, wife of the chief Caonabo . . . she was known for writing *areytos* [*sic*] or rhythms." The *Merriam-Webster* online dictionary defines *areíto* as "a ceremonial dance among the indigenous peoples of Spanish America; also: the songs and masks associated with the dance." In this manner, much like Curet Alonso, Anacaona is actually a composer. Salazar (2007, 40-42) describes how Anacaona was actually captured by Viceroy Nicolás de Ovando for whom she performed a majestic *areíto* only to be later assassinated.

The song, even though specifically dealing with the story of Anacaona, places the possibility of interpreting the case of Anacaona initially as a totem of Native roots, perhaps of only Taínos. There is also the possibility of understanding the song as an anti-colonialist declamation. This is particularly plausible taking into consideration the fact that this song is written by a Puerto Rican composer describing the suffering of a Dominican chief, thus expanding a pan-Caribbean sensibility against Spanish oppression. Worthy of note is the fact that Curet Alonso later wrote a song titled "Caonabo" describing the suffering of Anacaona's husband after her death. In joining and expanding these two songs, the anti-colonialist sentiment can be understood not only as the struggle between the Native population and the Spaniards, but as a reference to the colonial state of Puerto Rico's relationship with the United States, thus combining the contemporary with the historical. There is in this song and in "Plantación Adentro" a historic sensibility that places Curet Alonso as a virtual "griot" by telling the history of his people through song.

The song is introduced by the first chorus, where the lead character is placed after her capture. The chorus marks the primitive region as the native place of Anacaona, that is, the Caribbean basin. The verse shows the suffering and anger of Anacaona while associating her with an expectation of freedom. In the totemic image of Anacaona, the freedom can easily be understood in a larger colonial context.

"ANACAONA" AS PERFORMED BY CHEO FELICIANO

Coro: Anacaona, India de raza cautiva	**Chorus:** Anacaona, Indian woman of a captured race,
Anacaona, de la región primitiva.	Anacaona of the primitive region.
Anacaona, India de raza cautiva	Anacaona, Indian woman of a captured race,
Anacaona, de la región primitiva.	Anacaona of the primitive region
Anacaona oí tú voz,	Anacaona, I heard your voice,
Como lloró, cuanto gimió	How much it cried when it moaned
Anacaona oí la voz de tu angustiado corazón	Anacaona, I heard the voice of your anguished heart
Tu libertad nunca llegó	Your freedom never arrived[30]

The introduction of the chorus begins the call-and-response section, and includes the word *areíto*, thus playing on the fact that Anacaona wrote *areítos*, and that Curet's composition is itself an *areíto* dedicated to Anacaona. Feliciano's first pregón has a melancholic tone to it with the inclusion of the symbolic image of the "soul of a white dove" denoting Anacaona's purity and peace. The following pregones however, paint Anacaona as fierce since she does not forgive and was very brave. This emphasizes a contradictory spirit that is nevertheless part of her identity. It is also interesting to note the inclusion of the figure of the Black woman in this song as the song is dedicated to a Native woman. This detail was no doubt included to expand the relevance of the references to suffering giving the song a larger racial span and symbolizing the joint struggles of Black people next to the Natives under colonial rule. Following the instrumental interlude, the second chorus is once again introduced, and on this occasion Feliciano's pregones include historical details and the fact of the tribe's anger. There is once again an African racial component to this set of pregones:

Segundo Coro: Anacaona, *areíto* de Anacaona.	**Second Chorus:** Anacaona, song and dance of Anacaona.
India de raza cautiva,	Indian woman of a captured race
Alma de blanca paloma, Anacaona.	Soul of a white dove, Anacaona
Pero, India que muere llorando,	But, an Indian woman that dies crying,

Muere pero no perdona, no perdona no.	Dies but does not forgive, does not forgive, no
Esa Negra que es de raza noble y abatida	That Black woman of a noble and beaten-down race
Pero que fue valentona, ¡Anacaona!	But that was very brave, Anacaona!
Interludio instrumental	**Instrumental interlude**
Segundo coro: Anacaona, *areíto* de Anacaona.	**Second chorus:** Anacaona, song and dance of Anacaona
Oye, según la historia lo cuenta	Listen according to history
Dicen que fue a la cañona, Anacaona.	They say that it was full force, Anacaona.
La tribu entera la llora porque fue buena Negrona.	The whole tribe cries for her because she was a good Black woman.
Y recordando, recordando lo que pasó	And remembering, remembering what happened
La tribu ya se enfogona.	The tribe gets furious

Musically speaking, the arrangement is fairly sophisticated yet does not appear to contain any ethnic markers. Salazar (2007, 41) does, however, indicate that "in the musical arrangement stands out the jam or mambo, as it is called in the Salsa argot, a unirhythmic sound that possibly was utilized in the *areítos* according to what has been found by some researchers." While the point is contentious, as the actual components of the musical arrangement of *areítos* are ultimately unknown due to the Native genocide at the hands of the Spaniards, Salazar's idealistic intentions point to the intensity of the connection of the conscious Latino with their past. As I have already pointed out, this connection with the Native past of Latinos is quite important yet often set aside due to Eurocentric visions of belonging. Nevertheless, as per Salazar's account, and taking into account Bobby Valentín's

Figure 5. "Anacaona" *areíto* motif as described by Salazar.

(the arranger of the song) idealistic intentions, it seems fitting, given that such a type of device was ultimately used to develop some kind of ancestral connection to the Taíno realm.

The Poet of Salsa Consciente

As I have shown, Curet Alonso's work contains a great number of elements that qualify him not only as one of the main composers of the Salsa movement but as the key initial developer of Salsa consciente. Despite having found earlier occasions where Afro-Latino identity or social discourse had been presented as part of pre-Salsa, Curet Alonso quickly developed an early, profound, and consistent discourse regarding negritude, social, and ethnic issues.

I have remarked that Curet Alonso's discourse uses poetic indirection to exalt beauty rather than directly denouncing an issue. This can clearly be seen in songs such as "Pura novela," where poverty and disenfranchisement are glorified and equated with being "real." In the case of "Con los Pobres Estoy," there is a direct connection between place and being one with El Pueblo, The People. By the same token, the *arrabal*, the slum, is glorified in "Pura novela" as a place where the lead character wishes so strongly to return that she would give her castle and nobility title to be once again part of it.

Regarding the case of "Las Caras Lindas," there is direct praise of the beauty of the faces of Black people, consequently confronting the internalized Latin American racism and its denial of its African heritage. The racial issue is also brought up in "Sorongo," where Curet Alonso's unanswered question gives way to a lengthy reading and subsequent racial and historical speech by Calle 13.

Regarding the Indigenous issues, Curet Alonso brings his Native perceptions from a sociohistorical and, perhaps, anti-colonialist point of view, tying the historical into the contemporary and developing a timeless socio-historical discourse regarding Native issues. As shown previously, the idea of Latino unity is one where Curet Alonso developed part of his discourse, although not in the same direct manner or breadth as Blades did; the concept was still presented forthrightly as exemplified by the song "Pueblo Latino." The concept of Latinidad in Curet Alonso's oeuvre, however, is expressed ultimately in a very distinct manner that combines a number of elements with a very poetic language achieving a consistent concern and connection with being Puerto Rican, Black, Indigenous, Latin American, and Latino.

This look at a sample of Curet Alonso's work only does justice to a very small part of his effort. Curet Alonso's work still remains a large pool to explore as his oeuvre is enormous in terms of quantity and extremely profound in terms of quality. It is difficult, if not impossible, to think of another musician/composer who has had such an enormous impact on the output of a whole genre.

CHAPTER FOUR

Rubén Blades's Move into Salsa

I really think that music itself, being one of the greatest possible vehicles
for mass communication, should be probed to its extremes, to see how
effective it can actually become, which is one of the reasons why I became
also interested in presenting political points of view.

—Rubén Blades

Rubén Blades is without a doubt the most important artist of Salsa
consciente and has historically been, along with Curet Alonso, its
intellectual force. I am developing this section not only as a case
study on Rubén Blades, but also as a study of Salsa as a mainly oral, perfor-
mance-based art to its development as Salsa consciente stemming from a
compositional, written process. In this sense, Blades is not the creator but
one of the major theorists of Salsa consciente. Unlike Curet Alonso, however,
Blades worked as a performer and as such he became the catalyst for the
movement's surge in popularity. Additionally, Blades's position as a non-
Puerto Rican, but as a highly educated Panamanian and Latin American,
precipitates this change by including an internationalist and intrinsically
progressive discourse that moves beyond Lavoe's Puerto Rican signifiers,
and utilizes a larger, synthetized Latino/Latin American set of lyrical and
sonic markers that ground the musical output not as inward-facing, but
as a discourse engulfed in the progressive Latin American-based liberation
ideologies. In this manner, I analyze Rubén Blades's work through his

compositions rather than his performances, positioning Blades's work as the definitive means of development of Salsa consciente, as he not only addresses previous issues, but forges a number of new paths to produce a significant change in the conceptualizations of Salsa.

As I have done earlier in this study, I pursue this analysis from a Gramscian point of view, through which I consider Blades to be an anti-hegemonic cultural figure, specifically in regard to the norms and values imposed upon Latinos and Latin Americans by the power of the United States. Blades's work from early on displays a remarkable sensibility toward developing the value of Latino/Latin American culture as a working-class identity. He does this through his social role as an intellectual who employs Salsa as a medium to express a working-class culture.

In this sense, Blades is as much an educator as a musician, since it could be argued that much of his work is based upon that of Paulo Freire and the pedagogy of the oppressed, as well as Althusser's concept of interpellation, as he incites and educates Latinos and Latin Americans to participate critically in the changes experienced by Latino/Latin American societies. As such, Blades develops the Latin Americanist cause as parallel and consciously attached to the struggles of Latinos. This element likely stems from the fact that Blades is a highly educated Latin American born and raised in Panama.[1] Thus, he approaches his work from a perspective that in an initial stage sees the struggles of his country as part of Latin America, and then, upon his arrival in New York City, sees and connects the similarities of these struggles with those of Latinos in the city.

Blades's work adds to the discussion of the—thus far absent—concept of Latinos/Latin Americans and Salsa as related to specifically political endeavors. This contrasts with the idea of Salsa confronting social issues, as was the case in Curet Alonso's work, given that Blades immerses himself deep within the recent past of a Latin America that by the 1970s and 1980s had experienced—and still was experiencing—massive levels of violence, related mostly to dictatorships and invasions of Latin America often tied to the United States. In fact, Blades's compositions quickly question the almost assumed role of the United States in Latin America as a force of good and a role model that has the best interests of the region at heart.

Blades's journey, which is the driving idea behind the current and the next chapter, can be approached via his move into the Fania label as first and foremost a Salsa artist to his later move out of Fania and with it the development of a gradual move out of Salsa. While this is not an argument that says that Blades gave up on Salsa, it does present the idea of Fania Records owning Salsa in the commercial sense, while the growing politicization of Blades's compositional work eventually drove him out of the commercial Salsa mainstream.

Blades before Fania

Blades's early musical career included the release of a few singles and participation in a full-length recording with "Los Salvajes del Ritmo" in the 1960s in Panama. His abilities as a songwriter, however, began to emerge early as the group Bush y Su Nuevo Sonido featured a 45-rpm single with two of Blades's compositions, which even though he wrote he did not perform them with the group. Side A of the single included the song "9 de Enero" (January 9th) in which a young Blades began to make clear his position on social and political issues.

9 DE ENERO

This song is particularly poignant in Blades's work as not only did it mark one of his first occasions as a songwriter, but the piece has a strong sociopolitical tone referencing the events of January 9, 1964, in Panama. Cruz (1997, 8-9) describes the events as follows:

> One morning in January 1964, a few North American students attending Balboa High School in the Canal Zone refused to fly the Panamanian flag alongside the American, even though it was in violation of a United States-Panama agreement . . . The next day, in protest, two hundred Panamanian students from the national institute marched into the Canal Zone and tried to raise the Panamanian flag next to the American flag. The American Canal zone students again refused, and when a fight broke

out, the United States military was called to restore order. When police started attacking the Panamanian students with tear gas, a riot followed. Angry Panamanians stormed The Canal Zone . . . After four days of rioting, twenty-two Panamanians and three United States soldiers were left dead. Another five hundred Panamanian citizens were wounded and hundreds more were jailed.

"9 DE ENERO" COMPOSED BY RUBÉN BLADES, 1967

Nueve de Enero,	January ninth
Yo no te olvido,	I don't forget you
Ni al pueblo entero que con valor enfrentó	Or the people that bravely faced
A la metralla del "Buen Vecino,"	The machine gun of the "Good Neighbor"
Que en un momento sus promesas olvido.	That in an instant its promises forgot.
Orgullosa, sobre el plomo fue flameando mi bandera,	Proud, over the lead was flying my flag
En blanco, azul y con rojo, sangre de Ascanio Arosemena[2]	In white, blue and red, blood of Ascanio Arosemena![3]

While the song has a strong sociopolitical tone to it, it is a nationalist song, a topic that is not directly related to the larger argument of this book. I present this composition, however, as part of this analysis mainly to show Blades's early and explicit preoccupation with social issues. Regarding the song's connection to Salsa consciente, it shows Blades from the start utilizing key allegories that would later play important roles in his work. The use of the term *pueblo*, The People, for example, is a key marker of Salsa consciente as it determines the singer as part of and committed to a larger social group. The second important allegory here is the sarcastic use of "good neighbor" in reference to the United States. References of this type were repeatedly used by Blades, whether to refer to the United States or to the vision to which Latin America aspires. The idea of removing the mask of imperialism and showing it to Latinos became a crucial marker for Blades specifically and a part of his Salsa consciente discourse.

While in New York in 1970, Blades produced an early work as a leader entitled "From Panama to New York" alongside the orchestra of Pete "Boogaloo" Rodriguez. The record was released by Alegre Records the same year. This record, though ultimately not a critical symbol of Salsa consciente, introduced Blades as a songwriter, and presented the first layer of Blades's socially engaged discourse. Perhaps the most relevant track on this recording is the opening song called "Juan Gonzalez," the first song he ever wrote, in 1968. The track is based on the style of Cuban *son*.

JUAN GONZALEZ

Built around standard liberation ideologies, "Juan Gonzalez" is situationally and temporally displaced as its introduction denotes: "The story you are about to hear is a work of fiction. Any similarities with people dead or alive are just a coincidence." This disclaimer holds an important caveat, and can, perhaps in retrospect, be considered a satirical touch to the song. Within the statement, however, an idea that permeated most of Blades's work quickly presents itself: the creation of fictional places and/or characters that in some way or another are "real," tangible, or recognizable to a great majority of Latinos and Latin Americans and that act as clear markers of Latinidad.

The song tells the story of a fictional (but well-known) guerilla fighter with a name analogous to John Smith. The song thus draws on the current awareness that the guerrillas had become a mainstay in the Latin America of the period. Groups such as the Peruvian Ejército de Liberación Nacional (National Liberation Army), the Uruguayan Movimiento de Liberación Nacional Tupamaros (Tupamaros National Liberation Movement), or the Nicaraguan Frente Sandinista de Liberación Nacional (Sandinista National Liberation Front) had been in full force, and using this song Blades tells the story of one of their fighters being killed by the military.

"JUAN GONZALEZ" AS PERFORMED IN THE ALBUM *DE PANAMA A NUEVA YORK*

La patrulla ha llegado al pueblo con la noticia	The patrol has arrived in town with the news
Que acabaron con Juan González el guerrillero	That they finished off Juan Gonzalez the guerrilla fighter

| Que por fin el león de la sierra reposa muerto | That finally the lion of the mountains lies dead |
| La guerrilla murió con él grita un sargento | The guerrilla died with him yells a sergeant[4] |

What is potentially expected of a Salsa song produced in New York at this time was definitely not the story of a guerrilla fighter, much less one showing the guerrilla point of view. In the second verse, Blades shows the sadness of a woman who is potentially Gonzalez's partner and mother of his child. The section also notes the connection of Juan Gonzalez's efforts to those of the poor of the world, yet another pueblo marker:

En un bohío monte adentro se escucha el llanto	In a shack deep in the mountains you hear the crying
De una mujer con un niño que está en pañales	Of a woman with a child in diapers
Con ella lloran también los pobres del mundo	With her also cry the poor of the world
Los campos lloran la muerte de Juan González	The fields mourn the death of Juan Gonzalez

The arrival of the chorus ultimately paints Juan Gonzalez as an important figure for El Pueblo, as the mountains, the place where the guerrilla and the resistance would be located, "cry" at news of his demise. There is also a light yet important reference to Native people (Indians) as they also are seen to have shared pain and lost people in the same fight. Blades's pregones once again reinforce the idea of Juan Gonzalez as the hero of the story as well as showing a human side to Gonzalez by presenting him as a son and as a friend:

Coro: La Sierra viste de luto, mataron a Juan González	**Chorus:** The mountains are dressed for mourning, they killed Juan Gonzalez
...	...
Con él cayo Papo "El Indio" y el bueno de Claudio Fernández	Along with him fell Papo "The Indian," and good man Claudio Fernandez
Tiraron al león más bravo, al hijo de Juana Morales	They shot the bravest lion, the son of Juana Morales

El Indio solloza triste, mataron al tigre errante	The Indian weeps sadly, they killed the roaming tiger
Interludio instrumental	**Instrumental Interlude**
Coro: La Sierra viste de luto mataron a Juan González	**Chorus:** The mountains are dressed for mourning, they killed Juan Gonzalez
…	…
Tiraron al león más bravo al hijo de Juana Morales	They shot the bravest lion, the son of Juana Morales
Desde la sierra sale un grito, no has muerto en vano compadre	From the mountains comes a cry, you have not died in vain my friend

With the introduction of the half chorus, the song fades out, while gunfire eventually overpowers Blades's pregones.

Medio coro: Mataron a Juan González	**Half chorus:** They killed Juan Gonzalez
Tiraron al hijo de Juana Morales	They shot the son of Juana Morales
Que lo tiraron, que lo tiraron lo pillaron durmiendo	They shot him, they shot him sleeping
…	…
Que tiroteo, que tiroteo más grande se escucha.	What gunfire, what huge gunfire you can hear.

The Alliance with Willie Colón

After a brief stint as a mailman with Fania Records in the early 1970s, Blades was eventually hired to sing lead vocals with Ray Barretto, as background vocalist for several Fania recordings, as well as writing songs for numerous other Fania artists, among them Ismael Miranda, Andy Harlow, and Bobby Rodriguez y La Compañía.

By 1975 Rubén Blades began singing with trombonist Willie Colón, and in the end replaced the most iconic figure of Salsa, Puerto Rican singer Héctor Lavoe. This played out both positively and negatively for Blades, who must have been aware of the significance of stepping into the shoes of one of the most beloved Salsa icons in history. Not only is this important in Salsa history, as Blades had to be different enough from Lavoe, yet respectful enough of Colón's role as one of the definers of Salsa, but it is a fact that the Colón/Lavoe duo defined the sound of Salsa as a very Puerto Rican-centered endeavor. With Blades not being Puerto Rican, and a very socially and politically minded person, the nationalistic associations of the music shifted dramatically toward a Latin American social-centered discourse. This shift came rapidly, not only from Blades's positioning, but from the personal meltdown of Lavoe as the star of the Colón/Lavoe duo, allowing Blades as his replacement to be the catalyst of profound change in the social emphasis of Willie Colón's music.[5] This fact, coupled with the importance and fame of Willie Colón in the Salsa world, immediately lent an enormous amount of musical credibility to Blades's proposals. Throughout the rest of this chapter I elaborate on many of the propositions brought forth by the Colón/Blades collaboration, and analyze their impact on the overall development of Blades's work.

Blades's Fania period is clearly marked by a preoccupation with Latino/ Latin American issues at large, as his discography in general at this time discusses the connections, commonalities, and ways to improve mutual issues shared by Latinos and Latin Americans as a major point of contention. The Fania period of Blades can be understood initially in terms of Blades's recognition of El Pueblo, despite his "non-street" credentials. In a second stage, however, he delved into a discourse very much characterized by the idea of Latino/Latin American unity through the idea of The People, and he developed a discourse that approached Salsa from a more intellectual basis, thus attracting many listeners who had up to this point considered Salsa to be "low class" music.

The association with the well-known Willie Colón quickly established Blades as one of the top Salsa singers of the era, and it soon marked the arrival of a new stage in Salsa music. The release of their 1978 album *Siembra* marked a clear shift in the endeavors and role of Salsa, and established Salsa consciente as a pillar of the genre. Blades continued to work with Colón either as coleader or as producer for the next few years and released several other albums, such as *Maestra Vida* and *Canciones del Solar de los Aburridos*. The association with Willie Colón, however, led first to the release of *Metiendo Mano* in 1977.

METIENDO MANO (1977)

Metiendo Mano marked the official end of Héctor Lavoe as the lead singer of the Willie Colón band and gave Blades the complex task of replacing the highly beloved Puerto Rican as a lead vocalist in the ensemble. The release officially placed Blades alongside Salsa "royalty" such as Cheo Feliciano, Héctor Lavoe, and Celia Cruz. Sonically, the album mostly employs the Cuban musical models that had become standard in the Salsa of the time. As such it includes the styles expected in such a release: *son, guaracha, guajira, bolero,* and *guaguancó.* An exception to this is the inclusion of sonic markers, alongside very poignant lyrics, in the song "Plantación Adentro" (Deep inside the Plantation) composed by Curet Alonso.[6]

Most important with regard to Blades's contribution is his role as a composer/songwriter in the album. The four pieces Blades contributed to in the recording merit an in-depth analysis, as they stand out from most of the Salsa that had been released thus far and, partially thanks to Colón's fame, marked the arrival of a Latino consciousness to the mainstream Salsa scene.

In terms of social awareness, the most salient feature of the album is the repeated inclusion of the word "Pueblo" in both the opening and the closing tracks of the album. The use of this word is crucial in understanding Blades's discourse in general, as this is one of the key concepts of how he expresses Latinidad. It is in the idea of expressing an undetermined nationalist identity, as he is not singing to a town in particular but to "The People," where Blades thrives. This concept is repeated frequently throughout his discography and presents a clear push to help empower Latinos and Latin Americans not as separate nations but as unified.

While the concept of mixing sociopolitical issues and Salsa is not new, this release introduced the substantive understanding of such topics in a very direct and commercially popular manner. I include an analysis below of the song "Pablo Pueblo" as the most relevant song of the album. It contains myriad elements that make it critical within both Salsa consciente and Blades's work as a whole, such as very vivid description of places and the creation of one of the main characters of the "meta-barrio."

PABLO PUEBLO

"Pablo Pueblo" sees Blades, much as he did with "Juan Gonzalez," create a character that depicts not a person in particular but an iconographic image of the working man who aims to escape his reality, emphasized by his choice of names: Pablo Pueblo (Paul People). This image plays into the inclusion of urban characters that Blades developed in his work, with Pablo Pueblo the first urban character in a very long list to which Curet Alonso has also contributed. The lyrics of the song depict alongside Pablo Pueblo a clear view of the meta-barrio in which Blades, with his gift of description, paints a Latino meta-homeland with the streets that every Latino/Latin American that grew up in an urban area easily remembers.

The importance of such archetypical characters plays within the social discourse as it shows the realities of the everyday Latino/Latin American without the need to refer to specific nationalities. These types of signifiers, as I have already mentioned, are crucial to the development of Salsa consciente as a transnational phenomenon, since it links different nationalistic identities, not via heritage but through the common ground of social issues and general marginalization. Pablo Pueblo is one of the most crucial characters in the development of this transnational phenomenon as Salsa previously had mostly developed its conscious discourse either based on racial issues, or as an expression of a general disenchantment with the system. The use of archetypical characters and sets of realities, once again, founded on larger, internationally constructed signifiers was, if somewhat controversial, or not specifically relevant to the general Salsa audience of the United States, "permitted" to be released by the record company (Fania) as Salsa's popularity in dictator-ridden and disenfranchisement-laden Latin America had risen enormously, and these topics were apt to sell in that market.

The verse of the song paints a clear description of the meta-barrio, a place of poverty and social discrimination and a direct marker of pueblo identity. This barrio, with trash piles, political posters, dark alleys, and noisy bars, is a place known to the large majority of Latinos and Latin Americans. This barrio also connects the diaspora, as the large majority of the Latin American migrants in the United States had left their countries to directly escape this situation. In a way Blades reminds us that poverty has no nationality, as well as reminding us of misery, desperation, and hunger; and in that image, there is a clear and very purposeful connection of Blades's discourse to all of the working Latin American and diasporic Latino pueblo.

"PABLO PUEBLO"

Regresa un hombre en silencio	A man silently returns
De su trabajo cansado	From his work, tired
...	...
Lo espera el barrio de siempre	The usual neighborhood awaits him
...	...
Con la basura allá en frente	With the trash pile in front
Y el ruido de la cantina	And the noise from the bar
Pablo Pueblo	Paul People
Llega hasta el zaguán oscuro	Arrives at the dark entranceway
Y vuelve a ver las paredes	And sees once again the walls
Con las viejas papeletas	With the old flyers
Que prometían futuros	That promised futures
En lides politiqueras	In political matters
Y en su cara se dibuja	And his face is drawn with
La decepción de la espera	The deception of waiting
Pablo Pueblo	Paul People
Hijo del grito y la calle	Son of the yell and the street
De la miseria y del hambre	Of misery and hunger
Del callejón y la pena	Of the alley and sadness
Pablo Pueblo	Paul People
Su alimento es la esperanza	His nourishment is hope
...	...
Entra al cuarto	Comes into the room
Y se queda mirando	And looks
A su mujer y a los niños	At his wife and the kids
Y se pregunta hasta cuando	And asks himself how long?
...	...
Pablo Pueblo	Paul People

Hijo del grito y la calle	Son of the yell and the street
De la miseria y del hambre	Of misery and hunger
Del callejón y la pena	Of the alley and sadness
Pablo Pueblo	Paul People
Su alimento es la esperanza.	His nourishment is hope.

The chorus shows Pablo as a member of the family—my family and your family—by calling him "brother." He is my brother, your brother, our brother. Pablo Pueblo searches for relief in the usual ways, having drinks, playing dominoes, praying, and looking to change his luck playing the lottery. Not only is Pablo Pueblo depicted as one who is socially displaced, but he is shown as a politically disenchanted person who has experienced the empty promises of the politicians, has voted, and is still in the same situation:

Coro: Pablo Pueblo, Pablo hermano	**Chorus:** Paul People, Paul brother
Trabajo hasta jubilarse	Worked until retirement
Y nunca sobraron chavos	And never had extra dough (money)
Votando en las elecciones	Voting in the elections
Pa' después comerse un clavo	So he can afterwards eat nails (suck it)
Pablo con el silencio del pobre	Pablo with the silence of the poor man
Con los gritos por abajo	With the screams underneath
…	…
Echa pa'lante Pablito	Push forward Pablito
Y a la vida mete mano	And fight for life
A un crucifijo rezando	To a crucifix praying
Y el cambio esperando ¡ay Dios!	And waiting for change, dear God!
Mira a su mujer y a los nenes	Looks at his wife and kids
Y se pregunta hasta cuando	And asks himself, how much longer?
Interludio (instrumental)	**Interlude (instrumental)**
Coro: Pablo Pueblo, Pablo hermano	**Chorus:** Paul People, Paul brother
Llega a su barrio de siempre	Arrives at his old neighborhood
Cansa'o de la factoría	Tired from the factory
Buscando suerte en caballos	Searching for luck at the horse races

Y comprando lotería	And buying lottery tickets
Gastando su dinerito en domino	Spending his money in dominoes
Y tomándose un par de tragos	And having a couple of drinks
Hijo del grito y la calle	Son of the screams and the streets
De la pena y del quebranto	Of sadness and grief
Ay Pablo Pueblo	Oh, Paul People
Ay Pablo hermano.	Oh, Paul Brother.

"Pablo Pueblo" has no obvious musical signifiers that permit an extensive analysis of its sonic content. It is worth noting, however, the switching of rhythms from a Cuban *son* style to a Puerto Rican *bomba sicá*. This is not a particularly innovative device, as the very same Colon/Lavoe duo had already made use of this switch, but in this case it can be seen to include the style of *bomba* as a representative of the humble beginnings of both the style and of Pablo Pueblo, as well as drawing a connection to Puerto Rico as one of the main consumers of the music, and as a representation of the pan-Caribbean sensibility of the image of the common man embodied by Pablo Pueblo.

SIEMBRA: THE BREAKTHROUGH ALBUM (1978)

The album *Siembra* is not only one of the pillars of Salsa consciente but of Salsa itself.[7] Despite the fact that the album was released when the Salsa boom was fading, *Siembra* not only propelled Rubén Blades to Salsa stardom but it cemented Salsa as the main Latino/Latin American music genre of the late 1970s. The album's popularity in the United States and in Latin America was enormous. Rondón (2008, 276) indicated that *Siembra* was "an album that even amid the decline of the boom became the best-selling record in the history of Caribbean music." Sara Del Valle Hernández, writing in the Puerto Rican newspaper *El Nuevo Día*, confirms it as the bestselling Salsa album of all time, with over 30 million copies sold as of 2008, marking the thirtieth anniversary of the release of *Siembra*. In the same article, promoter and music historian Richi Vera pointed out that "the record showed the experiences of all of Latin America, everybody identified themselves in it."

Regarding the content of the album, *Siembra* was a very unusual release for its time: the themes are certainly not what was expected from such a popular album, since it contains references to social issues facing Latin America as well as Latinos in the United States. "Plástico," for example, denounces materialism and classism in Latin America as well as Latinos in the United States. "Pedro Navaja" presents life in the urban city via the lengthy story of an urban gangster against the sounds of New York police-car sirens opening the track. The story of "Maria Lionza" is based on a Venezuelan Indigenous religious figure, thus including Venezuela in the album, with the album eventually achieving enormous success in that country.[8] The pièce de résistance, however, is the track "Siembra," with its now-famous call to plant the seeds of the Latino future with faith and consciousness. I analyze "Plástico" and "Siembra" in detail in this chapter.

While the narration of social issues was not new, *Siembra* went beyond the specificity of C. Curet Alonso's African, Indigenous, and Puerto Rican pride, or the presentation of social issues such as Arsenio Rodriguez and his African-centered discussion. *Siembra* is unquestionably the first album to confront deep contemporary issues in Latinidad. Despite the fact that Larry Harlow's 1977 Grammy-nominated release *La Raza Latina* (The Latin Race) paid homage to Salsa and being Latino,[9] and even when Willie Colón and Héctor Lavoe furthered a pan-American sound by including rhythms and lyrics relating to countries other than Cuba and Puerto Rico, *Siembra* represents a quantum leap into issues of Latinidad, as Blades and Colón created what Blades (1983) referred to as "The Republic of Hispania" (La República de Hispania)—a place where the Latino and its issues exist every day. This concept is what I have already referred to as the creation of the meta-barrio—a place where the conceptualizations and commonalities of being Latino and/or Latin American are presented as a cohesive unit and the images, people, and places are recognized by everyone without being actually tied to any country in particular.

In a manner different from previous efforts, perhaps with the exception of some of Tite Curet's works, *Siembra* presents the beauty, joy, and a general celebration of being Latino. In addition, the album speaks of dictatorship, Latino unity, gangster life, prostitutes, the ambiguity of "success," and the idea of sowing the seeds for a better future. Though the album reads partially as a list of warnings, the success of the album clearly calls attention to the importance of the themes as something relevant and not just an alarmist call.

The sonic content was relatively progressive for Salsa standards as it contained harmonies and rhythmical developments that stretched the traditional tenets of the *sones* and *guarachas* played by other Salsa artists. With *Siembra*, there is a clear turn towards emphasizing sonic markers as part of the overall discourse. While the lyrics are still at the forefront of the display of social consciousness, the sonic aspect shows clear development. This was a true advancement for Salsa music, where historically, following the European models, the lyrical aspect of the genre had superseded the music, which mainly served as mere accompaniment to the lyrics. The length of every piece was a significant difference from previously recorded material, with the shortest piece of the album being just shy of five minutes, thus deviating from the three and a half to four minutes standard song length of the radio format of the times. The forms of the songs were also different compared with previous Salsa releases; the development of pieces was not necessarily based, as was traditional, on the repetition of the call and response of the chorus section, but mainly on the development of a long story or theme during the head of the song. One can thus say that the concept of Salsa as literary narrative can be attributed specifically to Blades's work.

The reception of the album, however, was not wholly positive. Aurora Flores in her Fania.com review of Blades's album *Maestra Vida* remarked that

> In those liberal New York times Blades stood out as artist/immigrant/ working class hero giving voice to the struggling Latino. In war torn Latin America, however, that same standing had a double edge as the military disrupted concerts while government controlled press interrogated rather than interviewed promoters and artists.

Another reason to consider this album as the pillar of Salsa consciente is the inclusion for the first time of the term *conciencia* (conscience/

consciousness) within the context of Salsa. The term is presented as the opening of the last track ("Siembra") where Blades famously proclaims "Usa la conciencia Latino, no dejes que se te duerma, no la dejes que muera" ("Use your conscience/consciousness Latino, do not let it fall asleep, do not let it die"), and in the closing of the album where both Blades and Colón in unison say, "Conciencia, familia" ("Conscience/consciousness family"). This lyrical theme not only opened the door to the style but attempted a unification of the Latino/Latin American experience by referring to everyone as a family.

Regarding the content and reception of the album, Willie Colón (in Del Valle Hernández, 2008) indicated that

> This was a concept album, not only a commercial project. It became a movement, a symbol of a Latin American hope . . . we could not have expected the response it had, what we were conscious of, however, was that we were using the record, the moment as a platform to make a socio-political proposal. It was an idea, of forming a brotherhood and solidarity between Latin Americans. The acceptance was so big and so logical that it broke many barriers of class.

In the same article, Blades mentioned that

> The argument of the content of the record never stopped being fresh. That is why it is remembered today. The ideas that are developed in each of the songs are still in full force. It was always an expression of the urban feeling, and in our cities, the basis of the existential human conflict has not really changed in 30 years.

Furthermore, Blades (1983) remarked that *Siembra*

> was a record where there was a lyrical production that was much more deliberate, and that in its moment represented a document that shook the institutions of Latin American popular music . . . *Siembra* was a slap in the face, if you will, to the apparently asleep popular sensibilities.

In analyzing the impact of *Siembra*, it is clear that the album shook the structures of the Salsa establishment, and that in this position it presented a transnational Latino/Latin American discourse that was to a large extent sociopolitically centered. The importance of this release cannot be over-emphasized; *Siembra* is arguably the most important Salsa release ever, not only thematically, but also stylistically, in terms of song length, lyrical storylines, orchestration, arrangements, inclusion of orchestral textures, development of the album as a larger interconnected conceptual album, and departure from the radio airplay mold, production, etc., all of which made the release unprecedented for Salsa standards. It could even be argued that it is the most important work in the history of Latino recording. I analyze some of these groundbreaking features below; however, I advise the readers to listen to the album as a whole, contextualize it themselves, and compare *Siembra* to other Salsa releases of the time.

PLÁSTICO

Along with "Pedro Navaja," this piece was one of the biggest hits of the album *Siembra*.[10] "Plástico" is a critique of not only materialism but also the loss of traditional Latin American values in the face of the market economy of the United States. In 1978 only a few countries in Latin America had a democratically elected government and political repression was at its peak. While some people were dying in violent dictatorships, others were enjoying a frivolous, opulent lifestyle as if nothing was happening. "Plástico" is based on critical references to class warfare and lifestyles built upon falsehood and superficiality versus the authenticity that, according to Blades, should prevail in the Latino community.

The piece begins by introducing the vain and consumerist "plastic girl," her partner the "plastic boy," the "plastic family," and the "plastic city." The piece questions the values of this family as based exclusively on appearances to keep their social status. The family is criticized as racist, elitist, and enthralled by vain consumerism financed by debt. This presentation offers a critique of the falsehood and deceit that consumerism and concern with appearances bring and how Latinos are positioned to be tricked into believing that this is the image of success and that it should be attained at any cost.

"PLÁSTICO" COMPOSED BY RUBÉN BLADES

Ella era una chica plástica de ésas que veo por ahí,	She was a plastic girl like others I see around,
De ésas que cuando se agitan, sudan Chanel No. 3.	Those girls that sweat Chanel No. 3 when they are agitated.
Que sueñan casarse con un doctor pues él puede mantenerlas mejor.	They dream of marrying a doctor because he can provide for them best.
No le hablan a nadie si no es su igual. A menos que sea fulano de tal.	They don't speak to anybody they don't consider their equal unless he is "Mr. So-and-So."
...	...
Él era un muchacho plástico de esos que veo por ahí.	He was a plastic guy like others I see around.
Con la peinilla en la mano y cara de yo no fui	Comb in hand and an "it wasn't me" expression,
De los que por tema en conversación discuten que marca de carro es mejor	Whose favorite topic in conversation is which car brand is the best?
De los que prefieren el no comer	He would rather not eat
Por las apariencias que hay que tener	To keep an appearance
Para andar elegantes y así poder a una chica plástica recoger.	And look elegant to be able to pick up a plastic girl.
Que fallo.	What a failure.
Era una pareja plástica de esas que veo por ahí	It was a plastic couple like those I see around,
Él pensando sólo en dinero	With him thinking only about money
Ella en la moda en París	And her only on Paris fashion,
Aparentando lo que no son	Pretending they are what they are not,
Viviendo en un mundo de pura ilusión	Living in a world of pure illusion
Diciendo a su hijo de cinco años	Telling their five-year old son
"No juegues con niños de color extraño."	"Don't play with kids of different color,"
Ahogados en deudas para mantener	Drowned in debts to sustain
Su estatus social en boda o coctel.	Their social status at weddings and cocktail parties.
Era una ciudad de plástico de esas que no quiero ver	It was a plastic city like those I'd rather not see,

De edificios cancerosos y un corazón de oropel	With cancerous buildings and a tinsel heart.
Donde en vez de un sol amanece un dólar	Where a dollar rises instead of the sun,
…	…
Gente que vendió por comodidad	People that sold out of convenience
Su razón de ser y su libertad	Their reason to live and their freedom.[11]

As the song continues, in direct contrast to the denunciation offered in the first verse, and following Althusser's concept of interpellation, the listeners are hailed (interpellated) and asked to be subjects in an explicit call to action/development of an ideology in which Latinos embrace their heritage, reject the value of material goods, and continue fighting against the ignorance that makes them mindless consumers of capitalism.

Oye Latino, oye hermano, oye amigo	Listen Latino, listen brother, listen friend,
Nunca vendas tu destino por el oro ni la comodidad	Don't ever sell your destiny for gold or convenience,
Nunca descanses pues nos falta andar bastante	Never rest because we have a long way to go
Vamos todos adelante para juntos terminar	Let's all go ahead so together we can get rid
Con la ignorancia que nos trae sugestionados	Of the ignorance that has us all obsessing
Con modelos importados que no son la solución	About imported designs that are not the solution.
No te dejes confundir	Don't let them confuse you,
Busca el fondo y su razón	Search for the bottom line and its reason
Recuerda se ven las caras	Remember we see the faces
Pero nunca el corazón.	But never the heart.

Following the first chorus of the song, Blades reminds the listener of the values that will prevail since "plastic melts down when the sun hits it directly," and incites the listener to study, work, and not allow himself to be led astray by false values. The final stanza of the section appeals for unity between Latinos, and Blades includes himself as one among them by using first-person plural form while at the same time asking them (us) to continue the fight as "in the end we shall overcome."

Coro:	**Chorus:**
Se ven las caras,	We see the faces,
Se ven las caras, vaya	We see the faces, hey
Pero nunca el corazón.	But never the heart.
…	…
Recuerda que el plástico se derrite si le da de lleno el sol	Remember plastic melts down when the sun hits it directly
Interludio instrumental	**Instrumental interlude**
Coro:	**Chorus:**
Se ven las caras,	We see the faces,
Se ven las caras, vaya	We see the faces, hey
Pero nunca el corazón.	But never the heart.
Estudia, trabaja y sé gente primero allí está la salvación.	Study, work, and be somebody first, that's where salvation lies.
…	…
Pa'lante, pa'lante, pa'lante y así seguiremos unidos y al final venceremos	Forward, forward, forward and so we shall remain united and, in the end, we shall overcome

With the introduction of the second chorus (a reduction of the first one), Blades does not sing but actually speaks and retells the listener that despite the consumerist society surrounding them, Latinos are full of hope and working for a united Latin America. He promptly returns to his singing and continues his praise, referring to Latin Americans as people who have not sold themselves and are proud of their heritage. In this section he includes a particular reference to the Venezuelan independence martyr Simón Bolivar (1783–1830), who helped many countries in Latin America in their respective quests for independence, and is still regarded as one of the most influential figures in Latin American history. Blades's reference recalls Bolivar's words regarding a unified Latin America.

Segundo coro: Se ven las caras	**Second chorus:** We see the faces
Hablado:	**Spoken:**
Pero señoras y señores, En medio del plástico también se ven las caras de esperanza, se ven las caras orgullosas que trabajan por una Latino América unida y por un mañana de esperanza y de libertad	But ladies and gentlemen in between the plastic we can also see the faces of hope, we see the proud faces that are working for a united Latin America and for a tomorrow full of hope and freedom
Se ven las caras del trabajo y del sudor	We see the faces of labor and sweat
De gente de carne y hueso que no se vendió	People of flesh and bone who did not sell themselves
De gente trabajando, buscando el nuevo camino	People working, searching for the new path
Orgullosa de su herencia y de ser Latino	Proud of their heritage and of being Latino
De una raza unida la que Bolívar soñó	Of one people united, like the one Bolivar dreamed of
Siembra!	Sow!

The final section of the song takes the form of a "roll call" of a united Latin America with the chorus answering "present" to each one of the calls to the respective countries. As an additional point, not only does this type of roll call echo taking attendance in a class, but this idea was also utilized in Latin America during meetings of people who opposed the dictatorships. At the beginning of the meeting, someone would call the name of a person who had been killed or disappeared by the military dictatorships, and the whole meeting would respond "present." Also worthy of note in this section is the inclusion of references such as "Nicaragua sin Somoza," a clear nod to the forty-three-year (1936-1979) U.S.-funded dictatorship of the Somozas in Nicaragua, "El Barrio" as the main Latino community in New York, as well as "La esquina"—the latter being the symbol of both the geographical and culturally constructed social space of "the corner" within the popular neighborhood and also as part of the meta-barrio.

The roll call initially did not include every country in Latin America. When analyzing live versions of the song, however, the call is often modified to include some of the countries left out in the original recording. The same section reflects a further call to Latin American unity as Blades oftentimes included as part of the roll call either "Latino América una" (Latin America [as] one), or simply: "Latino América."

Tercer coro: Presente	**Third chorus:** Present
Panamá	Panama
Puerto Rico	Puerto Rico
México	Mexico
Venezuela	Venezuela
Perú	Peru
República Dominicana	Dominican Republic
Cuba	Cuba
Costa Rica	Costa Rica
Colombia	Colombia
Honduras	Honduras
Ecuador	Ecuador
Bolivia	Bolivia
Argentina	Argentina
Nicaragua sin Somoza	Nicaragua without Somoza
El Barrio	El Barrio
La esquina	The corner

"Plástico" is a composition built upon three musical themes that express the different realities of the Latino community around 1978. The first theme is based upon disco music, the second one comprises the standard accompaniments of Salsa, and the third one is built upon the folkloric *bomba sicá* rhythm of Puerto Rico.

The first 36 seconds of the piece are centered around a rhythmic model centered on disco music, presented mainly by the bass and, unusual for Salsa, a drum set. This layer of music is positioned far from the popular Salsa songs of the time performed by artists such as Héctor Lavoe or Cheo Feliciano. Yet it ties directly into a critique of the plastic society symbolized by the disco era. It is worth noting that the release of "Plástico" and the movie *Saturday Night Fever* are only one year apart.

Figure 1. Accompanying bass and drums for the introduction of "Plástico."

The transition to the second theme (00:37–00:46) fuses the disco motif with an aspect of Latino reality by incorporating the violins that were heavily featured in the disco section over a Cuban *son*-based accompaniment. The section obliterates the drum set for the standard Salsa instrumentation of timbales, conga, and bongo and utilizes a clave-aligned bass accompaniment in the following manner:

Figure 2. "Plástico" clave aligned bass line.

The second theme (0:47–0:56) is based on one of the standard accompaniments of the Cuban *son* on all instruments. The section specifically utilizes the *son* formula with the anticipated bass on beat 4 and the piano anticipating the "and" of beat 4:

Figure 3. Piano and bass accompaniment of "Plástico" second theme.

The third theme (0:56–1:05) utilizes the folklore of Puerto Rico in the form of *bomba sicá.* While the piano and bass, as had already been done by Cortijo y su Combo, maintain a relatively consistent figure with that of the Cuban *son,* the percussion section shifts its patterns to the non-clave-based style of *bomba.* The shifting pattern of the second and third themes continues to alternate until (2:38) where the Cuban *son* structure prevails almost until the end of the piece where the *bomba sicá* is reintroduced (5:59).

In analyzing the shifts between these modes of accompaniment, one can see that they are not mere aesthetic choices as they signify location as well as define identity. The three modes of accompaniment of the piece thus speak to the shared reality of Latinos at the time when the urban disco theme places the situation in the United States; the contrasting Cuban *son* model places the city not only as dominated by the non-Latino disco music, but as a stronghold of Latino culture. At the same time, the contrast of the Puerto Rican *bomba sicá* speaks to the heritage of Latinos and the roots of their culture.[12]

More specifically, the disco music introduction locates the composition in the urban centers of the United States (i.e., New York), while at the same time presenting a frivolous context where the "plastic girl" and "plastic boy" can be found. However, the leitmotif of Salsa and perhaps that of Latinidad are presented by the inclusion of the *Bongó* within the disco texture. The transition to the second theme fuses the Latino within the urban reality of disco music as it is the only section that features the violins over the Salsa accompaniment. This section offers an analogy with the mixture of the trendy downtown, disco-laden area of New York, and the Salsa-grounded upper part of the city, for example, El Barrio, Spanish Harlem, and the South Bronx, where most Latinos lived at the time. Salsa's basic Cuban structures are clear in most of the song as a generic appeal to the dancing Latino audiences. But additionally, and as a reminder that they not forget their roots, the Nuyorican population, as an immigrant second generation, is used to foreground their heritage with the inclusion of the *bomba sicá.* Another notable musical fact is the disappearance of the disco music, the drum set, and the violins so heavily featured in the introduction, as if to denote that the consumerism represented by the style is finally overcome by the Latino heritage.

The ending of the piece as *bomba sicá* (where the Latin American "roll call" is executed) is again more than an aesthetic choice as it consciously evokes both a call for awareness of the cause of Puerto Rican independence as the only remaining colonized country in Spanish-speaking Latin America, and as an expansion of Salsa to determine identity beyond the music of Cuba with Puerto Rico—in this case, as the sonic totem of Latinidad.

"SIEMBRA," THE SONG OF FAITH

"Siembra" is a song of hope; it is not, as Blades has sometimes called his music, "an urban chronicle." In fact, the keyword of this composition is "faith." The song, as the title of the entire album underlines, sets the tone of what is to follow. "Siembra" speaks of consciousness, of conscience, of hope; it is thus offered as a manifesto for Salsa consciente, and thanks to the popularity of the whole album, the song has become, next to Tite Curet's "Pueblo Latino," a battle cry for Latino unity and consciousness.

As such, "Siembra" is the key piece in understanding the concept of the whole album. While it was not its biggest hit commercially, it anticipated Blades's future musical output. Alongside the word *Siembra* and the invitation to plant the seeds of the Latino future, the other keywords that play a prominent role in the song are the words *fe* and *conciencia* (faith and conscience/consciousness). Blades utilized the word *fe* (faith) both in the first chorus and during his pregones. The use of the word denotes emphasis on what he felt was necessary in the Latino community to move forward. Beyond the ideas of faith and conscience/consciousness, the song promotes belief in the true values of Latinos, and offers a very sharp critique of the superficial and capitalistic values of U.S. society as the example to follow.

The song begins with a spoken call for Latinos to be conscious, to not let their minds fall asleep. The invitation to be conscious, however, comes with—just like "Plástico," and again utilizing Althusser's interpellation concept—a recommendation (warning) that there is a need to plant good seeds—that is, to make sure that what we do today is worth it—as we are impacting not only our own futures but also those of our children.

"SIEMBRA"

Hablado: Usa la conciencia Latino, no la dejes que se te duerma, no la dejes que muera

Spoken: Use your conscience/consciousness Latino do not let it fall asleep, do not let it die

Siembra, si pretendes recoger,	Sow, if you intend to collect
Siembra, si pretendes cosechar.	Sow, if you intend to harvest.
Pero no olvides que de acuerdo a la semilla,	But do not forget that according to the seed,
Así serán los frutos que recogerás.	Will be the fruit that you will collect.
Siembra, si pretendes alcanzar,	Sow, if you intend to reach
Lo que el futuro te traerá.	What the future will bring you.
Pero no olvides que de acuerdo a la semilla,	But do not forget that according to the seed,
Así serán los frutos que recogerás.	Will be the fruit that you will collect.
¡Siembra!	Sow!

The introduction of the first chorus invites Latinos to trust what is being done as long as the seeds are planted with faith. It is around this word that the song revolves; it is ultimately a call to keep moving forward, carefully, and planting good seeds, but with faith.

During the call-and-response section, Blades claims first the need to let go of materialism in the same manner that he did with the song "Plástico," and asks Latinos to forget the plastic, that is, fake appearances. The second and third pregones make reference to fighting for the race (referring to the Latino "race"), and to not give up: "Always fight for your race, never give up" and "When bad things disturb you and cloud your heart, think of Latin America and repeat my song."

The closing pregón asks us to not forget Betances, as a direct reference to Puerto Rican listeners, since it refers to Puerto Rican nationalist Ramón Emeterio Betances y Alacán (April 8, 1827–September 16, 1898). Betances was the primary instigator of the *Grito de Lares* revolution and is considered the father of the Puerto Rican independence movement and nation (Rama 1980).

Coro: Con fe, siembra, siembra y tu verás.	**Chorus:** With faith, sow, sow and you shall see.
Con fe, siembra y siembra y tu va a ver	With faith sow and sow and you will see
Olvídate de lo plástico, eso nunca deja na'	Forget the plastic, that never leaves (you) anything

Siembra con fe en el mañana, nunca te arrepentirás	Sow with faith in tomorrow, you will never regret it
Recuerda que el tiempo pasa, no da fruto árbol caído,	Remember that time goes by, a fallen tree does not bear fruit,
Lucha siempre por tu raza, nunca te des por vencido	Always fight for your race, never give up
Cuando lo malo te turbe y te nuble el corazón, piensa en América Latina y repite mi pregón	When bad things disturb you and cloud your heart, think of Latin America and repeat my song
Prepárate	Get ready
Y de acuerdo a la semilla, así nacerán los frutos nunca olvides a Betances en la unión está el futuro	And according to the seed, the fruit will be borne; never forget Betances, in unity lies the future
Interludio instrumental	**Instrumental interlude**

Following the instrumental interlude, Blades once again addresses Latinos directly by asking them to have faith and move forward. This set of pregones (played over the half chorus) speaks of the differences between Latinos/Latin Americans, and how these variants should not be ones to hold the group back. This section includes both the idea of class awareness as noted by the presence of "forget appearances," and race/ethnicity as noted by the mentioning of the need to let go of "color differences." There is also a metaphorical "call to arms" in the fact that The People will eventually be called to actively participate. In this sense the discourse is strongly colored by revolutionary neo-Marxist ideological language and Latin American liberation philosophy (e.g., Freire 1970), interpellating and speaking directly to and for The People, the displaced, as the basis of the new society:

Hablado: Hermano Latino, con fe y siempre adelante	**Spoken:** Latino brother, with faith and always forward
Segundo coro (primera parte): Siembra, siembra y tu verás	**Second chorus (first part):** Sow and sow and you shall see
Segundo coro (segunda parte): Siembra, siembra y tu va a ver	**Second chorus (second part):** Sow and sow and you will see
Olvida las apariencias	Forget appearances
Diferencias de color	Color differences

Y utiliza la conciencia	And use your conscience/ consciousness
Pa' hacer un mundo mejor	To make a better world
Ya vienen los tiempos buenos	The good times are coming
El día de la redención	Redemption day
Y cuando llamen los Pueblos	And when The People call
Responde de corazón	Answer with the heart
Tu veras, tu va' ver, tu veras, tu va' ver, tu veras tu va' ver	You shall see, you will see, You shall see, you will see, You shall see, you will see
Interludio instrumental	**Instrumental interlude**

As the song continues, lyrically, the pregones that occur over the third chorus develop the idea of taking care of the seeds—that is, the children—and of being a good example to them.[13] It is also interesting to note here the appearance of the idiom "Travoltadas" ("Travoltisms") in reference to John Travolta's appearance in the 1977 film *Saturday Night Fever*. The presence of this idiom, as in the idea of leaving Travoltisms aside, points to a rejection of a materialist vision of the world exemplified by the values of a plastic society based on appearances. The appearance of this idiom also elaborates on the concept of the whole album as it is directly linked to the opening in which the song "Plástico" foregrounds disco music. Blades continues and again interpellates Latinos to face reality as a means to propel the expected shift and see and act beyond materialistic values. In this way people can move toward humility and love as the true essence of being Latino/Latin American so that the metaphorical seeds being planted will germinate and thereby be the best they can be:

Tercer coro (primera parte): Tu verás	**Third chorus (first part):** You shall see
Tercer coro (segunda parte): Tu va' ver	**Third chorus (second part):** You will see
La semilla son los niños que el tiempo hará crecer	The seed are the children that time will make grow
Pero hay que dar el ejemplo	But the example has to be set
Pa' que pueda suceder	So that it can happen

Olvida las Travoltadas	Forget the Travoltisms
Y enfrenta la realidad	And confront reality
Y da la cara a tu tierra y así el cambio llegará	And face your land and the change will come
Siembra cariño	Sow love
Siembra humildad	Sow humility
Y da frutos de esperanza	And bear fruits of hope
A los que vienen detrás	To the ones that come behind

The closing of the song and therefore the closing of the album sees Willie Colón and Rubén Blades thanking each other and in unison asking Latinos as a family to be conscious of the values associated in the album with their identity and in contrast to those of the United States.

Hablado: Gracias, Rubén, gracias, Willie. Conciencia familia	**Spoken:** Thanks, Rubén. Thanks, Willie. Consciousness/conscience family

Musically, the track "Siembra" is not as complex as other tracks from the same album such as "Plástico," with its signifying style changes, or "Pedro Navaja," with the rising key changes increasing the tension of the composition as the story is described. "Siembra" is constructed over the archetypal Salsa model, which takes most of its aesthetic cues from the Cuban *son*. It is interesting, however, to note the unusual nature of the choruses. The first is formed conventionally by a repeating section alternating in a call-and-response fashion with the lead vocalist singing the words "Con fe, siembra, siembra y tu verás. Con fe, siembra y siembra y tu va a ver." The call and response are exactly the same length of 4 claves each. However, the second chorus is a reduction of the first chorus through the use only of the words "Siembra, siembra y tu verás. Siembra, siembra y tu va a ver," with a total length of 4 claves for the call and response combined. This device is actually quite common in Salsa and often referred to as a half chorus (*medio coro*).[14] It is interesting to note, however, that the call-and-response section is now divided into two different parts with the lead vocals alternating between each part of the chorus. The chorus begins, *Siembra, siembra y tu verás,* with Blades interjecting his pregones. The chorus then changes and utilizes *siembra, siembra y tu va' ver*, with Blades interjecting a second set of pregones to complete the musical cycle. This section thus, because of its unusual nature, could be referred to as a double half chorus.

The innovation is taken even further through the development of the already truncated double half chorus into another half chorus that is still based on the original double half chorus. I employ the term "quarter chorus" (*cuarto de coro*) to denote the phenomenon.[15] This utterance is structured as a variation on the second chorus by using only the end parts of both the first and second parts of the second chorus: *tu verás* and *tu va' ver.* The total length of the chorus and lead interjections is actually 2 claves, with Blades freely singing lead over the chorus. While this device eventually became quite common, especially in the Cuban *timba* style, it is highly unusual for the time and demonstrates one of the musical innovations presented in the album.

The utilization of such devices represents a realization or acting out of the inevitability of the germination of the planted seed. The first chorus asks people to sow the seeds with faith as they will ultimately see the results. Once that stage has been passed, and the faith is integrated, the second chorus takes faith out of the equation and asks people to actively sow the seeds with the understanding that it is being done with faith, and still telling people that they will see what is to come. By the time the third chorus arrives, the seeds have been planted and all that is left is to wait and see the results.

CHAPTER FIVE

Rubén Blades's Move Out of Salsa

So that I saw music as a way of documenting realities from the urban cities of Latin America.

—Ruben Blades

R ubén Blades created a number of landmark albums in the years 1980 to 1991. Although Salsa was the basis on which his work was founded, eventually other elements were added in. In the following, I discuss Blades's development through the recordings he created, both with Fania Records and beyond.

Maestra Vida, the Solo Album (1980)

Maestra Vida—"Life the Teacher"—is a two-part/double LP concept album that is often recognized as the first all-original Salsa opera.[1] Although the album was produced by Willie Colón, this is truly Blades's first solo venture. It speaks to his genius that he followed an album as successful as *Siembra* with something so revolutionary, as *Maestra Vida* takes apart what had thus far become the standard conventions of Salsa. In her review of the release for the Fania website, Aurora Flores referred to the album as a "tour de force":

"Maestra Vida" deconstructs the Salsa formula of the times, creating a smooth fusion of classical, Latin music and urban mood settings . . . Lushly orchestrated and produced by Willie Colon who fuses and focuses on various Latin music genres including samba, bossa, plena, bomba and décimas along an Afro-Cuban matrix of metered beats and sounds, "Maestra Vida" goes beyond the predictably hard dance-style music into a more profound reflective level of art and culture.

Regarding the reception of the album, however, Rondón (2008, 287) indicated that

Blades inaugurated the 1990s [*sic*] with what would be seen as his most ambitious work . . . A great orchestra, singers, actors, and narrators all converged to create an immeasurably unique, inimitable work that today is still listened to with awe. At the time, however, it was a commercial failure of historic proportions, 180 degrees from the sales success of Siembra.

Originally released in 1980, the album traverses the lives and deaths of three characters from the Da Silva family. In the liner notes, Blades dedicates the work to his neighborhood in Panama, where he actually met many of the main characters of this story.[2] Regardless of its origin, this is probably the most crucial album evoking Latinidad within Blades's work, as it encompasses, literally and conceptually, the characters, places, and stories of the Latino meta-homeland. In this sense, Blades presents, at least in a literary manner, his home's reality as emblematic of Latin America. Musically, however, the approach is not as innovative as the literary conceptualization of the album. While the music is often quasi-symphonic, including strings, woodwinds, and brass, these sections function mainly as sonic interludes and ambiences. Interesting as the sections may be, they do not serve as cultural or identity markers. There are, however, instances of styles and rhythms that could potentially refer to Latin America at large, yet they are not always completely clear in terms of their significations, and they were likely not intended to be clear or understood in the same manner as were *Siembra*'s markers. Suffice it to say that the musical mold of the songs is mainly based on the same modernized Cuban or Puerto Rican forms that have already been analyzed in this book.

This album, however, is essential for developing a cohesive understanding of the concept of meta-barrio. In this release there is, as a central axis of the work, a continuum of characters and places that are shared within a larger Latino/Latin American urban context. The album can be understood as focused on a modern and popular history of the people of the barrio and nested within the works of Latin American literature, such as the magical realism of Gabriel Garcia Márquez's *One Hundred Years of Solitude* and the town of Macondo.[3] In this sense, *Maestra Vida* is more than a musical record; it is a musical addition to Latin American literature. I base my argument on the fact that three out of the four main markers of Salsa consciente intersect throughout the album: social and political issues and Latino/Latin American unity as told by a story based on "any place" in Latin America.

In expanding this understanding of the album as a crucial component of the many intersections of Latin American life, in her review of the album for the Fania website, Aurora Flores (n.d.) indicated that

> This is any story in Latin America. In this case the story of the sweet sastre (tailor) Carmelo, his love of Manuela, their courtship, marriage, childbirth of Ramiro and the hard times . . . Here, through Carmelo and Manuela, they tell of the trials and tribulations of the Afro-Caribbean people . . . In short, this is education through music: on the one hand, we can find meaning and direction for our own lives through the experiences of the protagonists; on the other, it demonstrates the proper construction and development of a good musical production.

It is relevant that on the record jacket notes Blades describes the album as a "drama-record Salsa Focila," thus distancing the album from being a standard Salsa release. He then directly addresses the audience, and writes,

> Dear audience:
> In this record-drama entitled "Maestra Vida" we present the word FOCILA (Latin city folklore) to describe and "baptize" a musical-social category

DIFFERENTIATING then in the global definition of SALSA the species from the genus.

Focila, argued Blades (1983), exalted the idea that music should be at the service of the expression of facts and urban life, with its daily affairs and contradictions, but that were so commonly avoided by the Salsa of the times. This is a very important definition, as it revealed Blades's desire to express a variety of interests, initially explored in *Siembra*, that go far beyond mere entertainment:

> Focila, Latin American city folklore, was born in Maestra Vida. This was probably the most anti commercial thing ever done in the world of Salsa. The record deals with the subject of death, a taboo topic thus far. The work begins with a classical overture and during its development one can hear some obscene words that eventually led to bannings. In Venezuela they pulled back the record because in one part it said "fag." In Puerto Rico there was also some agitation . . . the fact is that it was not accepted that a musical genre usually played to make people happy was used to speak of depressing subjects. The fact of the matter however is that in a musical field where 99% of the songs are about "come on baby let's dance," somebody had to show the flipside of the coin. I wanted to explore within the dynamics and realities of the urban [life], another type of stories, for example the one about the old folks that are alone in their houses waiting for the children that never arrive and end up dying in silence. There is also another series of images inside the work that makes people think about other things as well. (Blades 1983)

The recording begins with incidental music and the voice of journalist Cesar Rondón, author of the now famous *Book of Salsa* (1980/2008), describing the theme of the album:

> An April evening in 1975 finds Quique Quiñones full of memories drinking at one of the tables of the bar. He was the son of Vavá, eternal buddy of the legendary tailor Carmelo DaSilva. Today the usual beers and rum are

shared by Quique with his son Carlito Lito and with Rafael DaSilva, grandson of that irresistible Manuela. The story is the same as all the stories of this neighborhood. Maybe it is the same. Because of that, as usual, music is nothing else but an excuse.

The songs that I have chosen for analysis in this case include the closing track of the first part, "Déjenme Reír (para no llorar)" (Let me laugh [so I won't cry]), and the climax of part two—and arguably of the whole album—the song "Maestra Vida."

DÉJENME REÍR (PARA NO LLORAR)

This song closes the first of the two LPs, as well as the story of the first life cycle of *Maestra Vida*, that of the grandfather Carmelo DaSilva and the grandmother Manuela DaSilva, their life situation in Latin America of the 1920s, their courting, their marriage, and the birth of their son, Ramiro. The song in its entirety, especially in the first verse, shows a clear sense of class awareness as it depicts the frustrations of a middle-aged Carmelo, the tailor, the main character of the work and the archetypical character of the common man, coping with life in general, poverty, and the injustices to which he is submitted daily. Within the first verse there is a reference to his economic situation, as well as blame placed on the "thieving politicians." The appearance of the "out of tune" neighborhood choir in this section is relevant as it shows the situation as one that is shared by El Pueblo, represented by the neighborhood choir, and not unique to Carmelo. In this sense, the narration is tied to the tribulations of the previously mentioned character and song "Pablo Pueblo" (from the Blades/Colón Release *Metiendo Mano*) as the working man, disenchanted with the social situation that surrounds him and the empty promises of politicians:

Desde que nació Ramiro las cosas están más duras que ayer,	Ever since Ramiro was born, things are harder than yesterday
Yo lucho y yo trato y no puedo obtener lo que pa' vivir requiero.	I struggle and try and cannot get what I need to live on
Desde que nació Ramiro, le dije a Manuela: ¡"Esto está cabrón"!	Ever since Ramiro was born, I told Manuela: This is messed up!

No veo la manera ni la solución pa' pode' arreglar el pobre su situación	I do not see the way or solution for the poor man to fix his situation
Si el político ladrón nos entretiene con cuentos y estadísticas, diciendo:	If the thieving politician entertains us with stories and statistics, saying:
¡"La culpa es de la inflación"!	"Blame it on inflation"!
Coro de barrio responde:	**A neighborhood choir responds:**
No se pue' arreglá del pobre la situación	The poor man's situation cannot be fixed
Si el político ladrón nos entretiene con cuentos y estadísticas, diciendo:	If the thieving politician entertains us with stories and statistics, saying:
¡"La culpa es de la inflación"!	"Blame it on inflation"!

As the song continues, the second part of the verse develops the idea of the thieving and deceitful politicians who are only looking for votes. As the lead singer presents the story, the chorus responds behind by echoing the perceptions of the realities promised by politicians.

Cada cuatro años se aparecen,	Every four years they show up,
Cargando niños por el barrio;	Holding children in the neighborhood
Prometiendo;	Promising;
Saludando.	Saying hello.
El voto buscando (y robando)	Looking for the vote (and stealing!)
El voto buscando (y engañando).	Looking for the vote (and deceiving)
…	…
Y acaban las elecciones	And when the elections are over
Y al mirar las selecciones siempre ves	One looks at the chosen ones and always see
La misma gente (ja, ja, ja), sorpresa	The same people (ha, ha, ha), surprise!
Y el que votó esperanzado, sigue del gancho colgado,	And the one that voted full of hope is still hanging by a thread
…	…
(Amen), y entretanto, caballeros,	(Amen), and in the meantime, people,
El pobre sigue esperando.	The poor man keeps waiting
Coro: ¿Y el político qué? (Eso digo yo)	**Chorus:** And what about the politician? (that is what I say)

¿Y el político qué?	And what about the politician?
El voto buscando (¡y robando!)	Looking for the vote (and stealing!)
El voto buscando (y engañando).	Looking for the vote (and deceiving)
El voto buscando (¡y robando!)	Looking for the vote (and stealing!)
El voto buscando (y engañando).	Looking for the vote (and deceiving)

The third part of the verse revolves once again around the idea of the politicians, yet now there is also the involvement of the media machine, presenting conflicting issues to the public. The social distress caused by the politicians finally results in social revolt, only to end with the military eventually declaring a coup. While this coup might refer to the 1968 coup in Panama, there is no clear declaration of such an intention; meanwhile, almost all of Latin America had by 1980 indeed lived exactly the situation described, coups included.

Y el nuevo presidente, y el nuevo gabinete	And the new president, and the new cabinet
Hacen mil declaraciones	Make a thousand statements
La prensa da mil versiones	The press gives a thousand
Que enredan más a la gente;	Versions that confuse people even more;
Y de repente, comienzan las bolas, los bochinches, los rumores;	And suddenly come the fibs, the gossip, the rumors
"Fulanito va pa' fuera; cambio en las gobernaciones"—	"So and so is going out; changes in the government"
Y de pronto estalla la burbuja rosa	And all of a sudden the pink bubble explodes
Y queda el gobierno espantado con la noticia que marcha en las calles:	And the government is stunned with the news on the street
"¡Vamos a arreglá esta cosa!"	"We are going to fix this"
Orden de golpe de estado decretan los generales.	Order for a coup the generals decree

As the song returns specifically to the situation of Carmelo, the call-and-response section sees him lamenting his current situation and the general poverty in which the politics of "the country" have trapped him.

Carmelo sings, placing the blame directly on "the damned government that has been useless." The chorus at this point aids in the relief strategy of the poor man by accompanying him while he sings his lament, offering music as a relief for the marginalized, in the form of upbeat music, just so he can be allowed to laugh, so as not to cry:

Coro: Déjenme reír, para no llorar; déjenme cantar, pa' que las penas no duelan	**Chorus:** Let me laugh, so I won't cry; let me sing so the sadness does not hurt so much
Señores para empezar el culpable de mi infierno es	Gentlemen, for starters, the one guilty of my hell is
El maldito gobierno que ha resultado incapaz.	The dammed government that has been useless.
Ahora vuelvo a recordar aquellos días de infancia	Now I remember those childhood days when
En que viví la abundancia de amor de papa y mamá.	I lived in the abundance of love by mom and dad
Señores voy a reír ay disque pa' no llorar	Gentlemen I am going to laugh, oh, so I won't cry
Y el tiempo sigue pasando mi hermano	And the clock keeps ticking my brother,
Y no hay pa' papear.	And there is nothing to eat

The song develops over three musical themes: The Puerto Rican *bomba sicá*, Cuban *son*, and Puerto Rican *plena*. The song starts as *bomba sicá*, perhaps in reference to the popular nature of the rhythm as a marker of the common barrio/lower-class neighborhood where this style would be found, and to the same characteristics found within the characters portrayed in the album. Following the *bomba* introduction, the first part of the initial verse is developed within the structure of the Cuban *son*, yet this is truncated with the appearance once again of the *bomba* along with the words "the situation of the poor," probably referencing the often racialized and class-centered neighborhood associations of the *bomba*. This style, with the same class-based implications, is maintained as the neighborhood choir once again declaims about the situation of the poor and the lies of politicians.

The appearance of the descriptions of the politicians searching for votes is accompanied by the change of musical style as it moves toward the Puerto

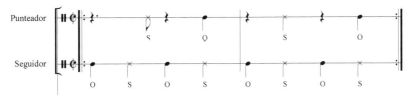

Figure 1. *Plena* rhythm.

Rican *plena*. This fact, more than just being a large identity marker, probably stems from the fact that the *plena* is actually used for political rallies in Puerto Rico. *Plena*, which is generally considered a "sung newspaper," is utilized in this section to declare not the news from the upper part of town, but the news from the slums as a marker of Pueblo identity. Tied to the appearance of *plena* in political rallies, there is the fact that *plena*, which is generally characterized by an upbeat and cheerful rhythm, is placed in this section as a satire of the deceit and eventual poverty caused by the politicians and the "damned government." While this rhythm is not uncommon in Puerto Rican Salsa orchestras, it is fairly infrequent in the general work of Blades as a non–Puerto Rican.

The closing of the song returns to the original tribulations of Carmelo and the use of the Cuban *son* as the main informant of Salsa aesthetics. It is briefly followed by the appearance of the *bomba* style over the development of the call-and-response section, denoting once again the idea presented in the title, where the celebration of life as understood through *bomba* assists in relieving the everyday hardships of the poor man.

MAESTRA VIDA: THE EMBLEMATIC LATINO STORY

"Maestra Vida" closes the album and is the climax of the whole work as it concludes the cycle of life and reflects on what was learned. At this point in the album Carmelo and Manuela, the main characters of the work, have died, and their son Ramiro reflects on the lessons that life, the teacher, has given him. Having returned to his neighborhood after leaving his parents for a long time, partially because of jail time and general rebelliousness, Ramiro stands on the corner and reflects on the death of his father. Ramiro's story, then, signifies the evolution of intergenerational poverty, and the cycles that continue to develop:

Hablado:	**Spoken:**
...	...
Con los ojos enterrados en el piso, sufriendo las malas jugadas de su existencia, Ramiro recorrió las calles del barrio.	With his eyes fixed on the floor, suffering from the bad moves of his existence, Ramiro walked the streets of his neighborhood.
La misma esquina con su mismo olor, todos los hechos lo condenaban, sin embargo, nadie hablaba de su soledad, de aquellos años en la cárcel, de las cosas que hizo y dejó de hacer, de su eterna mala suerte.	The same corner with the same smell, all the facts condemned him, nevertheless, nobody spoke of his loneliness, of those years in jail, of the things that he did and stopped doing, of his eternal bad luck.
Parado en la esquina Ramiro respondió las preguntas que jamás le hicieron.	Standing at the corner Ramiro answered the questions he was never asked.
...	...
Es una noche de Mayo de 1970	It is a night of May, 1970
Ramiro sigue en la esquina,	Ramiro is still on the corner,
Solo como siempre	Alone as usual

As the verse of the song actually begins, we see how Ramiro attempts to understand the meaning of his life as he recounts his passing through it. As he grapples with the concept, he realizes that life is ultimately composed of dark and bright, doubts and reassurances, justice and injustice. After experiencing the death of his father, Ramiro also begins to see that both sides, dark and bright, are intrinsic and necessary for the other to exist. Upon questioning his place and understanding of life, Ramiro reflects on the past and the life paths he has chosen. He questions his beliefs, and realizes that the inevitable advance of time sees it pass by everyone, including him. In this section there is thus a reflection on death, beauty, evil, war, and misery, but Ramiro also realizes the search for a higher truth after having witnessed life, with its joy and misery, in the form of a search for God. He, however, only searches for this spirituality in the face of the harshness of life, not in his happy moments. The third section of the verse, coupled first with the appearance of the musical style of *bolero*, and then followed by the resolution to *son* in the chorus, develops from the resignation to the drama of life, followed by the half chorus in which Ramiro realizes the inevitability of death and the passing of time. In this section Ramiro resigns himself to the ups and downs of life, realizes that despite the good things, time does not stop, and finally the death of his father, Carmelo, overcomes him as he yells out his name.

This focus on reflection is not one in which the sorrows highlighted are tied directly to the tribulations of the first part of the album, such as poverty, political disappointment, etc. Instead they show the intergenerational development of the "common family" and the many issues that such a family would be exposed to on a daily basis. It is interesting to contrast the concept of the "common family" and its relationship to previously explored themes in Blades's work such as "Plástico," where there is a condemnation of the "plastic family" and its values. I postulate that Blades's words as expressed in Ramiro's reflections are specifically geared toward a connection with the common man. These conceptions, connections, and dialectics, presented in this case as families with opposing points of view and with opposing values, are a very common and real sight in Latin America, as well as in the United States, where the levels of neoliberal-driven inequality have fragmented much of the realities for both families. The common family struggles and seeks to find a way out of the cycle of poverty, but the development and the opportunities associated with it (education, success, monetary rewards, etc.) are unlikely to arrive as the system perpetuates the disparities. In contrast, the "plastic family" is allowed to progress thanks to the systematic development of their already amassed, often intergenerational wealth. Such developments, vigorously sought by Ramiro and the "common family," are simply expected in a system where wealth is rewarded with opportunity. Despite the fact that the "people up top" might have some relation to many of these dynamics, many of the realities that Ramiro faces, such as exposure to misery, poverty, hunger, being jailed, and general suffering on a daily basis, are directly related to social discrimination, something that the "plastic family" may rarely, if ever, experience.

A tu escuela llegué sin entender porque llegaba.	At your school I arrived, without even knowing why I went.
En tus salones encuentro mil caminos y encrucijadas,	In your classrooms I find a thousand ways and crossroads,
Y aprendo mucho. Y no aprendo nada.	And I learn a lot, and then again, I learn nothing at all

Coro: Maestra vida camara' te da y te quita y te quita y te da

…

Paso afirmando, paso negando, paso con dudas,

Entre risas y amarguras, buscando el por qué y el cuándo

Coro: Maestra vida camará' te da y te quita y te quita y te da

Maestra vida de justicias e injusticias,

De bondades y malicias

Aún no alcanzo a comprenderte

…

Y vi espinas y vi rosas.

Vi morir seres queridos, vi bellezas.

Fui testigo de maldades y de guerras.

Vi lo bueno de la tierra, y vi el hambre y la miseria

Y, entre el drama y la comedia avancé entre agua y fuego.

Y en Dios me acuerdo primero

Sólo en trance de morirme,

A veces cuando estoy triste,

Mas nunca si estoy contento.

…

Interludio instrumental

Maestra vida, me voy persiguiendo al tiempo,

Chorus: Life the teacher, brother, it gives to you, and it takes away from you, it takes away from you, and it gives back to you

….

I go by being positive, I go by being negative, I go by with doubts,

And between the laughter and the sorrows, I look for the rhymes and reasons

Chorus: Life the teacher, brother, it gives to you, and it takes away from you, it takes away from you, and it gives back to you

Life the teacher of injustices and of justices

Of kindness and of malice

Yet I don't achieve an understanding of you

…

And I saw the thorns and the roses

I saw the death of loved ones, I saw beauty

I was a witness to the wickedness and to war

I saw the good of earth and I saw the hunger and the misery

And between the drama and the comedy I continued between the water and fire

And I remember God first

Only in the moment when I feel death coming

Or at times when I'm hopelessly sad

But never if I'm happy

…

Instrumental interlude

Life the teacher I leave chasing time

A ver si encuentro respuestas antes de la hora en que yo muera.	To see if I can find answers before the hour of my death
Aunque me estoy resignando a esta fatal realidad	Although for now I am resigning my self to this inevitable reality
Coro: Maestra vida camará' te da y te quita y te quita y te da	**Chorus:** Life the teacher, brother, it gives to you, and it takes away from you, it takes away from you, and it gives back to you
Segundo coro (medio coro): Te da y te quita y te quita y te da	**Second chorus (half chorus):** It gives to you, and it takes away from you, it takes away from you, and it gives back to you
…	…
Y el tiempo mira no se detiene	And look, time, does not stop
Ni por amor ni por dinero	Not for love nor for money
La muerte es compa'	Death is, my brother
La muerte es el mensajero	Death is the messenger
…	…
Cuando se murió Carmelo	When Carmelo died
Sentí un dolor tan profundo	I felt such a profound pain
Que no hallo nada en el mundo	That I cannot find anything in the world
Con que poder consolarme	By which I can be consoled
¡Carmelo, Carmelo!	Carmelo, Carmelo!

Within the song, there are three modes of accompaniment beyond the acoustic guitar introduction over the spoken section that serves mainly as a transitional element between tracks: Cuban *son*, Puerto Rican *seis*, and Cuban *bolero*.

These elements underline the Cuban *son*, the main aesthetic center of Salsa, as a signifier of the urban Latino/Latin American life. The appearance of this element in the music is always tied to the present tense, that is, the present urban life of the character conveyed in the lyrics. At the same time, the appearance of the Puerto Rican *seis*, a traditional rural style, is tied to the past tense and references to death in the lyrics to show the relevance of people and places from the past (i.e., a person's roots) in shaping the present. The accompaniment, although present in Salsa, is

Figure 2. *Seis* ostinato as performed in "Maestra Vida."

very uncommon in Blades's work. Figure 2 shows the basic ostinato used in the song's section.

The last sonic element is that of the *bolero*, which is used exclusively in the middle section of the song. *Bolero* is usually a style associated with dramas of love, yet in this case the style is utilized as a means to denote the drama of life as Ramiro, Carmelo's son, laments the death of his father and resigns himself to this inevitable reality.

THE CLOSING OF *MAESTRA VIDA*, THE ALBUM

It is important to mention that although not properly a song within the album, the recording closes the story by referring to Ramiro, who upon losing his father, leaves the old neighborhood in search of new life. The destiny of the son, however, ends tragically as he is gunned down by the police. The conclusion of the album is narrated as the introduction was by Cesar Rondón:

> Ramiro DaSilva and his common-law wife, Virginia Ocasio, lost their lives on Tuesday, July 4th, 1973. They were shot to death by police who were evicting squatters in the area known as "The Progress" (El Progreso). On the property of Mr. So-and-So, senator, millionaire, and member of the political party "steal as much as you can," currently in control of the country. They are survived by their sons Rafael, Naima, and Pablo, and hunger, misery, and hope.

This ending to the album shows once again the overarching link of Blades equating his "Panamanian reality" with that of Latin America. In this example he refers to the meta-barrio by the name of "El Progreso" (The Progress), which was also a common name given to marginal rural housing areas, and examples of areas called "El Progreso" can be found in El Salvador, Peru, and Guatemala. There is a reference to political resentment as the characters were evicted from the property of Senator "Mr. So-and-So," member of the ruling political party. There is also a reference, though subtle, to the United States, given the date of the deaths as July 4th. This story, with the United States included in the overarching scheme of repression, was repeated in Latin America in the 1970s and 1980s. Even though the dedication of the album might be to Panama, there is a significant parallel to be drawn with almost anywhere in the Latin America of this period.

Canciones del Solar de los Aburridos (1981)

The third album by the Blades/Colón duo, entitled *Canciones del Solar de los Aburridos* (Songs from the tenement of the bored), showcased once again Blades as the composer of almost all the pieces. Only "El Telefonito" and "Y Deja" were not composed by Blades. Recorded in 1981, the album was highly anticipated by the Salsa crowd, particularly after the success of *Siembra* and the complexity and lack of commercial success of *Maestra Vida*.

The album, however, stirred controversy almost from the beginning as some of the lyrics were very politically charged and directly critical of both the U.S. sociopolitical involvement in Central America and issues of class and race. Nevertheless, the album was nominated for a Grammy award; the tracks "Tiburón" and "Ligia Elena" became hits, and despite their topical content are still part of Blades's concert repertoire.

TIBURÓN

The opening track of *Canciones del Solar de los Aburridos*, "Tiburón" (Shark) criticized the U.S. military, political, and social involvement in Central America through the blood-seeking symbol of a shark lurking in the Caribbean waters. The piece has become somewhat of a battle cry for Spanish-speaking anti-hegemonic concerns as the image of the shark can certainly be expanded to many cases beyond the United States and Central America. Regarding the song, Blades indicated that

> the purpose of the song was to express my and our dislike for intervention. Now, US foreign policy has been intervening in the region all this time, so of course this song would directly be placed on the US. But then a funny thing happened; England had a problem also, with Argentina.[4] Then the song all of the sudden is not a song that can be applied exclusively to the US. I am also opposed, if the Russians would walk in, send an army and walk inside any Latin American country, you know like just walk in to put order and what not, I'd scream, of course I'd scream, because what's the difference between a Russian or a North American in terms of intervention? None! The problem that we've had in Latin America though has not been with Russian paratroopers or Russian marines. There weren't Russian marines who jumped in Panama in '64. There weren't Russian marines who jumped in Santo Domingo in '65. If there had been Russian marines, we would have thrown rocks at them too and asked them to get the hell out of there and get back to where they belong.
>
> All we want is to be left to deal with our own problems. I think that we have the capacity and at any rate we have the responsibility to do it for ourselves (in Mugge 1985 DVD).

In a performance of the song captured in the 1985 documentary *The Return of Rubén Blades*, he introduces the song as "Tiburón, against Intervention" (original in English), and more recently, in a 2006 concert in Cali, Colombia, with the phrase "About the empires, Latin America."[5]

As for the reception of the song, it remained controversial. Cruz (1997, 61) indicated that

> The song caused controversy in Miami's politically conservative Little Havana community. A popular Spanish-language radio station in Miami brought Blades to Miami to perform at a concert but asked him not to

sing "El Tiburón." Blades refused to be censored, however, and sang the song anyway while wearing a bulletproof jacket. The radio station claimed that they received bomb threats and banned "El Tiburón" from their programming.

Willie Colón (in Padura Fuentes 2003, 31) confirmed the fact and said "that type of composition caused us a lot of trouble, so much so that when we were doing 'Pedro Navaja' and 'Tiburón' with Rubén [Blades] we had to per-form in bulletproof vests." Similarly, in his review of the album for Fania. com, John Child (2013) remarked that

> Canciones del Solar de los Aburridos did not receive much air play in New York at the time of its release. This was largely due to deejays shying away from the opening cut "Tiburón" (literally meaning "Shark"; figuratively meaning "Imperialism"), arguably the duo's most contentious recording commenting on U.S./Latin American policy . . . the song led to accusations that he was a communist sympathizer and effectively alienated him from the Cuban community in Miami.

In the verse of the song, Blades presents both the location and the main character of the piece (the shark) as the focal centers of his argument. The shark is portrayed as a warrior fish that has no mercy for the life of its prisoners, and while everyone rests, the shark constantly lurks in nearby waters. The first chorus is offered as a question regarding the approach of the shark to the seashore. Not only is there a questioning of the shark's motives, but there is a direct addressing of the beast itself asking why it is approaching the shore. Much of the section is written in second person and in the form of direct questions, with the shark accused of having no limit to its carnage and being asked to respect the flag, that is, the sovereignty of the countries it is attacking. In this set of pregones comes the most important pregón of the song: the siren song. By equating the United States to a siren luring Latin America with her beautiful song toward a metaphorical ship-wreck, Blades implies that despite appearances, the imperialistic position of the United States is not one that in the long run will benefit the region.

The closing of the section also asks the countries being attacked to fight back and to hit the shark so that it realizes that these lands and their people are not passive in the face of invasion.

The second chorus develops from the closing of the first as it is designed to incite resistance in the form of hitting the shark, rather than tacitly accepting its wishes, while the pregones present a call to unity to defend the region. There are two Latin Americanist references in this section. The most direct one comes in the form of the mention of El Salvador, which at the time was engaged in a brutal civil war between the military government, sponsored in large part by the United States, and a coalition of left-wing guerilla movements. The American aid to the Salvadorian military government, along with the United States' involvement in Nicaragua, could be understood as proxy wars stemming from the Cold War, and the United States' fear of an emergent socialist, united Latin American movement. The second reference is linked to Puerto Rico's independence movement vis-à-vis its colonial relationship with the United States. The allusion comes in the form of a quote from the famous song "Que bonita bandera" ("What a Beautiful Flag") written by Florencio Morales Ramos, also known as Ramito, *El Cantor de la Montaña* (The Singer from the Hills). This song not only presents lyrical allegories to Puerto Rican independence, but it was used as a battle anthem by revolutionary Puerto Rican–centered groups such as the Young Lords. The closing of the song indicates Blades's concerns with the current situations in Latin America as, once the shark has been kicked out and peace has arrived, it invites all to work in the rebuilding of the region.

Ruge la mar embravecida	Growls the rough sea
Rompe la ola desde el horizonte	The waves break from the horizon
Brilla el verde azul del gran caribe	The blue green of the great Caribbean shines
Con la majestad que el sol inspira	With the majesty that the sun inspires
El peje guerrero va pasando	The warrior fish roams by
Recorriendo el reino que domina	Traversing the kingdom it dominates
Pobre del que caiga prisionero	Pity the one that becomes a prisoner
Hoy no habrá perdón para su vida	Today there will be no mercy for his life

Es el tiburón que va buscando	It is the shark that is searching
Es el tiburón que nunca duerme	It is the shark that never sleeps
Es el tiburón que va acechando	It is the shark that is lurking
Es el tiburón de mala suerte	It is the shark of bad luck
Solo el tiburón sigue despierto	Only the Shark is awake
Solo el tiburón sigue buscando	Only the Shark keeps searching
Solo el tiburón sigue intranquilo	Only the Shark is restless
Solo el tiburón sigue acechando	Only the Shark is still lurking
Primer coro: ¿Tiburón qué buscas en la orilla? Tiburón	**First chorus:** Shark, what are you looking for on the seashore? Shark
¿Qué buscas en la arena?	What do you search for in the sand
Lo tuyo es mar afuera	Your thing is offshore
Eh tiburón el canto de sirena	Hey Shark, the siren song
Serpiente marinera	Marine serpent
Ay tu nunca te llenas	Oh! You are never full
...	...
Respeta mi bandera	Respect my flag
Palo pa' que aprenda que aquí si hay honor	Hit him so it learns that here we have honor
Pa' que vea que en el caribe no se duerme el camarón	So he sees that in the Caribbean the shrimp does not fall asleep[6]
Segundo coro: Si lo ves que viene palo al tiburón	**Second chorus:** If you see it coming hit the shark
Vamo' a darle duro sin vacilación	Let's hit him hard without hesitation
En la unión está la fuerza y nuestra salvación	In unity is our strength and our salvation
Que bonita bandera que bonita bandera	What a beautiful flag, what a beautiful flag
Si lo tuyo es mar afuera que buscas aquí? So ladrón	If your thing is offshore what are you looking for here? You thief
Hay que dar la cara y darla con valor	We have to confront and do it bravely
Pa' que no se coma a nuestra hermana El Salvador	So it won't eat our sister El Salvador
Vamo' a darle duro sin vacilación	Let's hit it hard without hesitation
En la unión está la fuerza y nuestra salvación	In unity lies our strength and our salvation

Segundo coro: Si lo ves que viene palo al tiburón	**Second Chorus:** If you see it coming hit the shark
Pónganle un letrero que diga en esta playa solo se habla español	Put a sign that says "in this beach only Spanish is spoken"
Si lo ves que viene no se duerman mis hermanos pongan atención	If you see him coming, don't fall asleep my brothers pay attention
Palo palo pa palo pa' que aprenda que aquí si hay honor	Hit him, hit him so, hit him so he learns that here we have honor
Pa' que no se coma a nuestra hermana El Salvador	So he won't eat our sister El Salvador
Y luego a trabajar en la reconstrucción	And then off to work in the rebuilding
Hablado: Paz!	**Spoken:** Peace!

The song is remarkably well constructed, with the most prominent musical marker centered around the use of the *guaguancó*, a Cuban genre that could imply that the song may refer to the U.S. policy against Cuba. While Blades has indicated that the song was written in response to general intervention policies, the association with Cuba might have been connected to the recent events of the Cuban-American-organized Mariel boatlift of 1980.

LIGIA ELENA

"Ligia Elena" is a song constructed around two topics: racism and class. While Blades had already explored the idea of class disparity in songs such as "Plástico," racial topics are the exception rather than the norm in Blades's work. A clear contrast between the works of Curet Alonso and Blades in terms of their approach to race/ethnicity also lies in the fact that Alonso's discourse revolves around the idea of Black pride, while Blades's forays into racial issues usually revolve around denouncing racism.

The lyrics of "Ligia Elena" focus on the story of a well-behaved, élite white girl who falls in love and elopes with a trumpet player from the "hood." While Ligia Elena is seen to have spent her life being pampered, the trumpet player is in contrast both by being Black and coming from a "lowlife" background. The tone of the song is humorous, though it delivers a harsh critique of racial and social discrimination. While Ligia Elena's family cannot comprehend the desires of their daughter, her high-society friends wish for a love of their own that is as true as Ligia Elena's, one that does not know color or class differences. This song features the appearance of archetypical figures that tie this song to the meta-barrio. These include the common man (the trumpet player, who is tellingly a musician), akin to Pablo Pueblo, and Ligia Elena's family, akin to the plastic family represented in "Plástico." The song also contains a spoken section that closes the song and refers not only to racism in the form of the mother wishing for a grandson with "blonde teeth," but to American popular culture in the form of Troy Donahue.[7]

Ligia Elena, la cándida niña de la sociedad,	Ligia Elena the naive society girl
Se ha fugado con un trompetista de la vecindad.	Has run away with a trumpet player from the "hood"
…	…
De nada sirvieron regaños, ni viajes, ni monjas,	Useless were the scoldings, trips, and nuns
Ni las promesas de amor que le hicieran los niños de bien;	And the promises of love made to her by the rich kids,
Fue tan buena la nota que dio aquel humilde trompeta	The note that that humble trumpet player was so good
Que, entre acordes de cariño eterno, se fue ella con él.	That, among chords of eternal love she left with him
Se han mudado a un cuarto chiquito con muy pocos muebles,	They have moved to a small room with very little furniture
Y allí viven contentos y llenos de felicidad.	And there, they live happy and full of joy
…	…
Otras niñas que saben del cuento, al dormir, se preguntan:	Other girls that know the story, when falling asleep ask themselves
"¿Ay señor!, y mi trompetista cuándo llegará?"	"Oh Lord. When will my trumpet player arrive?"
…	…
Primer coro: Ligia Elena está contenta y su familia está asfixiá	**First chorus:** Ligia Elena is happy and her family is suffocatin'
…	…
Se escapó con un trompeta de la "vecindá"	She ran away with a trumpet player from the "hood"

...

"¿En dónde fallamos?," pregunta mamá. "Where did we fail?" Asks mom

Se ha colado un niche en la Blanca sociedad. A niche[8] has snuck into White society

Primer coro: Ligia Elena está contenta y su familia está asfixiá **First chorus:** Ligia Elena is happy and her family is suffocatin'

...

Eso del racismo, broder, no está en ná'. That racism thing, brother, that is not happening

...

Hablado: **Spoken:**

Mire doña Gertrudis, Look Mrs. Gertrudis

...

A mí lo que más me choca To me the most shocking part

Es que esa mal agradecida, Is that this ungrateful girl

Yo pensaba que me iba a dar un nietecito con, I thought that she was going to give me a little grandson with,

Los cabellos rubios, Blonde hair,

Los ojos rubios, Blonde eyes

Los dientes rubios, Blonde teeth,

Como Troy Donahue, Like Troy Donahue

Y viene y se marcha con ese . . . , And she comes and runs away with that . . .

¡Con esa tusa! With that worthless!

Blades after Fania

Following a bitter separation between Blades and Fania Records in 1984, due both to the unethical practices toward artists on the part of Fania, and Blades's efforts to unionize Fania-based musicians, Blades embarked on a career with Elektra Records as the first Latin American artist to be signed to a major U.S. label. In this post-Fania career of the 1980s, Blades was the biggest survivor of the 1970s Salsa boom, and its consequent explosion, and had the sole responsibility, whether he wanted it or not, of determining Salsa's direction. Since his interests were varied, he carved a particular path that led him to develop a form of sonic experimentation beyond Salsa. While at times he returned fully to a hard trombone-driven Salsa sound, such as in the Grammy-nominated 1988 release *Antecedente* and *Caminando* from 1991, the traditional definitions of Salsa seemed to be limiting to him. Along with graduating from Harvard Law School and being a successful Hollywood actor, Blades experimented during this decade not only with a more international sound, but also with the idea of crossing over to the Anglo market by producing a fully English-language album featuring music by Sting, and songs cowritten with Lou Reed and Elvis Costello. While his albums always contained Salsa in some shape or form, and his music was, as it has always been, remarkably innovative for Salsa standards, his endeavors widened; eventually, in 1994, he ran for president of Panama. Rondón (2008, 287) sums up the development of these stages as follows:

> Few of these experiments, however, were well received by the usual listeners to and dancers of Salsa. For them, the figure of Blades became more and more difficult to decipher (was he a film actor in Hollywood, presidential candidate in Panama, graduate student at Harvard, or . . . ?). Nevertheless, he was unquestionably one of the most important innovators to determine and influence all of the music known throughout the Caribbean in the second half of the twentieth century.

Defining Blades's music, following the release of *Caminando* in 1991, as exclusively Salsa or Salsa consciente is very difficult. While this shift became especially evident with the release of the 2002 album *Mundo*, where Blades purposely attempted a fusion of world music and his well-documented past as a Salsa musician, his experimentation has always been linked to Salsa in one form or another. Regarding Blades's lyrical discourse, it continued to develop, albeit not exclusively relating to Latino/Latin American sociopolitical issues. The more obvious shift in sound, however, is ultimately consequential in terms of using musical signifiers as markers of cultural identity, and might be related to a partial exhaustion of the traditional musical structures of Salsa as well as the exhaustion of the author.

But there is also the possibility that Blades understood the unlikelihood of every single Latino/Latin American being identified with a single musical genre, no matter how popular.

Aside from his change of sound, Blades continued to produce some remarkably profound records, both in terms of lyrics and musical performance. In terms of lyrical content the most important release of the post-Fania period was the Grammy-nominated *Buscando América* (in search of América).

Buscando América (1984)

Given the strength of the Salsa monopoly led by Fania during the 1970s, this album represented one of the first hints that a Salsa career outside of that label was possible. For the release, Blades assembled a new band. Breaking from the canons of the "Fania sound" and Willie Colon's trombone-driven concept, Blades's new sound was a modernized throwback to the 1960s' Joe Cuba sextet, replacing the horn section with a vibraphone. Thus the album introduces not only Blades's new sound but also Blades's new band, *Seis del Solar*.[9] The reception of the album was significant, as it gained a Grammy nomination and accolades such as "Time Magazine Ten Best of 1984" and "Village Voice Critic's Pick 1984."

After leaving Fania, Blades's work became very international in its reach, and by the time of *Buscando América*, Blades's sound, while remaining mostly Salsa-centered, included a reggae-based song titled "Desapariciones." And while reggae does not necessarily express Latinidad, the thematic focus in this album is not necessarily in the music but in the depth of the lyrics. This move by Blades toward internationalism was precipitated partially by the decline of Salsa's popularity in the mid-1980s, mainly due to its overexposure and by Fania's commercialist goals. His stylistic plurality continued to be used as a way to change the "provincially" based image of the Latino toward a larger *cosmopolatino* sensibility. These undertakings moved his aesthetic discourse beyond the limits of a single genre, expanding his vision toward a musically more progressive and international approach. The move, however, also marked a departure of the Nuyolatino-focused discourse, and while still maintaining a Salsa-centered sound, the lyrics reference the horrific sociopolitical situations of 1980s Latin America as their main point of focus.

The lyrical content of the album is remarkably powerful, and this is possibly Blades's most poignant recording with regard to political and social issues. While there is a clear hint at hope, and delineating a meta-homeland, the tone of the album is somber, with direct references to shootings, disappearances, murder, gagging, and torture.

The songs that I have chosen to analyze for this release are "GDBD," "El Padre Antonio y el Monaguillo Andrés," and "Buscando América." While the recording as a whole is a concept album that paints a grim picture of 1980s Latin America, these three songs offer a representative sample of the fundamental themes of the album.

GDBD

"GDBD" is the second track of *Buscando América*, and presents a dramatic shift from the lighter-themed and more danceable song that precedes it, "Decisiones." The song is based around the theme of people being disappeared in South America, and is constructed as a short story, a device that Blades used successfully throughout his career. According to the composer, "it's a story about disappeared persons, in Argentina, and all over Latin America. The title means 'Gente Despertando Bajo Dictaduras': 'People Awakening under Dictatorships'" (in Hamill 1986).

While the most common way of delivering such a piece would be from the perspective of the victims of the disappearances, as Blades does with the reggae-infused "Desapariciones" from the same album, in this song he switches the narrative to the voice of the perpetrator. In the lyrics one senses a Kafkian influence in the combination of shock used to understand the main character as a "normal person." Blades develops the bulk of the story around an individual engaged in the daily routines of life, just like anyone else. It is only at the end of the song that the plot becomes twisted, leaving the listener with a revolting sense of sympathy for a character who spends his life making people disappear.

Musically, "GDBD" is remarkably creative. It uses vocal percussion to re-create the rhythm of the *guaguancó* as a backdrop to the song, yet the main level of interest is in the lyrics.[10]

Despiertas.	You wake up
No has podido dormir muy bien.	Not having been able to sleep very well
Te levantas.	You get up.
Caminas y pisas uno de los charcos de orine que el nuevo perro ha dejado por toda la casa.	Walk and step in one of the urine puddles that the new dog has left all over the house
...	...
Vas hasta la bañadera blanca,	You go to the white tub,
Abres los dos grifos del agua	Open the two faucets
Y controlas la temperatura.	And control the temperature
Levantas la cosa esa que no sabes cómo se llama	You lift that thing that you don't know what is called
Y que hace que el agua salga por la regadera.	And makes the water come out of the shower
...	...
Cuando te estás afeitando, suena el despertador.	When you are shaving, the alarm clock sounds
Tu mujer abre los ojos.	Your wife opens her eyes
...	...
Se levanta, de su lado de la cama.	She gets up from her side of the bed
Cada uno tiene su lado de la cama.	Each one has their side of the bed
Cada uno tiene su lado en todo.	Each one has their side in everything
...	...
Te arde la cara.	Your face stings
Sales del baño.	You leave the bathroom
Pisas otra vez el orine del perro.	You step again on the dog's urine
Le mientas la madre, en voz alta.	You condemn her mother loudly
...	...
Vas al closet y sacas la ropa que te vas a poner.	You go to the closet and pull out clothes
Miras el reloj.	Look at the clock
Hueles el café.	Smell the coffee
...	...

Vas a la cocina.	You go to the kitchen
Tu esposa ya preparó tu desayuno.	Your wife prepared your breakfast
…	…
Ella, sin contestarte, te recuerda que hay que pagar la cuenta de la luz y la matrícula de la escuela de los chiquillos.	She, without answering, reminds you to pay the electricity bill and the registration for the kid's school
Cuelgas tu jacket del borde de la silla y te sientas en la mesa de la cocina.	You hang your jacket on the back of the chair and sit at the kitchen table
…	…
Suena el teléfono.	The phone rings
Tu esposa lo contesta.	Your wife answers it
Es para ti.	It is for you
De la oficina.	From the office
Hoy van a arrestar al tipo.	The guy is getting arrested today
Va un carro a recogerte.	A car is going to pick you up
Que lo esperes abajo.	Wait for it downstairs
Cuelgas el teléfono.	You hang up the phone
Vas a tu cuarto.	Go to your room
Abres la segunda gaveta del armario.	Open the second drawer of the closet.
Tu gaveta.	Your drawer
Sacas tu libreta y los lentes negros.	You get your notebook and your dark glasses
Vas a la cama. Levantas el colchón y sacas tu revólver.	You go to the bed, raise the mattress and get your gun.
Vas a la cocina, tomas tu jacket y lo pones todo en el bolsillo de adentro.	You go to the kitchen, take your jacket and put everything in the inside pocket
…	…
Abres la puerta y bajas por la escalera de madera,	You open the door and come down the wooden stairs
…	…
Llegas a la calle.	You arrive on the street
Ves al camión recogiendo la basura.	You see the truck picking up the garbage
Aún está oscuro, pero huele a mañana, varón.	It is still dark but it smells like morning, man.

This song clearly exemplifies Blades's preoccupation with the situation in 1980s Latin America. While the song illustrates a clear direct reminder of the disappearance of people at this time in Latin America, on a second analytical level the piece also reminds the listener that the people who enforced the disappearings were also engaged in commonplace life, and as such, it could ultimately be anyone, maybe even someone who does not appear to be involved in such brutality. On this second level, the song reminds us that the enforcers, killers, and torturers of the Latin American dictatorship cycle were and are actual people just like everyone else. In some ways, this song creates an additional character of the meta-barrio, that of the enforcer, one that exists and in many cases still roams the streets today freely. This is one character that we might want to forget, but as Blades reminds us in a later work, which I analyze further in this chapter, it is forbidden to forget, *Prohibido Olvidar*.

EL PADRE ANTONIO Y EL MONAGUILLO ANDRÉS

"El Padre Antonio y el Monaguillo Andrés" ("Father Anthony and the Altar Boy Andrés") is a song based on the murder of Salvadorian archbishop Oscar Arnulfo Romero y Galdamez on March 24, 1980. Romero was an important advocate of human rights in El Salvador, as well as a voice of resistance against the brutality of El Salvador's government. The song showcases the image of Romero, the liberation and the hopes of the people, while at the same time denouncing repression.

The symbolic image of the priest, though fictional and related to Romero, actually highlights the roles of many priests who, during the 1970s and 1980s in Latin America, offered their churches as safe havens from the violence. By extension, there were religious-based organizations formed to aid in the peace process. A clear example of this was the Vicariate of Solidarity (La Vicaría de la Solidaridad), a Catholic organization established during the Chilean dictatorship of Augusto Pinochet (1973-1990) that sought to stop the abductions, disappearances, and general violence against Chilean citizens.

Following the end of the dictatorship cycle in Latin America, Blades's position with regard to the aftermath of the brutal violence was succinctly foregrounded in the live version of this song released in Blades's 1990 album

Live!, where during the first musical interlude he poignantly declares: "And you know why? Because in Latin America they kill people but they don't kill the ideals."

Constructed around a fictional representation of Romero, the song describes the arrival in a Latin American country of an idealistic Spanish priest who believes in spreading the word of Christ via The People. His sermons condemn violence and aim to spread love and justice. The image of Andrés, though he was not based on a real altar boy, is poignant in its appearance, as his presence functions as a symbol of the thousands of people, including children, that were killed amidst the violence in El Salvador.

The second part of the verse shows the moment of the assassination, which occurred while Romero was giving Mass. There is in this section, reflecting the real assassination, a reference to the unresolved nature of the murder. While the murder was never resolved, BBC News (March 25, 2010) reported that for the thirtieth anniversary of Romero's assassination, an official state apology was given by Salvadorian president Mauricio Funes. Part of the apology indicated that those involved in the assassination acted with the protection, collaboration, or participation of state agents.

During the chorus section, several lyrical instances are relevant. Not only is the mention of Arnulfo Romero critical, as the song finally confirms its content, but there is a message of hope as the bells of Américan freedom toll for the end of the violence. The most relevant part of the section is a paraphrase of the now-famous anthem of The People, originally composed in Chile by the group *Quilapayún*, as part of the *nueva canción Latino Americana* movement, "El Pueblo unido jamás sera vencido" (The People united will never be defeated). This is not only relevant as a call to unity and to the strength of The People, which it is, but more importantly this plea was made in the midst of the Latin American dictatorship cycle (1984) and the interjection emotionally delivered what could not be said at the time:

El Padre Antonio Tejeira vino de España,	Father Antonio Tejeira came from Spain
Buscando nuevas promesas en esta tierra.	Searching for new promises in this land.

Llegó a la selva sin la esperanza de ser obispo,	Arrived in the jungle without the hope of becoming bishop
Y entre el calor y en entre los mosquitos habló de Cristo.	And amidst the heat and the mosquitos spoke of Christ
El padre no funcionaba en el Vaticano,	The father did not function in the Vatican
Entre papeles y sueños de aire acondicionado;	Among papers and air-conditioned dreams
…	…
El niño Andrés Eloy Pérez tiene diez años.	The child Andrés Eloy Pérez is ten years old
Estudia en la elementaria "Simón Bolívar."	And studies at the Simón Bolivar elementary
Todavía no sabe decir el Credo correctamente;	He still does not know how to say the Creed correctly
Le gusta el río, jugar al futbol y estar ausente.	Loves the river, playing soccer, and being absent.
Le han dado el puesto en la iglesia de monaguillo	They have given him the altar boy position at church
A ver si la conexión compone al chiquillo;	With hopes that the connection will fix the boy
Y su familia está muy orgullosa, porque a su vez	And his family is really proud, because at the same time
Se cree que con Dios conectando a uno, conecta a diez.	They believe that connecting one with God, they connect ten
…	…
El padre condena la violencia.	The father condemns violence
Sabe por experiencia que no es la solución.	He knows by experience that it is not the solution
Les habla de amor y de justicia,	He speaks to them of love and justice
…	…
Al padre lo halló la guerra un domingo en misa,	War found father Antonio one Sunday during mass
Dando la comunión en mangas de camisa.	Giving communion in his under shirt
En medio del padre nuestro entró el matador	In the middle of the Lord's prayer came in the killer
Y sin confesar su culpa le disparó	And without confessing himself shot him

Antonio cayó, ostia en mano	Antonio fell, host still in hand
Y sin saber por qué Andrés se murió a su lado sin conocer a Pelé.	And without knowing why, Andres died right next to him without ever meeting Pelé.
...	...
Y nunca se supo el criminal quién fue	And it was never known who the criminal was
Del Padre Antonio y su monaguillo Andrés.	Of father Antonio and the Altar boy Andrés
...	...
Interludio instrumental	**Instrumental interlude**
Coro: Suenan las campanas	**Chorus:** The bells toll
...	...
Por América	For América
...	...
Centroamericana	Central American
Por mi tierra hermana	For my sister land
Mira y tu verás	Look and you shall see
Mundo va a cambiar	The world is going to change
Interludio instrumental	**Instrumental interlude**
Coro: Suenan las campanas	**Chorus:** The bells toll
Para celebrar	To celebrate
Nuestra libertad	Our freedom
Porque un Pueblo unido	Because the people united
No será Vencido	Will not be defeated
...	...
Por un cura bueno	For a good priest
Arnulfo Romero	Arnulfo Romero
De la libertad	Of freedom
Por América	For América

While the song is constructed mostly around the structures of the Cuban *son*, there is a very specific musical signifier used throughout the introduction, interlude, and ending of the song. From the beginning until 0:25, then again between time markers 3:57–4:25, and finally between time marker

Figure 3. "South American" 6/8.

6:48 until the end of the song, there is a ternary rhythmic system that is actually not based on the traditional Afro-Cuban *bembé* that thus far had been the standard in Salsa. The section is instead founded on a form of playing ternary systems that is very common in South American styles such as Argentinian *chacarera*, Venezuelan *culo'e puya*, and Peruvian *vals*, yet not common practice in Afro-Cuban music. Since it is not clear where in South America this rhythm derives from, I have dubbed this performance style generically as "South American 6/8." This device is utilized to give location to the song, as one that is not centered in the Caribbean islands but on the continent. While the rhythm might not be connected directly to El Salvador, the concept of locating the song as not Afro-Cuban but pointing toward Central/South America is highly significant. It should be noted that during the introduction and the ending, the rhythm is actually played by a shaker and by a South American wooden bass drum that is also used in Salvadorian music, called *bombo leguero*. During the interlude, however, the congas imitate the rhythm, pointing to a potential overdub during the studio sessions.

BUSCANDO AMÉRICA

"Buscando América" is the closing song of the album of the same title and refers to the notion of América as a whole having "gone missing." This idea expressed a very clear Latin American view amidst the 1980s dictatorship cycle that was once again not tied to nationalist discourses, but rather, the song, and the album, were meant to express the larger reality of the region as a connected struggle. In the introduction to the live version of the song featured in the aforementioned *Live!* album released in 1990, Blades refers to the discussion Latin Americans have had for a long time against the idea of the United States taking the name of the whole continent, América, for the designation of their country.[11] This idea points to a continental understanding of the oppression imposed by the United States that, whether on purpose or not, is perpetuated every day:

> When I talk about América I talk about the continent and everybody who is born in the continent of América is an American. The more we think about it, the more sense it makes. Because we should be working together as opposed to against each other, and we have to talk and we have to deal with the fact that we are all here, nobody is going to leave and we might as well make the best of it. Let's play our strengths as opposed to our differences. With respect and we'll get somewhere. (Original in English)

"Buscando América" is a song based around the metaphorical concept that América, the continent, has gone missing, suggesting that the preferred name of the homeland has lost its referent. In the verse Blades declaims this search and his fear of not finding the continent. The fact that the song was written in the 1980s points to the idea of "the lost decade of Latin America" in which the 1980s are associated with widespread violence and chaos in the region. Blades points out that América has, like many of its citizens, disappeared at the hands of those afraid of the truth. América, in this case, stands for the concept of the continent but also the fight of its people to survive. This is specifically pointed out by the lyrics "Living in dictatorships, I look and cannot find you, your tortured body they don't know where it is," as this is not only a call to find América, but it is a literal call made by many Latin Americans echoing the fact that to this day they are still looking for their disappeared loved ones.

Within the second verse of the song there is also a message of hope through the idea of walking forward; even though América has been kidnapped, it is the role of The People, of which Blades counts himself by the use of "we are going to find you," to propel this shift.

The chorus section is a recapitulation of the already explored subjects of loss and hope in the verses. There are, however, two specific pregones that speak of Latinidad, as Blades indicates "Fighting for the people and our identity" in reference to "La raza Latina," The Latin People, and "this is my house" in reference to his identity as a Latin American.

Te estoy buscando América	I am searching for you América
Y temo no encontrarte,	And I am afraid I won't find you
Tus huellas se han perdido entre la oscuridad.	Your footprints have become lost in darkness.
Te estoy llamando América	I am calling you América
Pero no me respondes,	But you are not answering
Te han desaparecido,	You have been disappeared,
Los que temen a la verdad.	By the ones that are afraid of truth
…	…
Viviendo dictaduras,	Living in dictatorships
Te busco y no te encuentro,	I look and cannot find you
Tu torturado cuerpo,	Your tortured body
No saben dónde está.	They don't know where it is
Interludio instrumental	**Instrumental interlude**
Si el sueño de uno	If the dream of one
Es sueño de todos.	Is the dream of all
Romper la cadena	Break the chain
Y echarnos a andar.	And start walking
Tengamos confianza.	Let's trust
Pa'lante mi raza.	Let's move forward my people
…	…
Interludio instrumental	**Instrumental interlude**
Te han secuestrado América	You have been kidnapped América
Y han amordazado tu boca,	And they have gagged you
Y a nosotros nos toca	And we have to
Ponerte en libertad	Set you free
Te estoy llamando América,	I am calling you América
Nuestro futuro espera	Our future awaits
Y antes que se nos muera	And before it dies on us
Te vamos a encontrar.	We are going to find you
Interludio instrumental	**Instrumental interlude**
Coro: Te estoy buscando América.	**Chorus:** I am searching for you América.
Te estoy llamando América.	I am calling you América.
Oh, oh	Oh, oh.

Interludio instrumental	**Instrumental interlude**
Coro: Te estoy buscando América.	**Chorus:** I am searching for you América.
Te estoy llamando América.	I am calling you América.
Oh, oh	Oh, oh.
Luchando por la raza y nuestra identidad.	Fighting for the people and our identity
Esta es mi casa	This is my house
…	…
Te han desaparecido los que niegan la verdad	You have been disappeared by those who deny the truth
Y a nosotros nos toca, hoy, ponerte en libertad.	And we have to, today, set you free

Though not filled with specific musical indications of Latin America, as in "El Padre Antonio y el Monaguillo Andrés," "Buscando América" develops a unique set of musical features. The song begins with an instrumental piano introduction over a bass pedal, creating a dramatic tone that leads into a solemn snare march. The introduction is followed by Blades delivering the verse of the song over the often-used *guaguancó* rhythm. While the first part of the verse is developed over a style centered on percussion with sparse melodic-harmonic accompaniment, the second part of the verse switches toward a hopeful future, using a piano accompaniment reflecting the up-lifting Cuban-based *guajeos* typically used in Salsa.

Leading into the chorus (5:45–5:54) is one of the most famous rhythmic section breaks in Salsa. This break not only showcases the percussion, but it also shows that musically "Seis del Solar" had begun to push the boundaries of Salsa. These types of structures, ones that would likely throw the dancers off, show a preoccupation with musicianship as much as with the lyrics. Blades's band Seis del Solar was at this point a powerhouse of mature Salsa musicians who were not afraid to experiment beyond the set boundaries of Salsa; accordingly, throughout the song and album, there is a remarkable level of musicianship, making this band one of the best Salsa ensembles ever. Clearly, this stage of Blades's work did not have the dancer as its main audience, but rather an audience that would listen to the whole. But, despite this display of skill, Salsa will always be about the dancer. In this manner, the introduction of the chorus and the call-and-response section of "Buscando América" satisfies the commitment to dance that is characteristic of the music.

Caminando (1991)

The beginning of the 1990s saw the closing down of the oppressive and genocidal military dictatorships in Latin America, as well as the end of the Salvadorian civil war and the Nicaraguan revolution. The end of this cycle saw new hope following a very dark three decades for Latin America. The turn of the decade also saw Blades release the album *Caminando* (Walking) in 1991.

Along with the ending of the widespread violence in Latin America, it could be argued that with the release of *Caminando*, Blades also brought to an end much of his development using Salsa as his main means of expression. As such, the output of Salsa consciente as a genre was diminished significantly. Regarding the album *Caminando*, however, there is a very important song for understanding the closing of this period, both for Blades and Latin America: "Prohibido Olvidar"—"It is forbidden to forget."

PROHIBIDO OLVIDAR

This is a song of hope after the long-awaited arrival of peace in Latin America. While the song places much importance on the future, it contains a reflection on dictatorships, and an acknowledgment that everything happened as part of the historical processes of the countries. Through the verse, Blades makes a strong call that to be fully able to close the cycle, and for this not to happen again, we must acknowledge, and not merely forget, the brutal past as a main factor in the rebuilding of the countries. The construction of the very long verse revolves around the idea of a number of prohibitions enforced during military times, with a strong command in the form of the chorus claiming, "It is forbidden to forget!" closing every verse.

Following the instrumental interlude there is, in the same warning tone of "Siembra," a list of things that may come with the end of the violence and the arrival of liberal economic states, where drugs, corruption, and greed might become the easy way to achieve success. In closing the song, Blades makes an appeal to the people to not "sell" their country for this easy success. This figuration provides a note of hope for the future; at the same time it is a warning to a region that has seen its people and resources severely damaged, and is only beginning to rebuild itself:

Prohibieron ir a la escuela e ir a la universidad.	They forbade going to school and the university
Prohibieron las garantías y el fin constitucional.	They forbade warranties and the constitutional state.
Prohibieron todas las ciencias, excepto la militar.	They forbade all sciences except for military ones.
Prohibiendo el derecho a queja, prohibieron el preguntar.	They forbade the right to complain, they forbade questioning.
Hoy te sugiero, mi hermano, pa' que no vuelva a pasar,	I suggest to you today, my brother, so it does not happen again,
¡Prohibido olvidar!	It is forbidden to forget!
¡Prohibido olvidar!	It is forbidden to forget
Prohibido esperar respuestas.	It is forbidden to expect answers
...	...
Prohibida la libre prensa y prohibido el opinar.	It is forbidden to have free press and it is forbidden to have an opinion
...	...
¡Prohibido olvidar!	It is forbidden to forget!
¡Prohibido olvidar!	It is forbidden to forget
Prohibido el derecho a huelga y el aumento salarial.	It is forbidden to strike and raise salaries
Prohibieron ir a la calle y al estado criticar.	They forbade going to the streets and criticizing the government.
...	...
Yo creo que la única forma de darle a esto un final es:	I believe the only way to put an end to this is:
¡Prohibido olvidar!	It is forbidden to forget!

Prohibido olvidar

...

Prohibieron el rebelarse contra la mediocridad.

Prohibieron las elecciones y la esperanza popular.

Y prohibieron la conciencia, al prohibirnos el pensar.

Si tú crees en tu bandera y crees en la libertad:

Prohibido olvidar

Interludio instrumental

Pobre del país donde lo malo controla,

Donde el civil se enamora de la corrupción.

Pobre del país alienado por la droga,

Porque una mente que afloja, pierde la razón.

Pobre del país que, con la violencia crea

Que puede matar la idea de su liberación.

Pobre del país que vea la justicia hecha añicos

Por la voluntad del rico o por orden militar.

Cada nación depende del corazón de su gente.

¡Y a un país que no se vende, nadie lo podrá comprar!

Coro: No te olvides

It is forbidden to forget

...

They forbade rebelling against mediocrity

They forbade election and popular hope,

And they forbade conscience, by forbidding us to think

If you believe in your flag and you believe in freedom:

It is forbidden to forget

Instrumental interlude

Unfortunate is the country where evil controls,

Where the civilian is infatuated by corruption

Unfortunate is the country alienated by drugs

Because a mind that lets up, loses reason

Unfortunate is the country that believes that with violence

The ideas of liberation can be killed

Unfortunate is the country that sees justice shattered

Because of the will of the rich or military decree

Each nation depends on the heart of its people

And a country that is not for sale no one will be able to buy

Chorus: Don't forget

While the song is still based on the standard rhythmic forms of the Cuban *son*, and therefore contains no particular sonic identity markers, it is not centered on the development of the call-and-response section as a main focal point, but over a very long verse where, despite the fact that the song maintains a dance feel, the expected chorus-singer interaction never arrives. While the chorus does exist, it is only repeated once at the end of each verse, with the exception of the end, where the chorus is repeated while the song fades. Yet at this point, the lyric-based call-and-response section is obliterated and replaced by a trombone solo. This sets the song apart from standard Salsa, and indicates Blades's utmost concern with the audience understanding the lyrics very closely. The lack of chorus forces the listener to pay closer attention to the words of the verse rather than mindlessly repeating the song's "hook" while the words of the lead singer go by.

Blades's Musico-Political Development

In closing, I would like to expand upon the idea of Salsa consciente as a literary development as opposed to oral-based "traditional" Salsa. In this sense, I categorize Blades's oeuvre as resting upon a literary foundation where his development of themes—as main arguments of his literary work, characters, and place—fit into a larger narrative of the meta-barrio and show a level of interconnectivity among much of his work. As such, I argue that Blades's work as a whole is connected by an overarching conceptualization of a Latino/Latin American sense of urban folkloric chronicling, where each one of the characters interacts as part of the everyday of the meta-barrio. In order to clarify the endeavor, I will first classify the analyzed songs into thematically based categories, and then develop an analysis of these categories and places as described by Blades. The themes are

1. Racial
2. Political
3. Latino/Latin American unity
4. Urban places/urban characters
5. Social
6. Latino life.

This categorization is by no means exhaustive or exclusive, as several other classifications could be developed. I do, however, assert that much of the data that has been discussed in this chapter can be analyzed from the point of view of these categories. It is necessary to add that the songs presented are not exclusive but rather intersectional in terms of their categories. While a song might be largely about racial issues, it can at the same time deal with social issues. In these cases, I pursue a hybrid categorization. The readings that I give to the songs reflect my own analysis of Blades's work, and as such other possibilities of how to approach the issues exist. I invite other scholars to further develop this thought.

The first category, racial issues, is presented in the song "Ligia Elena." The song describes both an interracial and interclass relationship between a Black trumpeter "from the hood" and a white girl from high society. It deals with a dose of humor yet contains a critique of the latent racism and class warfare in Latin America. While the main theme of the song has to do with racial issues, there is a great deal of emphasis on the idea of so-cial—and in this particular case, class—issues as presented by the rejection of Ligia Elena's choice of partner on the part of her family. Furthermore, "Ligia Elena" adds another dimension to the analysis since the song also fits within the category of urban places and urban characters. This last part appears in Ligia Elena in several forms. The idea of the common man, in this case the humble trumpet player, is akin to the archetype used in "Pablo Pueblo," while the rich high-society family of "Ligia Elena" can be compared to the family of "Plástico," telling their five-year-old child not to play with children of strange colors.

The second category, political issues, quickly emerges given the fre-quency of the theme in most of Blades's work. I have decided to include in this category songs that deal with the struggle between The People and government forces at large. Janson Perez (1987, 154) refers to these types of pieces as "sociopolitical Salsa." Regarding the political content of his music, Blades stated the following:

> Now, within the Latin American society, politics are very important and
> they permeate society. I mean whether you like it or not you are involved

in what's going on. Some are passive, others are active but I mean we are all involved. Political consequences affect us all. (In Mugge 1985 DVD)

In the case of this category, I have included Blades's first recorded piece "9 de enero" describing the fight between Panamanian students and the U.S. troops stationed in the Canal Zone in 1964. The song "Déjenme Reír (para no llorar)" from the *Maestra Vida* album also fits into this category as its main argument is the lying and stealing of politicians. The other song that clearly fits in this category is "Tiburón," where Blades takes a clear stab at the United States' intervention in Latin America. The song eventually had its meaning expanded as a general critique of the concept of intervention, yet the core argument is still a political one. Additionally, the song produced political ripples within the Cuban community of Miami, eventually leading to Blades's refusal to perform in that city.

Within this category, *Buscando América* is clearly the deepest politically minded album produced by Blades, and also provides the most Latin American-based content in the subject matter. The song "GDBD," for example, deals with the disappearances of people by their own governments in South America. Meanwhile, "El Padre Antonio y el Monaguillo Andrés" shows a real-life connection to political issues at large regarding the life of Archbishop Oscar Arnulfo Romero and his fight against the Salvadorian government's repression and violations of human rights that eventually led to his assassination as described in the song. From the same album, the song "Buscando América" speaks of the general political state of Latin America in the 1980s in which direct references are made to disappearances, gagging/censorship, and torture. At the same time, the idea of Latin American identity and unity are highly present in this song, as Blades refers not to single countries but to many issues that were commonplace at the time. The last song to include this political discussion is "Prohibido Olvidar," released in 1991. A year earlier, Augusto Pinochet was finally ousted from power in Chile, thus ending the last of the 1960s/1970s/1980s South American dictatorships. The song, timely released, revolves around the idea of not forgetting the concepts that were described in an album such as *Buscando América* as the country moves forward and rebuilds itself.

The third category, Latino/Latin American unity, encompasses the discussion of subjects that are created through a shared imaginary of concepts that in turn demonstrate the idea that the commonalities rather than the differences between Latinos/Latin Americans should be more relevant. In the case of Blades, this is relevant in the hopes that a united Latin America will make for a stronger identity and Latinidad. While this category can be constructed as somewhat controversial since it negates the national identities of countries, it has nevertheless been a prevalent issue discussed in Blades's work. An interesting point to analyze here is the position of Blades's music with regard to including or excluding Latinos born in the United States. While early on he presented the subject with a more open focus, as in "Siembra," where the general call to unite is fairly open, eventually the topics presented shifted to Latin Americans and first-generation immigrants as a main focus. This is the case in the album *Buscando América*. In turn, the reception of Blades's work became more international. Regarding the issue, Blades (1983) stated that

> When I arrived here and talked with the people, I realized that the themes that I was presenting were very foreign, and it was then that I understood the difference between the points of view of an American-Latin and a Latin American . . . You talk to the people here of a curfew and they do not know what that is, maybe they saw it in a movie like "Missing," but they don't have a true concept of what it means. I don't want to say either that life is a curfew but if I write a song with that subject or with any other that reflects the situation of our countries, I will have an international reception much larger than what I would have in the USA. Here only the ones that have migrated recognize what I'm saying, meanwhile the ones that have been raised here don't understand certain subtleties and ironies, certain humor or pain that is manifested in my song, that are the product of my having been born and raised in a Latin American country.

The Latino/Latin American unity category is a very common theme within Blades's work, with the album *Siembra* being essentially a call for a united Latin America. Songs from this release include "Plástico," with the now famous roll call of Latin American countries; although not all were included in the original release, live versions have certainly made up for that omission. Within the same song, it is interesting to note the inclusion of El Barrio in New York as part of the roll call, thus identifying the city as an important Latino enclave. Within the same album, the most direct song in this category is certainly "Siembra," where Blades invites Latinos to sow the seeds of the Latino/Latin American future. There is a message of looking at Latin America as a main point of reference and of the essence of what Latinos are and should be, or how they can improve upon that essence. Proclamations such as "When bad things disturb you and cloud your heart, think of Latin America and repeat my song," or "face your land and the change will come" are clear markers of Latinidad and ideals of unity that are not specified by country.[12] Both of these songs contain a spoken section addressed to the mainly Latino/Latin American listener. "Plástico" places the idea of a united Latin America front and center with the following: "But ladies and gentlemen in between the plastic we can also see the faces of hope, we see the proud faces that are working for a united Latin America and for a tomorrow full of hope and freedom."[13] "Siembra," in turn, offers three instances of spoken word, first in the opening with the wording that arguably names the movement of Salsa consciente: "Use your conscience/ consciousness Latino, do not let it fall asleep, do not let it die," later followed by the familial address of "Latino brother, with faith and always forward," and closing with "Conscience/consciousness, family."[14] These addresses are clearly directed to the listening Latino/Latin American and show the neo-Marxist and Bolivarian ideals of a unified Latin America, which if one follows the roll call of "Plástico" includes the Latino diaspora of El Barrio in New York City. By the same token, "Buscando América" does not present such an explicit call to Latin American unity as "Siembra" or "Plástico," but it does speak of a search for América, a search for an identity and a path that is about a continent and not a country.[15]

The fourth category, urban places/urban characters, plays again on the idea of commonalities of Latinos/Latin Americans. The reason for this categorization derives from the many instances in Blades's work that push the idea of a shared Latino deterritorialized meta-barrio—named after the historical

New York Latino neighborhood El Barrio as a place where Latino encounters, stories, histories, places, and characters share a common Latino reality. While this category could probably be subsumed under the theme of urban chronicling, I believe that the specific pointers of places and characters provide a framework that allows for a more detailed examination of the phenomenon.

Blades's work often presents the category by means of the creation of fictional archetypical characters and places. These archetypes are based on commonplace people and occurrences within Latino communities, whether diasporic or national. In Blades's case, despite not describing a place or a person in particular, these archetypes capture the essence of being in and from Latin America as these characters and places are found in any and all neighborhoods where Latino communities are located, thus becoming a part of the Latino meta-homeland. In this analysis, for example, I have delved into some of these archetypes, including the common man presented in "Pablo Pueblo," and the plastic family and city from "Plástico."

The case for this analysis lies in the fact that Blades has created throughout his work a series of places and characters that are literally fictitious but figuratively real. I argue that Blades's descriptions of places and people are not only vivid but capture the essence of the archetypes of Latinidad. In this category is "Juan Gonzalez," which is the image of the guerilla fighter ubiquitous to the Latin America of the time. Then the common man represented by "Pablo Pueblo" and the trumpet player of "Ligia Elena" are mocked with disdain by the plastic family from "Plástico" and the rich high-society family and rich kids of "Ligia Elena." Clearly the mainstays in this categorization are the characters of *Maestra Vida*. Throughout the whole album the Da Silvas (Carmelo, Manuela, and Ramiro) represent the poor family/El Pueblo. Meanwhile in "Déjenme Reír (para no llorar)" Blades presents the lying and stealing politicians blaming the problems on inflation. Another important character in the same song is the neighborhood choir that actually sings much of the song. This group of people is the archetype of El Pueblo, The People, and there is a specific reference to them in the song "Plástico": "People of flesh and bone who did not sell themselves, people working, searching for the new path, proud of their heritage and of being Latino." This is a particularly important reference as it ties The

People, El Pueblo, with the people as the true people, Latinos. This group of characters as a whole represents the people of the meta-barrio.

The other part of this equation is actually the "physical" space of the meta-barrio: the urban places. Within this small sample of Blades's work, the first chronological reference is to the mountains of "Juan Gonzalez" and where the guerrilla lives. In later compositions, the concept is developed further, and one of the songs that clearly references spaces and places is "Pablo Pueblo." In this song we find first and foremost "the usual neighborhood . . . with the street lamp in the corner, with the trash pile right across and the noise from the bar," followed promptly by his arrival at "the dark entranceway, and . . . the walls with the old flyers that promised futures in political matters." The picture is completed by "the courtyard . . . with the screaming underneath, the clothes there in the balconies and the wind drying it," to finally arrive at "his old neighborhood tired from the factory." The other archetypical place that emerges from this analysis is the "plastic city" that is very well described in the song "Plástico." "It was a plastic city like those I'd rather not see, with cancerous buildings and a tinsel heart. Where a dollar rises instead of the sun, where nobody laughs and nobody cries." This plastic city is at the same time referenced in "Ligia Elena" as the luxurious mansions of society. In direct opposition to the plastic city, the space of the corner makes an appearance during the roll call in "Plástico" as a symbol of popular neighborhood encounters. Last but not least, *el barrio* (as well as El Barrio) makes its appearance both in "Plástico" and "Déjenme Reír (para no llorar)" as a space where El Pueblo lives. There certainly is a deliberate ambiguity here as it is unclear if Blades meant El Barrio in New York City or *el barrio* as in any neighborhood in Latin America, or both.

In reading Blades's work at large, there are many other characters and places that could be added to this list; among them the most known are Pedro Navaja (the gangster), the prostitute, and the drunk (all of them from the song "Pedro Navaja"), but that is beyond the scope of this analysis. For reference, I have compiled the characters and places of Blades analyzed in this book (table 1).

Category number five, social issues, is one of the main topics not only in Blades's work but in Salsa consciente in general. In the case of this analysis,

Table 1: Characters and places of Rubén Blades

Song	Characters	Places
Juan Gonzalez	• The Guerrilla Fighter	• The mountains
Pablo Pueblo	• The Common Man • The People	• The usual/old neighborhood with the street lamp in the corner and the trash pile • Dark entranceway • The courtyard • The factory
Plástico	• The Plastic Family (including the plastic boy and the plastic girl) • The People	• The plastic city • The corner • El Barrio
Ligia Elena	• The Daughter of the Plastic Family (Ligia Elena) • The Common Man (the trumpet player) • The Plastic Family (Ligia Elena's family)	• The plastic city (luxurious mansions of society) • El barrio/El Barrio
Déjenme Reír (para no llorar)	• The Poor People (Carmelo, Manuela, and Ramiro) • The people (The neighborhood choir) • The lying politicians	• El barrio

the category transverses the following issues: poverty, materialism, classism, and violence. In the case of "Pablo Pueblo," the idea of poverty is prevalent as the song shows the common man and his family struggling to survive, with only hope for nourishment. The matter of poverty is certainly tied to the idea of classism present in both "Ligia Elena," and "Plástico." In the case of "Ligia Elena," the idea of the daughter running away with a low-society Black musician produces horror in the mother. At the same time, "Plástico" shows the plastic girl who does not "speak to anybody they don't consider their equal unless he is 'Mr. So-and-So.'" "Plástico" makes heavy reference to materialism and the idea of keeping up appearances for the sake of social status. The song, on the other hand, ultimately invites listeners to be, and shows Latinos as, the "real people" that shall not be fooled by plastic.

The last song that I include under the category of social issues is "El Padre Antonio y el Monaguillo Andrés." This song speaks first and foremost of the prevalent violence in the Latin America of the 1980s. The song deals directly with the assassination at the altar of the character that Blades calls Father Antonio. This character is later revealed by his pregones in the same song to be Archbishop Oscar Arnulfo Romero. The case of this priest and the fact that Blades wrote a song about his death is not a coincidence. During the 1970s and 1980s Latin American dictatorships, several priests played large roles in the development of the eventual demise of the military governments, whether by aiding talks between parties, advocating for human rights, or allowing churches to be safe havens from the violence. Archbishop Romero's story is, however, a fitting choice to be told as his killing at the altar was particularly symbolic.

The last theme in this analysis is Latino life. While the concept might seem to be a generalization, the idea of chronicling Latino life is perhaps the most prevalent topic in Blades's work. In this manner, the song and the whole album *Maestra Vida* can be understood as the primary source to reach a unified Rubén Blades theory. Blades's 2009 record *Cantares del Subdesarrollo* (Songs of underdevelopment) further supports the thought of *Maestra Vida* as the key recording in understanding the overall concept of Blades's work. Blades writes: "This work is a continuation of the arc of the characters and events originally described in the history of *Maestra Vida*, which unites all of my production, from 1969 to the present 2009."

The album *Maestra Vida* is the keystone of Blades's concept, as his discourse is centered on an anthropological and sociological chronicle of Latino life. As such, all the songs analyzed and potentially all of Blades's work would fall under this category. The output, however, as I have shown here, can be specifically categorized into subsections of Latino life, yet they include crucial aspects that tie them back into the idea of life—of being, and to the idea of being Latino, and Latin American, of being conscious of that Latino/Latin American existence and in being conscious of the issues of that Latinidad. The consciousness is shared by all Latinos. This Latinidad—or to quote Padilla, "Latino ethnic consciousness," is full of joys, sorrows, poverty, relationships, classism, violence, characters, etc. All of these experiences are what makes *Maestra Vida* the most crucial album for understanding the consciousness of that experience. Blades's work has been to put that experience into song.

Conclusion

We are all in this together, we have fought military dictatorships, we fought repression, we have fought brutality, we have fought rape, violations, the robbery of our sovereignty, the robbery of our identity, we have fought this to a standstill, now what we have to do is consolidate ourselves as a group, so that Honduras is not allowed to happen, so that we can remove the blockade from Cuba, so that Brazil can come forward as one of the great nations in the world, so that Puerto Rico can become independent, and trade itself, and form its own contracts, and have its own currency, so that Ecuador does not have to sell its prime biosphere to the oil interests, so that Chile can continue its road.

—Felipe Luciano (2013)

In many ways, this book started as a personal quest to understand my own position today. I am after all a Latino/Latin American and professional musician specializing in the performance of Salsa. I grew up under a brutal dictatorship, listening to Rubén Blades's lyrics and thinking that his songs were dedicated to my reality, my everyday, and my country. I migrated to the United States almost twenty years ago and have made a life here; I became one more Latino in the mix. Salsa consciente as I had known it became a music that, as I discovered, spoke to a lot of my peers in an incredible number of ways, regardless of our nationalities. In an attempt to understand my role as a Latino, I was helped by the music to connect to my immigrant status and relationships with Latinos and Latin America as a whole. Salsa consciente allowed me to approach the consciousness of the immigrant in relation to the idea of being Latino outside of the motherland, Latin America.

Throughout this book, I have attempted to convey various dimensions of the Latino conscience/consciousness movement that I have argued is enveloped in the discourse of Salsa consciente. I have discussed Salsa as an amalgam of musics that are related to the Latino/Latin American experience, and consciente as a taxonomy that encompasses the discussion of the heightened social awareness presented in the music. In this manner, I followed the development of such a discourse in Salsa to finally analyze through case studies the work of C. Curet Alonso and Rubén Blades as the two most relevant artists within the movement.

This book has also documented the development of Salsa consciente as part of a movement intrinsically tied to Latinidad insofar as this Latinidad is related to class consciousness. Latinidad as described by Padilla (1985) is best understood from the position of two or more Spanish-speaking groups in the United States joined by migration-related issues such as poverty, discrimination, etc. In the case of Salsa consciente, however, this Latinidad is expanded to include a transnational understanding where the socioeconomic issues referred to by critics such as Padilla relate to the development of a shared ethnic consciousness based on the same set of values but this time with and within the people of Latin America. As such, Salsa consciente functions as a transnational phenomenon that exploits the concept of a shared Latino/Latin American heritage connected via class consciousness.

In categorizing the consciousness of Salsa consciente, the African and Indigenous ethnic components are utilized as delineating features of Latinos and Latin Americans. Salsa consciente approaches these issues not necessarily by denouncing racism, but by asking Latinos to see themselves as a product of colonialism, slavery, and the assassination of the Native people. Curet Alonso's inclusion of the negritude and Indigenous components in his music plays a large role in the development of a discourse that accepts the Native and African heritages as intrinsic to the Latino ethnic categorization as opposed to certain ethnocentric Western values based on colonialist considerations that see African and Native as backwards, and White as the model for advancement. At the same time, the presentation of Native and African heritages as a common element of the Latino/Latin American population, no matter the nationality, aims at a deconstruction of the status quo of a Latino/Latin American ethnic identity as a model based on nationalistic divisions imposed by the rule of the Spaniards that does not consider Indigenous ethnicities.

The second categorization, political consciousness, which as I have argued before is mostly present in Rubén Blades's work, stems from his positions as a lawyer and as a Latin American, and is aimed directly at the region as a central concern of the discourse. The situations in Latin America regarding dictatorships and violence in the 1970s and 1980s, much of it related to the United States, were a central topic for Blades during this period. The inclusion of Latin America as a region that shared not only a racial/ethnic component but also a political one is based on a joint relevance in the same manner as the previously mentioned history of Spain as the initial colonizer. But Blades goes one step further to present and analyze the eruption of the imperialistic forces of the United States in Latin America. He then utilizes a Latin American Marxist conception to elucidate what Dussel (n.d.) refers to as the second emancipation of Latin America.[1] This second emancipation is grounded on the Latin American People becoming liberated not only from U.S. imperialism, but also from Western bourgeois ideals as a main point of reference for advancement. This emancipation is ultimately achieved by acknowledging and advancing a united Latin America, including Latino communities, as a sociopolitical People-based movement beyond national identities.

With regard to social issues, there is an understanding in Salsa consciente that the music comes from The People and it is for The People; therefore, this music in its original form, the Nuyolatino form, is not one where the realities of the working class are hidden; they are often exalted as a measure of "realness" in both the performers and the music. An often-heard popular expression in Salsa parlance is that of "tener calle" or "ser calle," that is, "to have street credibility." This manifestation speaks of the initial realities of the music, where the performers walked the streets—not the big avenues, but the streets of The People. This expression is utilized as a measure of the grittiness and general gusto of performers, since a Salsa musician who does not "have street" is ultimately not able to express the music at a proper level. This signification points to class awareness as one of the main tenets of the music, not only in the lyrics, but relating to the music as something that cannot be learned in school, but rather must be learned in the streets.

The concept of El Pueblo as one of the main identity factors of the movement plays a major role in understanding the associations of the music with The People at its core. Despite the fact that this concept is mostly tied to the social aspects of the music, it also showcases the transnational possibilities of the music as it ties in the analogical hegemon (Dussel 2008) of El Pueblo as one united fight where racial, ethnic, political, and social realities intersect. As such, Salsa consciente's discourse and understanding of Latino/Latin American consciousness at large is based on an acknowledgment and valuation of "the other history" as one where the social movements of El Pueblo that took hold in the 1970s expanded the popular collective Latin American imagination where racial concerns, be they Native or African centered, are intersected with the social and political concerns of The People. The movement that Salsa consciente then instigates is one where ethnicity/race is joined with class and sociopolitical struggles and considered a common fight. This is ultimately a fight against the conceptions of modernity established and imposed by Eurocentric social, racial, and political models, wherein Western-based civilization and the superiority of the White race/ethnicity are assumed as "natural" despite being social constructs.

Regarding the concept of Latino unity, while this might negate nationalistic identities, the precept of Latino unity in Salsa consciente aims to join people, not nationals, under one cause in which the advancement of Latinos and Latin Americans is intrinsically connected across borders. The concept of Latino/Latin American unity would have been particularly difficult to pursue from Latin America if it had not derived from the Latino community in the United States. The everyday national realities, including divisions often inherited either from the colonialism of Spain or from conflicts associated with war among Latin American countries, would probably not have resulted in a project of unity. Salsa consciente as a U.S. product, however, can maintain a broader view since the perspective of U.S. Latinos is removed from Latin America so they can see the everyday interactions of different Latin American nationalities in the United States without the restrictive barriers of national divisions. This issue, as I have shown in earlier chapters, is one that is relevant in the case of Rubén Blades.

This understanding stems from Blades's experience, where his views as a Panamanian and Latin American are merged with the Puerto Rican milieu of New York. These levels of interactions are new to Blades, who upon his arrival in New York City realizes the overarching power of his newly formed Latino shared consciousness; yet for Puerto Ricans in New York, given their migrant status and their vast and early social networks in the city, this consciousness is understood as everyday "Puerto Rican" life, thus reducing their ability to make a transnational connection.

In conceptualizing Salsa consciente, I posit that not only is the music a vehicle to chronicle the shared lives of Latinos and Latin Americans around the world from a critical perspective, but also this genre has been the engine behind the creation and development of a modern shared Latino/Latin American consciousness. Salsa consciente as a movement discusses crucial subject matters beyond the often explored traits of joy, treason, and disillusion as related to love. As such, Salsa consciente informs, shapes, questions, speaks of, and narrates the identities of The People, El Pueblo. Salsa consciente explores life as full of questions, joys, sorrows, and experiences by embracing all of these issues as part of a narrated reality. In this sense, I argue that the key album for understanding the concept of Salsa consciente is *Maestra Vida*, which portrays a family that "does not exist" yet is my family. It is the family of the Mexican laborer in the fields, the Puerto Rican dishwasher, the Salvadorian busboy. It is the family that ultimately shares *Una Sola Casa*: the family is all under the same roof. This album shows Latino/Latin American life and the awareness of the everyday, of being Latino and Latin American in all of its dimensions. Salsa consciente in this understanding is ultimately the lived, and not imagined, realities of the everyday Latino—and by association every Latin American—in music.

Salsa consciente showcased, among Latinos and Latin Americans alike, the importance for this population of acknowledging their culture not as a second-class product, but one where the realities facing The People are paramount. The production of Salsa toward the end of the 1970s boom aimed at standardizing Latino/Latin American experience and struggles as a commodity, since such precepts would be well received in the Latin American market. This selling of popular culture eventually negated the social, racial, and political discourses as true expressions of The People, and replaced them with the impositions of a system that exoticized the realities of the working people through and in favor of commercialism. This fact was eventually one of the main causes of the collapse of the Fania Records Salsa monopoly by the mid-1980s. The 1980s also saw the end of the burning of the Bronx and increased diversification of Latin New York with a growing Dominican population in Manhattan.[2] Consequently, Dominican merengue soon became the most promoted and popular Latin music coming out of New York. Despite the fact that Rubén Blades produced much of his crucial Salsa consciente output during the 1980s, a considerable amount of his work was directed toward a Latin Americanist project centered largely around the dictatorship cycle that continued to plague Latin America in the 1980s. It is in this deviation from Blades's original work with Fania, and also because of the record label's failure to deliver a quality product past the Salsa boom, that the understanding of Salsa consciente's discourse became somewhat separate from the U.S. Latino realities. While many other Salsa artists continued to produce records during the 1980s, eventually the success of the hard-driving Salsa of the 1970s in the United States faded, and the advent of the 1990s saw the rise of the formulaically produced, commercially standardized, musically sanitized "romantic Salsa/*Salsa romantica*," which was mostly devoid of social content.

Romantic Salsa as the main Salsa product of the 1990s did achieve great popularity; however, the image of Latinos became once again, in the vein of Desi Arnaz, stereotyped by the hyper-eroticized and highly produced looks of what is now known as Latin-pop, driven by artists such as Jennifer Lopez or Ricky Martin. The *Salsa romantica* movement, unlike the original 1970s Salsa, was built on the formula of producing and promoting artists mostly based on their looks and possibilities of commercial success rather than the development of a grassroots movement. As such, Salsa consciente was displaced from marketing strategies as too controversial, and Salsa became a popular cultural phenomenon sold as a commodity merely for the purpose of entertainment and profit.

Salsa as a movement in general, however, has always been based on understanding and respecting the music of the past to inform the future.

Thus, despite the formulaic standards of the 1990s, with the arrival of the twenty-first century, Salsa has seen a revival of the hard-driving sounds of the 1970s with groups such as the Spanish Harlem Orchestra, alongside the commercial success of Marc Anthony playing the role of Salsa legend Héctor Lavoe in the movie *El Cantante*. The reference point for this nostalgic revival, however, is almost exclusively the sound of the 1970s, and not the lyrical references that marked the Latino discourse of the Salsa consciente movement. While it could be argued that this sonic, as opposed to socio-musical, point of reference is related in particular to the fact that Latino struggles in the United States have shifted toward more nationalistic endeavors due to the shifts in modern migration patterns, and that, consequently, nationalistic Latin American alliances have formed beyond being "Latino," there are still a number of remarkably poignant issues such as immigration, political representation equity, inclusion, general discrimination, police brutality, and racism, to name a few, that affect Latino communities in the United States as a whole. Yet the current Salsa movement fails to a large degree to reflect those realities. This is not to say that Salsa consciente has ceased to exist, but the movement has undoubtedly lost much of its original drive. There are still, however, pockets of critical discourse in Salsa, as demonstrated by groups such as Orquesta Salsa con Conciencia (Orquesta SCC, formerly known as La Excelencia) with very poignant titles to their albums such as *Salsa con conciencia* (Salsa with a conscience) and *Mi Tumbao Social* (My Social Groove). As an example, I analyze here one of the cuts included in the CD *Mi Tumbao Social* titled "American Sueño," which is based on the topic of immigration and the questioning of the immigrant's dream as a central axis. It is interesting to note that, much in the vein of Salsa from yesteryear, the song is based on the form of the traditional lament, in this case the lament of the immigrant. Lyrically, the song makes a strong political statement as it contrasts the realities of the immigrant against the dream that a migration to the United States is expected to bring. There are also other references to darker realities, including the deadly risks that this decision may bring; the abuse and neglect of the government toward, and because of, the uncertain status of undocumented immigrants; the abuse of employers regarding overwork and underpay, which is a very common fact of life for undocumented workers; as well as a reference to immigration raids and searches. This lament contrasts the plight of the immigrant as an honest person who is only searching for ways to improve the living conditions of their family with someone who came to the United States to cheat and steal, as well as highlighting the positive drive and resistance of the undocumented worker. Additionally, it is worth remarking on the spoken section of this song, as it offers a continuation of the Salsa consciente tradition I have outlined via the recordings of the 1970s. As we have seen, these often contained spoken sections, and here the segment speaks of an anti-systemic resistance that must be launched. This section is thus very much akin to the focus of Curet Alonso and Blades on the raising of a Latino consciousness. In the case of "American Sueño" the identification with Latinos is implied by the Spanish used in the title and in the song and in the idea of class consciousness, which marks this release as a direct descendant of the 1970s movement.

"American Sueño" Composed by Julian Silva

Amigo, escuche lo que le estoy diciendo	My friend, listen to what I'm saying,
Yo no aguanto más este sufrimiento	I cannot take this suffering anymore
Y aunque me toque un futuro incierto	And even if I have an uncertain future
Yo me voy de aquí y ya no vuelvo	I am leaving and not coming back
Dejo atrás a mi familia	I leave my family behind
A mis queridos viejos	My dear mom and pop
Si es por ellos que tomo este riesgo	It is for them that I take this risk
Si por alguna razón la vida pierdo	If for some reason I was to lose my life
Ya son dos años en este nuevo pueblo	It's been two years in this new town
Y como un ladrón me tienen corriendo	And like a thief they have me running
Esta libertad le juro que no la entiendo	This freedom, I swear to you, I cannot understand it
Trabajo día y noche y casi no duermo	I work day and night and almost don't sleep
Y aun aquí yo sigo sufriendo	And I am still here suffering
Sin importarle a este bruto gobierno	Without this stupid government caring

Porque me fui de mi país ya no recuerdo	Why did I leave my country I cannot even remember?
Este no puede ser el American sueño	This cannot be the American dream
Coro: Me empujan y me empujan, pero no me caigo	**Chorus:** They push me and push me but I don't fall down
…	…
Voy en busca del billete para alimentar mi hogar	I am looking for the money to feed my household
Mi madrecita querida dime quien la va a cuidar dime pana mío ¿quién será?	My dear mother who is going to care for her? Tell me my friend, who will it be?
Inmigración me persigue y no sé qué pasará	Immigration chases me and I'm not sure what will happen
Lamento del inmigrante	The lament of the immigrant
Segundo coro: No, no me caigo	**Second chorus:** No, I don't fall down
No sé por qué me persiguen si yo vine a trabajar	I don't know why they chase me if I came to work
Yo no vine a hacerles daño, tampoco vine a robar	I did not come to hurt them nor to steal
Ay, solo quiero el billete para alimentar mi hogar	Oh, I just want the money to feed my household
Yo te digo caballero que yo no vine a hacer mal	I am telling you people that I did not come to do harm
Solo quiero que respeten que yo vine aquí a buscar	I only want you to respect that I came here looking for
Un futuro más seguro pa' mis hijos y mi hogar	A more secure future for my children and my household
…	…
Hablado:	**Spoken:**
Yo no creo en guerra	I do not believe in war
Sin embargo, yo sé que creer solamente en la paz	But I know that believing only in peace
Seria ignorar las injusticias que existen en nuestras tierras	Would be to ignore the injustices of our homelands
Ignorar las injusticias que existen en nuestra sociedad	Ignoring the injustices of our society
Y por esa razón y esa razón única	And for that reason, and that reason only

Levanto un puño al aire para gritar resistencia	I raise my fist up in the air to cry resistance
Contra un sistema que solamente me quiere callar	Against a system that only wants to silence me[3]

While some of the new generation of Salsa musicians are still carrying the torch of the Salsa consciente movement, they are the exception rather than the rule. There is, however, another genre that actually developed parallel to 1970s Salsa, and partially in the same neighborhoods: rap. Rap has served as a grassroots movement generating socially conscious music very much under the same tenets that Salsa has done since its creation. A comparison between Chuck D of Public Enemy and Rubén Blades is quite possible, yet here I simply wish to note that much of the new Latino/Latin American urban youth has now turned on a massive scale toward Spanish-language rap. Young Latinos and Latin Americans view rap's significations, along with its political, social, and racial, as well as entertainment implications, very much in the same manner that the Latino and Latin American youth of the 1970s and early '80s regarded Salsa as its music. The later popularity of rap in Latin America and with Latinos stems chiefly from the fact that rap music had been produced, until recently, largely in English, thus not allowing Spanish-speaking youth to identify with it.

Within Spanish-language rap there is a subgenre called *Rap consciente* or *Rap conciencia* (conscious rap). This movement has a remarkable number of similarities with the 1970s and '80s discourse of the Salsa consciente movement, as the new carriers of the torch of social consciousness have found a new way to express Latino/Latin American struggles. This development can be partially related to the development of the spoken word as a popular means of expression in the New York Latino communities of the 1980s. Luciano (2013) indicated that

> the energy went from music to spoken word. Slowly we begin to provide a new matrix for the politics and culture of our people . . . The cumulative effect [of the actions] was that people now were talking and were using it, because it wasn't in the music, so we took it and went into spoken word.

Regarding the influence on such a movement of Salsa consciente, there is great significance in the fact that many of the artists working on Spanish-language Rap consciente have come to express their consciousness not from the point of view of a Latino, but from the point of view of a Latin American or from the point of view of their own nationalities. It can thus be said that the seeds planted by the original 1970s Salsa consciente have sprouted and produced a new generation of Latin Americans that have digested Blades's and Curet Alonso's music, alongside the *nueva canción Latino Americana*, and now are able to raise their voice, or their metaphorical fists, from a Latin America that has gotten up and rebuilt itself in the aftermath of the dictatorships and violence of the past decades. Among these artists of myriad nationalities are Franco-Chilean Anita Tijoux, Peruvian-born Immortal Technique, and Puerto Ricans Residente/Calle 13 and Tego Calderón. It should be noted that despite my definition of these artists as part of rap/ urban music, as highly creative artists they have also found many ways to confront the ideologies and stereotypes associated with rap, and as such they defy the idea of genre based on a musico-cultural set of aesthetics. With this brief section, I strive to demonstrate the heritage of Rap consciente as one partially stemming from Salsa consciente, and not exclusively from socially conscious rap in English, as well as to highlight some of the connections of their discourses. The section also functions as a measure of the health and prevalence of many of the ideals set forth by the Salsa consciente movement, and their contemporary significations.

Franco-Chilean artist Anita Tijoux was born in France after her family was exiled during the dictatorship of Pinochet in the 1970s and '80s in Chile. Her political discourse is highly intellectually developed and touches upon ideas of feminism, Indigeneity, and Latin America's contemporary past. As an example, her song "Shock" makes reference to Naomi Klein's book *The Shock Doctrine*. In this song, Tijoux criticizes corruption and far-right Catholicism (Opus Dei), and directly criticizes Chile for still maintaining a constitution that was written during Pinochet's regime.[4] She contrasts these concepts with The People's movement and the popular expression of "rayar muros": the act of writing (politically minded) graffiti on the city's walls.

"Shock" as Performed by Anita Tijoux	
Constitución Pinochetista	Pinochet's constitution
Derecho opus dei, libro fascista.	Laws drawn by the Opus Dei, a fascist book
Golpista disfrazado de un indulto elitista	Participants of the coup disguised behind an elitist pardon
…	…
La calle no calla, la calle se raya.	The streets are not silent, the streets have writing on their walls.[5]

Another very important artist within the conscious rap movement is Peruvian-born Immortal Technique. He was born during the 1980s conflicts in Peru that saw the activism of the Communist revolutionary organization of the Shining Path (Sendero Luminoso) become the central axis of anti-dictatorial movements, as well as opposition to the 1978 version of the Peruvian constitution, and the "election" of Belaúnde Terry in 1980. Immortal Technique migrated to the United States (Los Angeles) at an early age, and developed his discourse from a Latino point of view, but primarily in English. In this manner, his appeal is directly to the English-speaking market and to Latinos who speak English. Immortal Technique grew up during the 1980s and 1990s in Los Angeles, and his music takes much from the L.A.-born gangsta rap of the era. His discourse references a great deal of violence, likely as a means to shock his audience, and includes a level of swearing that has promptly disqualified him from large commercial success. Despite his development within the "gangsta ideals," Immortal Technique does not focus his work on the racial conflicts of Los Angeles, as NWA or Ice Cube did. His work is also not based on a Latin American or nationalistic point of view, but instead he produces a sociopolitical critique regarding, among other topics, poverty, racism, class warfare, and the realities of the contemporary Latino in the United States. His song "3rd World" is a clear example of his ideals.

"3rd World" as Performed by Immortal Technique

Lock and load your gun where I'm from, the Third World, son
Been to many places, but I'm Third World born
Guerrillas hit and run where I'm from, the Third World, son
You polluted everything and now the Third World's gone
The water is poison where I'm from, the Third World, son
700 children died by the end of this song
Revolution'll come where I'm from, the Third World, son
Constant occupation leaves the Third World torn

I'm from where the catholic church is some racist shit
They helped Europe and America rape this bitch
They pray to white Spaniard Jesus, whose face is this?
But never talk about the black Pope Gelasius
I'm from where soviet weapons still decide elections
Military is like the mafia: you pay for protection[6]

Regarding the work of Residente/Calle 13 and Tego Calderón, the music
of these artists is based on very similar values as those of Salsa consciente,
which had cemented its role in relation to Puerto Rico and the Puerto Rican
diaspora. Salsa was the music of these contemporary artists' parents and
they grew up listening to people such as Rubén Blades and Ismael Rivera.
Tego Calderón, for instance, participated in the aforementioned tribute to
C. Curet Alonso, and is a self-declared fanatic of Puerto Rican icon Ismael
Rivera, the interpreter of "Las Caras Lindas" and a strong admirer of his positions on being Black and Puerto Rican. In continuing this legacy, Calderón
presents a modern rap-based discourse that is as much based on racial
issues as the original Salsa consciente discourse explored by Curet Alonso.
Mendoza (2008, 19) indicates that Tego Calderón's music centers itself on

issues of racial pride and socio-economic inequality within Puerto Rico. His
articulation of Latino identity is based on a racialized and gendered performance of an identity that actually revises the stereotypes attached to his

real physical presence as a Black Puerto Rican while using his music as his most brutal opposition to oppressive powers inside and outside the island.

Calderón also indicated the following in an interview with National Public Radio: "I started to make music from a Black rhythm so Black People would be proud of being Black."[7] As an example of these negritude, or Africanness, ideals, the number "¿Por qué?" (Why?) pays homage to the Afro-descendant people of Puerto Rico by utilizing the music and the associated Blackness aesthetics of *bomba*, in this case the styles of *cuembé* and *yubá*, to develop his rhymes along the same paths that Rafael Cortijo and Curet Alonso had marked out in the 1960s.

"¿Por qué?" as Performed by Tego Calderón

¿Por qué? ¿Por qué?	Why? Why?
Porque me gusta la bomba, repiquen barriles	Because I like bomba. Sound the drums.
¿Por qué? ¿Por qué?	Why? Why?
Africano Boricua, Africano con su aché	African Puerto Rican, African with their ashé[8]

One other artist that is very relevant to mention here is the group Calle 13 led by urban artist Residente. The Puerto Rican ensemble, which also participated in the DVD produced as an homage to Curet Alonso, has gained an enormous amount of exposure all over the world. They have won twenty-two Latin Grammys and three "regular" Grammys, as well as many other accolades. Their discourse is particularly revolutionary in the Latin American sense, and directly linked to the Salsa consciente discourse as their lyrics are very much based, although not exclusively, on socially conscious topics. The conscious discourse presented by Residente/Calle 13, however, often presents a transnational discourse and represents, in a Hegelian sense—and also in the same type of development that Blades showcased within Salsa—a development of the linguistic dialectics within conscious rap.

Mendoza (2008, 19) indicates that not only are the lyrics of Calle 13 quite relevant to this discussion, but they integrate sets of sonic markers very much in the same vein as Salsa consciente:

> They use violent lyrics to showcase deviant behaviors that are an expression of their frustration with U.S. intervention in Latin American politics and the immigrant experience. In their incorporation of different Latin American sounds such as Colombia's cumbias, Argentina's tangos, Mexico's rancheras, New York-based Salsa, and Andean rhythms of Peru and South America, they convey their belief that Pan-Latino solidarity can counteract the globalization of U.S. values.

A very poignant song, yet not as violent as the one Mendoza describes, is the song "Latinoamérica," which in the same vein as Blades's work exalts the beauties, joys, sorrows, and sentiments of the region within its lyrics. This song is tied to Bolivarianism as a precept that could be understood as one of the main concepts underlining both Salsa and Rap consciente's Pan-Latino ideals. Bolivarian concepts include forming a union of Latin American countries, providing public education, negotiating equitable distribution of (South America's) vast natural resources, and enforcing sovereignty to fight against foreign invasion.

The song makes direct references to the historical past of Latin America as a region by including a host of allusions, including ones to colonialism, by talking about the pillage of Latin America at the hands of (mainly) Spaniards; the exploitation of farms and farm workers at the hands of the first world; the Latin American dictatorship cycle of the 1960s, 1970s, and 1980s; and the role of the United States in those dictatorships via Operation Condor. It recalls the missing persons of the era and how their photos are still used to keep the memories of the disappeared alive. The song also mentions the Falkland Islands conflict between Argentina and the UK, and the pride felt by South America in the 1986 soccer World Cup when Argentinian soccer star Diego Armando Maradona scored two goals against the English national team. Despite the topics, much of the song also focuses on the beauty of the region in a transnational manner by highlighting the mountains, the Caribbean sea, the vineyards, and the African traditions of the region, and equates them with a notion of reality that connects Latin America and its people to being part of the soil.

This song made particular strides in the Latin American world as it was a commercial hit, and was recognized with the Latin Grammy award for best song of the year. The song was performed, along with a full symphony orchestra conducted by Venezuelan Gustavo Dudamel, at the 2011 Latin Grammys. As a side note, the album *Entren Los Que Quieran*, where the song appears, won best record of the year, in addition to eight other Latin Grammy awards for the band in different categories in the same year. The success of this work clearly demonstrates the well-being, as well as the heritage and the contemporary relevance, of the very same set of ideals that were brought forth by the artists I have analyzed throughout this book.

"Latinoamérica" as Performed by Calle 13

Soy, soy lo que dejaron	I am, I am what they left
Soy toda la sobra de lo que se robaron	I'm all the leftover of what was stolen.
…	…
Mano de obra campesina para tu consumo	A peasant working hand for your consumption
…	…
Soy la fotografía de un desaparecido	I'm the photograph of a missing person.
…	…
Soy Maradona contra Inglaterra	I'm Maradona against England
Anotándote dos goles	Scoring two goals.
Soy lo que sostiene mi bandera	I'm that which holds my flag,
La espina dorsal del planeta es mi cordillera	The backbone of the planet is my Andes.
Soy lo que me enseño mi padre	I'm that which my father taught me,
El que no quiere a su patria	Who doesn't love his motherland
No quiere a su madre	Does not love his mother.
Soy América latina	I'm Latin America,

Un Pueblo sin piernas pero que camina	People without legs but can walk
...	...
La nieve que maquilla mis montañas	The snow that puts makeup on my mountains.
Tengo el sol que me seca y la lluvia que me baña	I have the sun that dries me and the rain that washes me
...	...
Los versos escritos bajo la noche estrellada	The lines written under the starry night.
Una viña repleta de uvas	A vineyard filled with grapes.
Un cañaveral bajo el sol en Cuba	A sugar cane plantation under the Cuban sun.
Soy el mar caribe que vigila las casitas	I'm the Caribbean Sea watching over the houses,
Haciendo rituales de agua bendita	Performing rituals with holy water.
El viento que peina mi cabello	The wind that combs my hair.
Soy todos los santos que cuelgan de mi cuello	I'm all the saints that hang from my neck.
El jugo de mi lucha no es artificial	The juice of my struggle is not artificial,
Porque el abono de mi tierra es natural	Because the fertilizer of my land is natural.
...	...
La operación cóndor invadiendo mi nido	Operation Condor is invading my nest.
Perdono, pero nunca olvido.	I forgive, but I'll never forget![9]

I posit that Rap consciente is truly a continuation of the work of Salsa consciente, particularly that of Curet Alonso and Blades in lyrical terms. As such, I consider it very relevant to mention the makings of the current frameworks of Latino/Latin American consciousness in music, even if Salsa consciente has been mostly set aside at this point in time. The messages of Rap consciente directly continue and show clear links to the work of Salsa consciente by elaborating further upon Latino realities and their modern significations. Among these significations, Rap consciente develops its frameworks by utilizing the same levels of Latino/Latin American consciousness, be they racial, social, ethnic, Latino, or those of Latinidad.

The message is still relevant, and the seeds continue to germinate. The examples of Rap consciente shown here are simple snippets of a much larger movement that requires further exploration in a different volume.

As my focus on Rap consciente and its success shows, Latinos are still strongly linked to the idea of a shared consciousness. Politically this has also been demonstrated by the recent discussions about immigration reform in the United States. A united Latino movement is arguably stagnant in part due to the great diversity of new Latino immigrants in the United States. While this diversity has developed the unique, nation-centered cultural identities of every country represented, it has also divided a united Latino front as a movement of sociopolitical resistance. While the original New York–based push of the Salsa consciente movement was generated under the guise of the Puerto Rican social movements, today the diversity has created divisions within the Latino community. While this is an incredibly poignant issue, music has yet to play a major role in the development of a contemporary united Latino movement. Salsa, having declined in popularity, does not have the same relevance for the Latino community today as it did in the 1970s.

There is still a lack of education among Latinos and Latin Americans as regards the history of colonialism and slavery. Issues such as the still existent internal racism of Latinos that see Spain as the motherland, a "single mother" at that, present matters that need to be understood in order to develop an identity that assumes and advances not only a discourse established on Western-based constructs, but also one that takes history and a true acknowledgment of the past as part of that identity.

In conjunction with the idea of nationalist identities, specifically in U.S. Latino communities, there is a significant memory loss in regard to contemporary history in Latin America. The brutal violence of recent history, and the United States's frequent involvement in such violence in almost every country in Latin America, has seemingly been forgotten or deemed nonrelevant in the formation of Latino identity. This fact seems almost incomprehensible to me as a Latin American, yet issues of these types are rarely if ever discussed in the makeup of Latino identity.

Politically today, in the United States, there is much talk about the

Latino vote. Despite the efforts of U.S. political parties to group Latinos in this way, the idea of the Latino vote has not been proven empirically. The divisions regarding the positions the United States takes toward Latin America have fundamentally split the population. Among Puerto Ricans there is an important debate regarding its commonwealth status vis-à-vis the idea of Puerto Rico becoming a state or an independent country. Latino political alliances, however, despite Blades's left-leaning discourses, are not necessarily formed on ethnic relationships but rather on ideological grounds, and these differ greatly among Latinos. There is, however, a shared consciousness that has developed mainly via disenfranchisement and the valuation of Latinos as second-class citizens unable to adapt to the U.S. culture; while this might have political repercussions with regard to the ideology expressed in the phrase "I stand with my people," the outcome is more likely to prompt social mobilization rather than political unity.

In part, becoming a generic Latino, as opposed to a particular nationality, opens the possibility of a new life; hence, leaving the violence of the past behind seems a natural move. Yet, there is still much to do to advance the Latino community in the United States. There is an enormous commonality among Latin American histories and its recent pasts, the Latino/Latin American present, and its futures. Despite the fact that national agendas need to be acknowledged, many of the sociopolitical issues of Latinos are the same, and they are specifically treated as the same by U.S. policymakers. Maybe the new Latino life needs to acknowledge Latino ethnic consciousness in a new light and utilize the term to its advantage.

Throughout these chapters, I have pointed to further avenues of research along the lines outlined above. I have remarked that the lack of socio-musical biographies of artists such as C. Curet Alonso, Rubén Blades, Rafael Cortijo, Cheo Feliciano, etc., constitutes a research gap in the study of Salsa in general. There is also a great deal of work to be done regarding Salsa's impact in Latin America. Publications by Berríos-Miranda (1999) and Waxer (2002a), dealing with Venezuela and Colombia respectively, are certainly excellent starting points; however, a study of Salsa's impact in Peru, for example, popularly referred to today as the capital of *timba*, is still lacking. In terms of aesthetics, there needs to be a serious study conducted on the history and development of Salsa through the lens of its arrangers. While publications such as *The Latin Real Book* (Sher Music 1997) have partially shown the richness of the aesthetics of Salsa through sheet music, a study of the people involved, the developments, histories, and stories behind these works, is still lacking. This book has begun to address certain significant gaps, but clearly more work remains to be done.

Regarding Salsa consciente, there is also a great need to develop a comprehensive study of the lyrical content of Rubén Blades's music, its impact on Latino communities as well as its impact in Latin America. Regarding the work of C. Curet Alonso, Salazar (2007) has certainly advanced our understanding of his legacy; yet, C. Curet Alonso's massive output remains underanalyzed, and Salazar's publication is only available in Spanish. Probably the most important missing link in the study of Salsa, however, is one that analyzes in depth the social and musical aesthetics of Puerto Rican Salsa—that is, island-based, not New York-based, Salsa.

In this book, I have worked under the main assumption that Salsa is ultimately inclusive of all Latinos. While Salsa allows for a broad understanding of being Latino, it still leaves out Hispanic-based national identities and assumes that Latinos as a whole identify with Salsa. I have tried to circumvent this issue by arguing that Salsa is the only Latin-based music that has had such a large musical and social impact in Latin America as a whole, overcoming divisive nationalisms as a product developed in the United States. The overarching issue of Salsa as a signifier of Latinidad can be debated, particularly on the basis of nationalistic ideologies; however, the shared Latino consciousness is ultimately related to language and disenfranchisement as its main connectors.

There is an intrinsic point of contention in the way I have discussed the movement while not fully acknowledging the possibility of the movement being called *Salsa con conciencia* (Salsa with a conscience). While this is certainly a possibility, as it could be considered only a slight difference, the term *Salsa con conciencia* brings forth a reading of a Salsa for entertainment as the main axis of the movement along with the possibility of having critical consciousness. I have chosen the term Salsa consciente (conscious Salsa) as a stronger determinant of the critical consciousness of the music, as I consider it intrinsic and not optional to the overall discourse. There is the possibility of understanding Salsa, the sound, and not the consciousness as the main axis of the movement, and such an understanding potentially creates a discussion regarding the intrinsicness of critical consciousness in Salsa.

Another point of contention in this book stems from the partial tension between industrial mass culture and élite/literary cultural nationalism. While I acknowledge this contradiction, I understand this strain as a possible explanation of the eventual receding of Salsa consciente from its 1980s apogee. This is true of all social systems: Salsa consciente had a beginning, middle, and an end. This tension is arguably related to the fact that the seeds of Salsa consciente as a mass commercial product germinated into Rap consciente, a genre that despite some degree of commercial success remains largely an underground movement.

This book ultimately uncovers an understanding of Salsa from the perspective of being Latino. In this sense, I have positioned Salsa consciente as a popular cultural phenomenon that moves beyond mere entertainment to influence the masses of Latinos. As such, Salsa consciente opens a window for understanding the dynamics of a group that presents a number of disjointed nationalistic identities. There are many histories conveyed in being Latino. I have sought to present them as unified, yet I do acknowledge the dissimilar factors that make the population both united and disparate. There is yet much to do to deliver such a complex analysis in these ever-proliferating dimensions.

Throughout this work, it has become clear to me that there is still a vast absence of understanding among Latinos and Latin Americans as to who we are. This, in my opinion, stems fundamentally from a lack of education, and a partial denial of our history. I hope that through this work I can help my own Latino/Latin American communities understand, acknowledge, and educate themselves about who we are and why we are Latino América *Una Sola Casa*.

Cross-Referenced Table of Songs Included in This Book

Song	Composer	Performer	Year	Album	Lyrical Markers	Sonic Signifiers	Notes
Canto Karabali	Ernesto Lecuona	Machito	1947–1949	*Freezelandia 1947–1949*	N/A	None/mambo	
Chango Ta'beni	Justi Barretto	Machito	1947–1949	*Freezelandia 1947–1949*	Use of Yoruba (Lucumí) Language	None/mambo	
Ebo	?	Machito	?	*Ritmo Caliente*	Use of Yoruba (Lucumí) Language and Santería references	Use of Afro (siguaraya) rhythm.	
Zambia	Mario Bauza	Machito	?	*Ritmo Caliente*	N/A	Lengthy drum solos	
Mi Padrino me manda		Cuarteto Caney	1939–1940	*Cuarteto Caney (1939–1940) Featuring Machito*	Use of Yoruba (Lucumí) Language and Santería references	Use of Afro (siguaraya) rhythm in the introduction	
Ariñañara		Tito Puente	1949	*The Best of Tito Puente.*	Use of bozal	Use of *guaguancó*/ Lengthy drum solos	
Babarabatibiri		Tito Puente	1949–1955	*The Complete 78's Volume 1 1949–55*	Use of bozal	None/Mambo	
Dance of the Headhunters	Not Listed/ Arranged by Tito Puente	Tito Puente	1960	*Tambó*	N/A	Free use of Afro-Cuban traditional rhythms	
Call of the Jungle Birds	Not Listed/ Arranged by Tito Puente	Tito Puente	1960	*Tambó*	N/A	Free use of Afro-Cuban traditional rhythms	
The Ceremony of Tambó	Not Listed/ Arranged by Tito Puente	Tito Puente	1960	*Tambó*	N/A	Free use of Afro-Cuban traditional rhythms	
Ritual Drum Dance	Not Listed/ Arranged by Tito Puente	Tito Puente	1960	*Tambó*	N/A	Free use of Afro-Cuban traditional rhythms	

Song	Composer	Performer	Year	Album	Lyrical Markers	Sonic Signifiers	Notes
Witch Doctor's Nightmare	Not Listed/ Arranged by Tito Puente	Tito Puente	1960	*Tambó*	N/A	Free use of Afro-Cuban traditional rhythms	
Voodoo Dance at Midnight	Not Listed/ Arranged by Tito Puente	Tito Puente	1960	*Tambó*	N/A	Free use of Afro-Cuban traditional rhythms	
Chen-cher en guma		Tito Rodríguez	1949–1958	*Nostalgia con Tito Rodríguez (Recordings from 1949–1958)*	"Tumba caña en la colonia mi semana." Use of Bozal language	None/Mambo	Based on a Palo (Congo) song entitled Yenyere Guma
Boco boco	Chano Pozo	Tito Rodríguez	1949–1950	*Mambo Mona (1949–1950).*	Use of Bozal	None/Mambo	Originally made famous by Chano Pozo
Yambere	Tito Rodríguez	Tito Rodríguez	1958	*Three Loves Have I*	Use of Bozal	None/Mambo	
Me boté de Guaño	Arsenio Rodríguez	Arsenio Rodríguez	1949	*El Alma de Cuba: Grabaciones completas RCA Victor Volumen 3 1940–1956*	Abakua References/ References to urban toughness	None/Son Montuno	
Bruca Maniguá	Arsenio Rodríguez	Orquesta Casino de la Playa	1937	*Beyond Patina Jazz Masters: Orquesta Casino de la Playa*	Use of Bozal	Use of Afro (siguaraya) rhythm	Juxtaposition of Ki-Congo language with Spanish (Boza.)
Aqui como Allá	Arsenio Rodríguez	Arsenio Rodríguez	1950	*El Alma de Cuba: Grabaciones completas RCA Victor Volumen 3 1940–1956*	Use of "Ay dios" (oh God) in a lament form. Unity of Black people around the world by mention of many different countries	Drum roll signifying solemnity	

Song	Composer	Performer	Year	Album	Lyrical Markers	Sonic Signifiers	Notes
Yo Nací del Africa	Arsenio Rodriguez	Arsenio Rodriguez	1960	Cumbanchando con Arsenio Rodriguez	Yo no soy Rodriguez. Tal vez sea Lumumba.	None/Son Based	
La democracia	Arsenio Rodriguez	Arsenio Rodriguez	mid 1960s (1964?)	Never released. Available at the Smithsonian Folklife Archives	N/A	N/A	Never released. Available at the Smithsonian Folklife Archives
El Negro Bembón	Bobby Capó	Rafael Cortijo	1960	Baile con Cortijo	Racialized discussion delivered semi-comically/satirically	Quote to funeral march	
El Tema del Apollo	Eddie Palmieri	Eddie Palmieri y La perfecta	1965	Azucar pa'ti	El tema del Apollo, pa' que gocen los niches! (The theme of Apollo for the Black folk to enjoy)	None/Son montuno cha-cha-cha	
Ordinary Guy	Joe Bataan	Joe Bataan	1968	Riot!		Mix of Soul and Latin music unifying the realities of Harlem/Bronx	
Muchacho Ordinario	Joe Bataan	Joe Bataan	1973	Salsoul			Spanish version of Ordinary Guy
Subway Joe	Joe Bataan	Joe Bataan	1968	Subway Joe		Mix of Soul and Latin music unifying the realities of Harlem/Bronx	
Bang Bang	Jaime Sabater/Joe Cuba	Joe Cuba Sextet	1966	Wanted Dead or Alive (Bang! Bang! Push, Push, Push)	N/A	Son Montuno base with a backbeat	Lyrics are mostly in English

Song	Composer	Performer	Year	Album	Lyrical Markers	Sonic Signifiers	Notes
El Pito (I'll never go back to Georgia)	Jaime Sabater/Joe Cuba	Joe Cuba Sextet	1966	*Estamos Haciendo Algo Bien! (We Must Be Doing Something Right!)*	Quote to "I'll never go back to Georgia" by Gillespie	Son-based with "Soul claps"	Dizzy Gillespie utterance "I'll never go back to Georgia"
¿Y tu abuela dónde está?	Jaime Sabater	Joe Cuba Sextet	1966	*Estamos Haciendo Algo Bien! (We Must Be Doing Something Right!)*	Discussion of race/ Latino self-whitening	None/Son based	Based on a poem of the same name by Fortunato Vizcarrondo
Willie Baby	Willie Colón	Willie Colón	1967	*El Malo*			
Skinny Papa	Willie Colón	Willie Colón	1967	*El Malo*			
Willie Whopper	Willie Colón	Willie Colón	1967	*El Malo*			
Borinquen	D.R. (Derechos reservados/ Reserved rights)	Willie Colón	1967	*El Malo*			
El Malo	Willie Colón	Willie Colón	1967	*El Malo*		Use of bomba sicá rhythm to denote Puerto-Ricanness	
The Hustler	Willie Colón	Willie Colón	1968	*The Hustler*			Album abandons I lyrics
Eso se baila asi	Willie Colón	Willie Colón	1968	*The Hustler*	Boogaloo no va conmigo	Tracks starts boogaloo-like and ends moving away from the style	Album abandons I lyrics
Guisando	Willie Colón/ Héctor Lavoe	Willie Colón	1969	*Guisando Doing a Job*			

Song	Composer	Performer	Year	Album	Lyrical Markers	Sonic Signifiers	Notes
Oiga señor	Willie Colón/Héctor Lavoe	Willie Colón	1969	Guisando Doing a Job		Use of bomba sicá rhythm to denote Puerto Ricanness	
Che che colé	Willie Colón	Willie Colón	1970	Cosa nuestra	Pan-Latino unity by mention of Venezuela. Inclusion of African heritage to unite Latin America. Use of Ewe language	Use of gangá rhythm to denote African influences. Use of non-Cuban centered piano ostinato	Based on a Ghanaian children's song. Opened the doors of Panama, France, Colombia, Venezuela, and Peru
Ghana'e	Willie Colón/Héctor Lavoe	Willie Colón	1971	The Big Break La Gran Fuga			
Pa' Colombia	C. Curet Alonso	Willie Colón	1971	The Big Break La Gran Fuga			
Panameña	Willie Colón/Héctor Lavoe	Willie Colón	1971	The Big Break La Gran Fuga	Beauty of Panamanian, Dominican, and Puerto Rican women. Lavoe refers to aguinaldo as La Salsa de Puerto Rico	Nuyoricanized Danzón. Inclusion of Aguinaldo	
Barrunto	C. Curet Alonso	Willie Colón	1971	The Big Break La Gran Fuga			
No olvido a Caracas		Ray Barretto	1969	Together	Inclusion of Venezuela		
De donde vengo?	Louis Cruz & C. Fernandez	Ray Barretto	1969	Together	Questioning of Adam and Eve being White/hegemonic religious discourse		
Justicia	Ismael Quintana, Eddie Palmieri	Eddie Palmieri	1969	Justicia	mention of "the unfortunate"		Arguably the first mention of class consciousness in Salsa

Song	Composer	Performer	Year	Album	Lyrical Markers	Sonic Signifiers	Notes
Revolt La Libertad Lógico	Eddie Palmieri	Eddie Palmieri	1971	Vámonos Pa'l monte	Being mistreated because of ethnic conflict; stated by the sentence "This is where I was born." Being a slave to a system dictated by capitalism in "Economically, your slave."		
Jíbaro, my pretty nigger	Felipe Luciano	Felipe Luciano	1972	Live at Sing Sing Volume 1			
Las Caras lindas	C. Curet Alonso	Ismael Rivera	1978	Esto si es lo mío	Exaltation of beautiful Black faces	Lack of use of Afro–Puerto Rican music	
Sorongo	C. Curet Alonso	Rafael Cortijo	1968	Sorongo	Use of Sorongo as euphemism for "Black" Comparison of White vs. Black	Specific rhythm designed for the song	
Anacaona	C. Curet Alonso	Cheo Feliciano	1972	Cheo	Use of Anacaona the Indian chief. Use of Areíto. India de raza cautiva (Indian of a captive race) in reference to the Native genocide of colonial times.		
Plantación Adentro	C. Curet Alonso	Rubén Blades	1977	Metiendo Mano			
Juan Albañil	C. Curet Alonso	Cheo Feliciano	1980	Sentimiento tu	Notes discrimination and classism by the use of "no puede entrar" (he cannot go in)		

Song	Composer	Performer	Year	Album	Lyrical Markers	Sonic Signifiers	Notes
Con los Pobres Estoy	C. Curet Alonso	Roberto Roena	1972	Roberto Roena y Su Apollo Sound 4	Identification with poor people "Con Los pobres Estoy donde quiera que voy" (with the poor people I stand wherever I go). Use of Versos Sencillos by Jose Martí		
Lamento de Concepción	C. Curet Alonso	Roberto Roena	1978	Roberto Roena y Su Apollo Sound X–El Progreso			Based on the true story of Billy Concepción
Pura novela	C. Curet Alonso	Ray Barretto	1980	Giant Force– Fuerza Gigante	You would give up the castle and the nobility to be again a part of these slums		
Pueblo Latino	C. Curet Alonso	Fania All Stars/ Pete "El Conde" Rodriguez	1973	Fania All Stars Live at Yankee Stadium	Call to unity of Latinos of any city or barrio		
9 de enero	Rubén Blades	Bush y Su Nuevo Sonido	Unknown	Lo mejor de Bush y Su Nuevo Sonido	Sarcastic use of "El buen vecino" (the good neighbor) in reference to the United States		
Juan Gonzalez	Rubén Blades	Rubén Blades/Pete Rodriguez	1970	De Panama a Nueva York			
Pablo Pueblo	Rubén Blades	Willie Colón/ Rubén Blades	1977	Metiendo Mano			

Song	Composer	Performer	Year	Album	Lyrical Markers	Sonic Signifiers	Notes
Plástico	Rubén Blades	Willie Colón/ Rubén Blades	1978	Siembra		Use of Disco, Son, Bomba	
Siembra	Rubén Blades	Willie Colón/ Rubén Blades	1978	Siembra		Reduction of choruses	
Maestra Vida	Rubén Blades	Rubén Blades	1980	Maestra Vida		Use of Son Bolero Musica Jibara	
Déjenme reír para no llorar	Rubén Blades	Rubén Blades	1980	Maestra Vida	Inclusion of "the lying politicians"	Use of Bomba, Plena	
Tiburón	Rubén Blades	Willie Colón/ Rubén Blades	1981	Canciones del Solar de los Aburridos	Comparison of the United States to a shark lurking in the waters of Latin America	N/A	
Ligia Elena	Rubén Blades	Willie Colón/ Rubén Blades	1981	Canciones del Solar de los Aburridos		N/A	
El padre Antonio y el monaguillo Andrés	Rubén Blades	Rubén Blades/Seis del Solar	1984	Buscando América		Use of "South American 6/8"	
GDBD	Rubén Blades	Rubén Blades/Seis del Solar	1984	Buscando América		N/A	

Song	Composer	Performer	Year	Album	Lyrical Markers	Sonic Signifiers	Notes
Buscando América	Rubén Blades	Rubén Blades/Seis del Solar	1984	*Buscando América*			
Prohibido olvidar	Rubén Blades	Rubén Blades/Seis del Solar	1991	*Caminando*			
American Sueño		Orquesta Salsa con Conciencia (Formerly La Excelencia)	2009	*Mi Tumbao Social*			
Latino America	Calle 13		2010	*Entren Los Que Quieran*		Use of "South American 6/8"	

Table Showing the Album Personnel and Arrangers of the Songs Analyzed

Song	Album	Composer	Performer	Year	Album Personnel	Arranger
Canto Karabali	*Freezelandia 1947–1949*	Ernesto Lecuona	Machito	1947–1949	*Alto Saxophone*: Fred Skerrit, Gene Johnson *Baritone Saxophone*: Leslie Johnakins *Tenor Saxophone*: José "Pin" Madera *Trumpet*: Bobby Woodlen, Frank Davila, Mario Bauza *Bass*: Roberto Rodriguez *Bongos*: José Mangual *Claves*: Machito *Congas*: Luis Miranda *Maracas*: Machito *Piano*: René Hernandez *Timbales*: Ubaldo Nieto *Vocals*: Machito	Unlisted. Likely Mario Bauza
Chango Ta'beni	*Freezelandia 1947–1949*	Justi Barretto	Machito	1947–1949	Same as Canto Karabali	Unlisted. Likely Mario Bauza
Ebo	*Ritmo Caliente*	?	Machito	?		Unlisted. Likely Mario Bauza
Zambia	*Ritmo Caliente*	Mario Bauza	Machito	?		Marcus Persiani
Mi Padrino me manda	*Cuarteto Caney (1939–1940) Featuring Machito*		Cuarteto Caney	1939–1940		Unknown
Ariñañara	*The Best of Tito Puente*		Tito Puente	1949		
Babarabatibiri	*The Complete 78's Volume 1 1949–55*		Tito Puente	1949–1955		

Song	Album	Composer	Performer	Year	Album Personnel	Arranger
Dance of the Headhunters	Tambó	Not Listed/ Arranged by Tito Puente	Tito Puente	1960	Leader, Timbales, and Marimba: Tito Puente Trumpet: Doc Severinsen, Bernie Glow, Ernie Royal, Pedro "Puchi" Boulong, Jimmy Frisaura, Pat Russo Trombone: Seymour Berger Conga drums: Carlos "Patato" Valdez, Ray Barretto	Tito Puente
Call of the Jungle Birds	Tambó	Not Listed/ Arranged by Tito Puente	Tito Puente	1960	Leader, arranger, and Timbales: Tito Puente Flute: Alberto Socarras Flute and tenor sax: Rafael Palau Flute and Alto sax: Peter Fanelli Baritone sax: Shepp Pullman Piano and Arranger: Gilberto Lopez Bass: Bobby Rodriguez Conga drums: Carlos "Patato" Valdez, Ray Barretto, Catalino Relon Bongo drums: Jose Mangual Sr., Chickie Perez	Tito Puente or Gilberto Lopez
The Ceremony of Tambó	Tambó	Not Listed/ Arranged by Tito Puente	Tito Puente	1960	Same as "Dance of the Headhunters"	Tito Puente
Ritual Drum Dance	Tambó	Not Listed/ Arranged by Tito Puente	Tito Puente	1960	Same as "Dance of the Headhunters"	Tito Puente
Witch Doctor's Nightmare	Tambó	Not Listed/ Arranged by Tito Puente	Tito Puente	1960	Same as "Call of the Jungle Birds"	Tito Puente

Song	Album	Composer	Performer	Year	Album Personnel	Arranger
Voodoo Dance at Midnight	*Tambó*	Not Listed/ Arranged by Tito Puente	Tito Puente	1960	Same as "Dance of the Headhunters"	Tito Puente
Chen-cher en guma	*Nostalgia con Tito Rodriguez (Recordings from 1949–1958)*		Tito Rodriguez	1949–1958		
Boco boco	*Mambo Mona (1949–1950)*	Chano Pozo	Tito Rodriguez	1949–1950		
Yambere	*Three Loves Have I*	Tito Rodriguez	Tito Rodriguez	1958	*Leader:* Tito Rodriguez *Saxes:* Jerry Sanfino, Aaron Sache, Peter Fanelli, Dave Kuntzer, Frank Soccolow *Trumpets:* Al Stewart, Mario Alvarez, Harold Wegbrigt, Gabriel Gonzalez *Timbales:* Federico Pagani Jr. *Bass:* Julio Andino *Conga:* Narcissus Torres *Bongo:* Manny Oquendo, Victor Gonzalez *Piano:* Arthur Adwizeimer *Chorus:* Vitin Aviles, Yayo El Indio	Unlisted: Either Rene Hernandez, Artie Azenzer, or Harold Wegbreit
Me boté de Guaño	*El Alma de Cuba: Grabaciones completas RCA Victor Volumen 3 1940–1956*	Arsenio Rodriguez	Arsenio Rodriguez	1949		
Bruca Maniguá	*Beyond Patina Jazz Masters: Orquesta Casino de la Playa*	Arsenio Rodriguez	Orquesta Casino de la Playa	1937		

Song	Album	Composer	Performer	Year	Album Personnel	Arranger
Aqui como Allá	El Alma de Cuba: Grabaciones completas RCA Victor Volumen 3 1940–1956	Arsenio Rodriguez	Arsenio Rodriguez	1950		
Yo Nací del Africa	Cumbanchando con Arsenio Rodriguez	Arsenio Rodriguez	Arsenio Rodriguez	1960		
La democracia	Never released	Arsenio Rodriguez	Arsenio Rodriguez	mid 1960s (1964?)	N/A	N/A
	Available at the Smithsonian Folklife Archives					
El Negro Bembón	Baile con Cortijo y su combo	Bobby Capó	Rafael Cortijo	1960	Unlisted	Unlisted
El Tema del Apollo	Azucar pa'ti	Eddie Palmieri	Eddie Palmieri y La perfecta	1965	*Bongos, Timbales:* Manny Oquendo *Piano:* Eddie Palmieri *Vocals:* Ismael Quintana *Trombone:* Barry Rodgers, Jose Rodriguez *Flute:* George Castro *Conga:* Tommy Lopez *Bass:* Andy Gonzalez/Dave Perez	Either Eddie Palmieri or Barry Rogers
Ordinary Guy	Riot!	Joe Bataan	Joe Bataan	1968	*Bass:* Louie Devis *Bongos:* Milton Albino *Congas:* Lorenzo Galen *Coro:* Ralph Iguartua *Percussion [Bell]:* Richie Cortez *Piano:* Tito Gonzalez *Timbales:* Eddie Nater *Trombone:* Joe "Chickie" Fuentes, Rubén Hernandez *Vocals:* Joe "Mr. Soul" Bataan	

Song	Album	Composer	Performer	Year	Album Personnel	Arranger
Muchacho Ordinario	*Salsoul*	Joe Bataan	Joe Bataan	1973	*Bass, Flute, Saxophone, Percussion:* Bobby Rodriguez *Congas:* Joe de Leon *Coro, Saxophone:* Dennis Harris *Coro, Trombone:* Eddie Hernandez *Drums:* Rick *Guitar:* William Howes, Jr. *Leader, Vocals, Piano:* Joe Bataán *Timbales:* Vito de Leon *Trumpet:* Willie	
Subway Joe	*Subway Joe*	Joe Bataan	Joe Bataan	1968	*Bass:* Louie Devies *Congas:* Lorenzo "Chino" Galan *Lead Vocals* [Spanish]: Tito Ramos *Piano, Vocals* [English]: Joe Bataan *Percussion [Bell]:* Richie Cortez *Timbales:* Eddie Nater *Trombone:* Joe "Chickie" Fuente, Rubén Hernandez	
Bang Bang	*Wanted Dead or Alive (Bang! Bang! Push, Push, Push)*	Jaime Sabater/ Joe Cuba	Joe Cuba Sextet	1966	Unlisted	Unlisted
El Pito (I'll never go back to Georgia)	*Estamos Haciendo Algo Bien! (We Must Be Doing Something Right!)*	Jaime Sabater/ Joe Cuba	Joe Cuba Sextet	1966	Unlisted	Unlisted

Song	Album	Composer	Performer	Year	Album Personnel	Arranger
¿Y tu abuela dónde está?	Estamos Haciendo Algo Bien! (We Must Be Doing Something Right!)	Jaime Sabater	Joe Cuba Sextet	1966	Unlisted	Unlisted
Willie Baby	El Malo	Willie Colón	Willie Colón	1967	*1st Trombone Leader*: Willie Colon *Trombone*: Joe Santiago *Timbales*: Nick Marrero *Conga*: Mario Galagarza *Bongos*: Pablo Rosario *Piano*: Dwight Brewster *Bass*: Eddie Guagua *Bass*: James Taylor *Vocals*: Héctor Lavoe, Yayo El Indio, Eliot Romero *Recording Director*: Johnny Pacheco *Produced by*: Jerry Masucci *Audio Engineer*: Irving Greenbaum *Cover Photo*: Irv Elkin *Cover Design*: Shelly Schreiber	Unlisted. Like.y Willie Colón
Skinny Papa	El Malo	Willie Colón	Willie Colón	1967	Same as Willie Baby	Unlisted. Like.y Willie Colón
Willie Whopper	El Malo	Willie Colón	Willie Colón	1967	Same as Willie Baby	Unlisted. Like.y Willie Colón
Borinquen	El Malo	D.R. (Derechos reservados/Reserved rights)	Willie Colón	1967	Same as Willie Baby	Unlisted. Like.y Willie Colón

Song	Album	Composer	Performer	Year	Album Personnel	Arranger
El Malo	*El Malo*	Willie Colón	Willie Colón	1967	Same as Willie Baby	Unlisted. Likely Willie Colón
The Hustler	*The Hustler*	Willie Colón	Willie Colón	1968	*Bongo:* Pablo Rosario *Conga:* Héctor "Bucky" Andrade *Timbal:* Nicky Marrero *Bass:* Santi González *Piano:* Mark "Markolino" Dimond *Valve Trombone:* Joe Santiago *Valve Trombone:* Willie Colón *Lead Vocals:* Héctor Lavoe	Unlisted. Likely Willie Colón
Eso se baila asi	*The Hustler*	Willie Colón	Willie Colón	1968	Same as The Hustler	Unlisted. Likely Willie Colón
Guisando	*Guisando Doing a Job*	Willie Colón/ Héctor Lavoe	Willie Colón	1969	Unlisted	Unlisted. Likely Willie Colón
Oiga señor	*Guisando Doing a Job*	Willie Colón/ Héctor Lavoe	Willie Colón	1969	Unlisted	Unlisted. Likely Willie Colón
Che che colé	*Cosa Nuestra*	Willie Colón	Willie Colón	1970	*Trombone:* Eric Matos *Timbales:* Little "Louie" Romero *Congas:* Milton Cardona *Bongo, Cowbell:* José Mangual Jr. *Bass:* Santi González *Piano:* Professor Joe Torres *Producer:* Jerry Masucci *Recording Director:* Johnny Pacheco *Audio Engineer:* Irv Greenbaum *Original Album Design:* Izzy Sanabria *Original Album Photography:* Henri Wolfe	Unlisted. Likely Willie Colón

Song	Album	Composer	Performer	Year	Album Personnel	Arranger
Ghana'e	The Big Break/La Gran Fuga	Willie Colón/ Héctor Lavoe	Willie Colón	1971	*Leader, First Trombone:* Willie Colón *Second Trombone:* Willie Campbell *Conga:* Milton Cardona *Timbales:* Louie "Timbalito" Romero *Bongo:* José Mangual *Piano:* Joe "Profesor" Torres (Disputed by Kent "Kenny" Gomez on Wikipedia listing himself as pianist) *Bass:* Santi González *Lead Vocal:* Héctor Lavoe	Unlisted. Likely Willie Colón
Pa' Colombia	The Big Break/La Gran Fuga	C. Curet Alonso	Willie Colón	1971	Same as Ghana'e	Unlisted. Likely Willie Colón
Panameña	The Big Break/La Gran Fuga	Willie Colón/ Héctor Lavoe	Willie Colón	1971	Same as Ghana'e	Unlisted. Likely Willie Colón
Barrunto	The Big Break/La Gran Fuga	C. Curet Alonso	Willie Colón	1971	Same as Ghana'e	Unlisted. Likely Willie Colón
No olvido a Caracas	Together		Ray Barretto	1969	*Bass:* Andy Gonzalez *Bongos:* Tony Fuentes *Congas:* Ray Barretto *Design:* Izzy Sanabria *Piano:* Louis Cruz *Timbales:* Orestes Vilato *Trumpet:* "Papy" Roman, Roberto Rodriguez *Vocals:* Adalberto Santiago	

Song	Album	Composer	Performer	Year	Album Personnel	Arranger
De donde vengo?	Together	Louis Cruz & C. Fernandez	Ray Barretto	1969	Same as No Olvido a Caracas	
Justicia	Justicia	Ismael Quintana, Eddie Palmieri	Eddie Palmieri	1969	*Piano & Leader:* Eddie Palmieri *Trombones:* Lewis Kahn, José Rodriguez, Mark Weinstein, Julien Priester *Trumpet:* Armando "Chocolate" Armentero *Guitar:* Bob Bianco *Bass:* David Hersher *Percussion:* *Timbales:* Nicky Marrero *Conga:* Francisco Aguabella *Conga & Bongos:* Chino Pozo, Ray Romero *Bongos:* Manny Oquendo *Claves:* Roberto Franquiz *Chorus:* Elliot Romero, Justo Betancourt, Jimmy Sabater, Arturo Campa, Carlos "Caito" Diaz (Courtesy of La Sonora Matancera)	

Song	Composer	Album	Performer	Year	Album Personnel	Arranger
Revolt La Libertad Lógico	Eddie Palmieri	*Vámonos Pa'l Monte*	Eddie Palmieri	1971	*Vocals:* Ismael Quintana *Chorus:* Elliot Romero, Justo Betancourt, Marcelino Guerra, Mario Munoz (Papaito), Santos Colon, Yayo El Indio *Claves, Chorus:* Arturo Franquiz *Congas:* Eladio Perez *Congas, Timbales:* Nick Marrero *Piano:* Eddie Palmieri *Percussion:* Monchito Munoz *Producer:* Miguel Estivill *Tenor Saxophone:* Pere Yellin *Trombone:* Jose Rodriguez *Trumpet:* Alfredo Armentereos, Charles Camilleri, Victor Paz *Baritone Saxophone:* Ronnie Cuber	
Jibaro, my pretty nigger	Felipe Luciano	*Live at Sing Sing Volume 1*	Felipe Luciano	1972	N/A	N/A
Las Caras lindas	C. Curet Alonso	*Esto Si Es Lo Mío*	Ismael Rivera	1978	*Chorus:* Rubén Blades *Congas:* José Luis González *Saxophone:* Manolin Gonzalez *Bongos:* Victor González *Chorus:* Héctor Lavoe *Timbales:* Carlos "Rigo" Malcolm Quinto *Claves, Director, Guiro, Maracas, Vocals:* Ismael Rivera *Chorus:* Nestor Sanchez *Chorus:* Adalberto Santiago *Arranger, Musical Director, Piano:* Javier Vasquez *Bass:* Victor Venegas *Trumpet:* Héctor "Bomberito" Zarzuela	Javier Vazquez

Song	Album	Composer	Performer	Year	Album Personnel	Arranger
Sorongo	*Sorongo*	C. Curet Alonso	Rafael Cortijo	1968		
Anacaona	*Cheo*	C. Curet Alonso	Cheo Feliciano	1972		Bobby Valentín
Plantación Adentro	*Metiendo Mano*	C. Curet Alonso	Rubén Blades	1977		
Juan Albañil	*Sentimiento Tu*	C. Curet Alonso	Cheo Feliciano	1980		
Con los Pobres Estoy	*Roberto Roena y Su Apollo Sound 4*	C. Curet Alonso	Roberto Roena	1972		
Lamento de Concepción	*Roberto Roena y Su Apollo Sound X - El Progreso*	C. Curet Alonso	Roberto Roena	1978		
Pura novela	*Giant Force–Fuerza Gigante*	C. Curet Alonso	Ray Barretto	1980	*Trumpet:* Ray González *Trumpet:* Dominik Aloi *Trumpet:* José Jerez *Trumpet:* Angel Fernández *Trombone:* Joe De Jesús *Trombone:* Dale Turk *Piano:* Oscar Hernández *Bass:* Eddie Resto *Timbal:* Ralph Irrizary *Bongo:* Luis González *Conga:* Ray Barretto *Maracas:* Eddie Temporal *Vocals:* Ray de la Paz, Eddie Temporal *Coro:* Rafael de Jesus, Eddie Temporal, Luis Gonzalez, Ray de la Paz	Gil Lopez

Song	Album	Composer	Performer	Year	Album Personnel	Arranger
Pueblo Latino	*Fania All Stars Live at Yankee Stadium*	C. Curet Alonso	Fania All Stars/ Pete "El Conde" Rodriguez	1973		
9 de enero	*Lo mejor de Bush y Su Nuevo Sonido*	Rubén Blades	Bush y Su Nuevo Sonido	Unknown		
Juan Gonzalez	*De Panama a Nueva York*	Rubén Blades	Rubén Blades/ Pete Rodriguez	1970		
Pablo Pueblo	*Metiendo Mano*	Rubén Blades	Willie Colón/ Rubén Blades	1977		
Plástico	*Siembra*	Rubén Blades	Willie Colón/ Rubén Blades	1978	*Vocals:* Rubén Blades *Piano:* Jose Torres "Profesor" *Bass:* Salvador Cuevas, Eddie Rivera *Bongo, Maracas:* Jose Mangual Jr. *Conga:* Eddie Montalvo *Timbales:* Jimmy Delgado *Drums:* Bryan Brake *Maracas:* Adalberto Santiago *Trombones:* Leopoldo Pineda, Jose Rodriguez, Angel Papo Vásquez, Sam Burtis, Willie Colon *Chorus:* Willie Colon, Rubén Blades, Jose Mangual Jr., Adalberto Santiago *Musical Director:* Willie Colon	Luis Ortiz
Siembra	*Siembra*	Rubén Blades	Willie Colón/ Rubén Blades	1978	Same as Plástico	Carlos Franzetti

Song	Album	Composer	Performer	Year	Album Personnel	Arranger
Maestra Vida	*Maestra Vida*	Rubén Blades	Rubén Blades	1980	*Vocals, Acoustic Guitar, Maracas, Percussion*: Rubén Blades *Piano*: Jose Torres *Congas, Claves*: Milton Cardona *Bongo*: Jose Mangual Jr. *Bass*: Salvador Cuevas *Timbales*: Johnny Andrews *Trombones*: Leopoldo Pineda, Jose Rodriguez, Lewis Khan, Reynaldo Jorge, Willie Colon *Coros*: Milton Cardona, Jose Mangual Jr., Willie Colon, Rubén Blades *Principal Narration*: Cesar Miguel Rondón *Producer*: Willie Colon	Marty Sheller
Déjenme reír para no llorar	*Maestra Vida*	Rubén Blades	Rubén Blades	1980	Same as Maestra Vida	Improvised Arrangement
Tiburón	*Canciones del Solar de los Aburridos*	Rubén Blades	Willie Colón/ Rubén Blades	1981	*Vocals*: Rubén Blades *Congas*: Milton Cardona, Joe Santiago *Bass*: Salvador Cuevas, Andy Gonzalez *Piano*: Joe Torres *Trombones*: Reynaldo Jorge, Lewis Kahn, Willie Colon, Jose Rodriguez, Sam Burtis *Timbales*: Johnny Andrews, Jimmy Delgado	Unspecified. Either: Rubén Blades Willie Colon Luis Cruz Héctor Garrido Marty Sheller Javier Vazquez

Song	Album	Composer	Performer	Year	Album Personnel	Arranger
Ligia Elena	Canciones del Solar de los Aburridos	Rubén Blades	Willie Colón/ Rubén Blades	1981	Same as Tiburón	Unspecified Either: Rubén Blades Willie Colon, Luis Cruz Héctor Garrido Marty Sheller Javier Vazquez
El Padre Antonio y el monaguillo Andrés	Buscando América	Rubén Blades	Rubén Blades/ Seis del Solar	1984	*Vocals:* Rubén Blades *Bass:* Mike Viñas *Piano:* Oscar Hernandez *Congas:* Eddie Montalvo *Bongos:* Louie Rivera *Timbales:* Ralph Irizarry *Vibraphone, synthesizer:* Ricardo Marrero Drum set: Ray Adams *Chorus:* Rubén Blades, Mike Viñas, Eddie Montalvo, Louie Rivera, Ricardo Marrero	Oscar Hernández
GDBD	Buscando América	Rubén Blades	Rubén Blades/ Seis del Solar	1984	Same as El padre Antonio y el monaguillo Andrés	Rubén Blades
Buscando América	Buscando América	Rubén Blades	Rubén Blades/ Seis del Solar	1984	Same as El padre Antonio y el monaguillo Andrés	Ricardo Marrero

Song	Album	Composer	Performer	Year	Album Personnel	Arranger
Prohibido olvidar	*Caminando*	Rubén Blades	Rubén Blades/ Son del Solar	1991	*Vocals*: Rubén Blades *Trombones*: Reinaldo Jorge, Angel Vasquez *Piano and synthesizer*: Oscar Hernandez *Synthesizer and programming*: Arturo Ortiz *Bass*: Mike Viñas *Drums*: Robbie Ameen *Bongos*: Ray Colon *Congas*: Eddie Montalvo, Marc Quinones *Timbales*: Ralph Irizarry *Background Vocals*: Tito Allen	Unknown: either Angel Papo Vásquez; Mike Viñas; Oscar Hernandez
American sueño	*Mi Tumbao Social*	Julian Silva	Orquesta Salsa con Conciencia (Formerly La Excelencia)	2009	*Bass*: Jorge Bringas *Bongos*: Charles Dilone *Congas*: Jose Vázquez-Cofresi *Lead Vocals*: Edwin Perez, Gilberto Velazquez *Piano*: Willy Rodriguez *Timbales*: Julian Silva *Trombone*: Jack Davis, Ronald Prokopez, Tokunori Kajiwara *Trumpet*: Jonathan Powell, Sam Hoyt, Willie Oleneck	Likely Jorge Bringas

Song	Album	Composer	Performer	Year	Album Personnel	Arranger
Latinoamerica	Entren Los Que Quieran	Calle 13	Lead Vocals: Rene Perez Guest artists: Susana Baca, Maria Rita, Totó La Momposina Coros: Ileana Cabra, Gabriel Cabra, Daniela Buscaglia, Ismael Cancel, Edmanuel Gonzalez, Joanne Herrero, Kiani Medina, Carlos Lamboy, Ricky Morales, Rafael "Rafa" Arcaute, Pedro Tirado, Vicente Portalatin Bass: Eduardo Cabra. Francisco Fattoruso, Mariano Dominguez Congas: Rafael Rojas Camilo Piano: Edgar Abraham Tambora: Darío del Rosario	2010	Rene Perez	Edgar Abraham

Song	Album	Composer	Performer	Year	Album Personnel	Arranger
			Trompa: Raimundo Diaz *Guira*: Radames Travieso *Guitar*: Omar Rodriguez *Strings*: Edgard Marrero Cotte, José Daniel DeJesús, Arnaldo Figueroa, Yahaira O'Neill *Ronroco*: Gustavo Santaolalla *Ukulele*: Dan Warner			

Notes

PREFACE

1. My capitalization of Salsa emphasizes its distinctiveness as a musical genre (as opposed to a generic spicy condiment) and as a key political component of *Latinidad* (Latin identity) in the United States.

2. The title of this album can be parsed as a command, meaning "to sow or plant [the seeds]." Taken as a noun it could refer to the time of sowing/planting. A third possibility, consistent with the tone of the record as a whole, is a truncation of the biblical proverb about reaping what you sow.

3. The term *consciente* applied to Salsa allows several translations. One possibility evokes the idea of self-consciousness or class consciousness in the Marxist sense (see Lukács's *History and Class Consciousness*, 1971). Alternatively, the idea could be closer to Salsa with a conscience, i.e., a Salsa that is not self-absorbed in consumerist individualism but morally aware of the existence of others in society. The ambiguity may have been intentional on the part of the artists.

4. I introduce the term *Nuyolatino* adapted from the somewhat analogous term of *Nuyorican* to refer to the Latino diaspora that makes New York its home. As Nuyorican is to *Salsa*, so Nuyolatino suggests the sense of a deterritorialization, which strongly marks the phenomenon of Salsa consciente. I choose the spelling *Nuyolatino* instead of *Newyolatino* in order to emphasize the Spanish or Hispanicizing milieu of this transcultural and transnational phenomenon (see Acosta 1997, García 2006, Manuel 1994).

5. I introduce the concept of *meta-homeland* to denote a hybrid concept of the homeland as conceived in diaspora.

6. This phenomenon supports the view of Simon Frith, who claims that "the issue is not how a particular piece of music or a performance reflects the people, but how it produces them, how it creates and constructs an experience" (1996, 109). It also fits well with the distinction made by Roman-Velazquez, following Hall, between new and old ethnic identities: "Here, the old 'ethnic identity' refers to a Latin music as located in Latin America, the new ethnicities and identities refers to the possibilities that occur as salsa music is made and remade" (1999, 117-118).

7. For discussions of gender in Salsa, refer to Aparicio 1998 and 2004; Boggs 1992, 107-118; and Washburne 2008, 151-164.

8. For example through the exploration of multi-tonic systems in pieces such as "Giant Steps," and "Central Park West," and also through his later work exploring the improvisational possibilities of modal music.

9. Excellent examples of this are his explorations of music and spiritual dimensions with recordings such as *A Love Supreme*, and his exploration of Pan-Africanism in *Kulu se mama*, which was steeped in African spiritual sensibilities and socio-musical metaphors.

Section One. Performing Consciencia: Salsa as a Chronicle of El Pueblo

1. The other two levels of Latino ethnic consciousness include class consciousness and Trans-Latino ethnic consciousness. I address the concept of class consciousness in chapter 2. The third level, Trans-Latino ethnic consciousness, is addressed in chapters 3, 4, and 5 as related to the music of Tite Curet Alonso and Rubén Blades.

2. I develop and define this concept further in chapters 1 and 2.

CHAPTER ONE. SALSA AS CLASS CONSCIOUSNESS

1. See the introduction to the book for further basic details.

2. The capitalization of El Barrio denotes the uniqueness of Spanish Harlem as a Latino social migrant construct. There is no other place that could be referred to as El Barrio (with the emphatic capitalization) with which this Latino migrant construction could be confused. With this status, the capitalized article "El" defines the place as different from any barrio in Latin America, which in general tend to have a surname attached (e.g., el barrio de Jesus Maria in Havana Cuba).

3. For further analysis regarding *mambo*, see Cano 2009, García 2004, Gartner 2001, Hutchinson 2004, Kent 2005, Leymarie 2003, Loza 1996 and 1999, Manuel 1991, Mauleón 1993, Roberts 1979, Rondón 2008, etc.

4. For further analysis of the early presence of Latin music in the United States, see Roberts 1979.

5. For further reference see Mauleón 1993, Sher 1997, Moore 2010, 2012, etc.

6. For an excellent, detailed study on clave, see Peñalosa and Greenwood 2009.

7. The letters underneath the notes indicate the strikes to be played: F = fingers, I = Index finger, T = Thumb, O = Open strike.

8. Just as with the bongo, the letters underneath the notes indicate the strokes to be played. H = Heel, T = Toe, S = Slap, O = Open strike.

9. The letter B underneath the conga notation refers to the bass sound of the drum.

10. For further explanation, see Moore (2010).

11. For discussions of the origins of *mambo*, see Acosta 2004a, Boggs 1992, Cano 2009, García 2004, Glasser 1997, Hutchinson 2004, Leymarie 2003, Roberts 1979, Rondón 1980, Salazar 2002, Sublette 2007, and Waxer 1994.

12. The title is a vernacular Spanish way of referring to drums. The form is a shortened "street" way of saying *tambor*—lit. drum.

13. Musically, the work of Arsenio Rodriguez is still highly understudied. Kevin Moore's 2013 work deals with the renovation of the Cuban music bass lines that Rodriguez singlehandedly developed. As far as I am aware this is the most detailed study dealing specifically with Rodriguez's musical aesthetics.

14. García (2006) is the most in-depth English-language scholarly work to date to deal with this fact.

15. From the compilation *Arsenio Rodriguez: Complete RCA Recordings 1940–1956*. Originally recorded November 9, 1950.

16. From *Cumbanchando con Arsenio Rodríguez*, 1960.

17. Despite its relevance, Rafael Cortijo's work is a topic that has not really been explored to a great degree. Further information can be found in Juliá 2004, and Berríos-Miranda and Dudley 2008.

18. Composed by Bobby Capó. From Rafael Cortijo's 1960 release *Baile con Cortijo*.

19. See www.fania.com for an image of the cover.

20. *Cocolo* is a Puerto Rican slang term used to refer to a Black person. The term later became associated with people who liked Salsa music (as opposed to rock) as many of them were actually Black.

21. From the 1966 release *Estamos Haciendo Algo Bien! (We Must Be Doing Something Right!)* Composed by Jimmy Sabater. Sung by Cheo Feliciano.

CHAPTER TWO. SALSA AS THE ENGINE OF LATINO CONSCIOUSNESS

1. Salsa has a good number of references to "La Raza Latina"—the Latin race—with Larry Harlow's 1977 Salsa suite titled *La Raza Latina* likely the most famous incarnation of the term. Despite the idea of categorizing Latino as a race, Africa as evoking a musical pathos filtered through Cuban music makes a strong appearance on the first track of the recording.

2. This expression (*tener calle, ser calle*) is commonly used in Spanish slang. The expression refers to the idea of having significant experience in honing one's craft, in a "been there, done that" type of statement. The term, however, also refers to the idea of street knowledge as opposed to something that can be learned in school. In the case of Salsa, and in tandem with hip hop culture, being "street" often denotes a type of attitude and grittiness in the performance that can be acquired only "in the streets." Willie Colón, being a South Bronx native, initially utilized his upbringing as a way to denote the "realness" of his music and to achieve recognition with The People.

3. For a full analysis of this piece, see chapter 3.

4. "Let's all dance African style." (*Vamos todos a bailar, al estilo Africano.*)

5. In the 1970 Fania release *Cosa Nuestra*; composed by Willie Colón.

6. For further studies regarding Salsa and gender, see Aparicio 1998 and 2004; Aparicio in Waxer 2002b, 135–160; Boggs 1992, 107–118; and Washburne 2008, 151–164.

7. From the 1969 Fania release *Together*; sung by Adalberto Santiago; composed by Louis Cruz and C. Fernandez.

8. In the 1969 Tico Records LP *Justicia*; lyrics by Ismael Quintana; music by Eddie Palmieri.

9. Composed by Eddie Palmieri. From the 1971 Tico Records release *Vámonos Pa'l Monte*.

10. Volume 2 of this recording was released in 1974, though it was recorded on a different date.

11. *Jíbaro* refers to Puerto Rican countryside peasants. Transcriptions and live performances of this piece by Luciano himself are readily available on the Internet.

12. Curet Alonso's work is extensively analyzed in chapter 3. I bring him up here only to show the importance of the *Salsa consciente* discourse within the concepts analyzed within the ethos of the Fania All Stars. The reason for not choosing the appearance of Curet Alonso as a cutoff point lies in the fact that his works were performed mostly by people other than himself. Despite the fact that Curet Alonso's discourse was often very clear in terms of social consciousness, the output of the musicians who performed his compositions did not always display the same commitment to social issues.

13. See chapters 4 and 5 for a detailed analysis of the works of Rubén Blades.

14. The half-chorus device is a standard use in Salsa and is easily traceable to the Cuban *son*. The earliest use of this device in Latin America, however, can be traced to music of African origin, such as the music of *Santería* in Cuba.

15. Sung by Pete "El Conde" Rodriguez; composed by Catalino "Tite" Curet Alonso. Released in *Fania All Stars Live at Yankee Stadium, Vol. 1* (1975).

CHAPTER THREE. THE WORKS OF CATALINO "TITE" CURET ALONSO

1. "Tite Curet Alonso es el padre de la Salsa," special available on YouTube.com, https://www.youtube.com/watch?v=_2-W8l3tSqU&t=4s.

2. Referring to the Puerto Rican rural peasants.

3. The specific issue of Latino identity in the music of Curet Alonso is not present in this chapter as it has been previously analyzed in this work as related to the song "Pueblo Latino" performed by the Fania All Stars (see chapter 2).

4. Literally "John Construction Worker" in reference to Curet Alonso's song. The song is analyzed later in the chapter.

5. In reference to Curet Alonso's song "La Tirana" popularized by La Lupe.

6. For a full definition of Blades's concept of *Focila*, see chapter 5.

7. Rafael Cortijo was a Puerto Rican musician and bandleader who is often quoted as responsible for popularizing the often marginalized musical style of *bomba*. His band participated as the house band for the television show *La Taberna India* in the late 1950s.

8. Cortijo's band was named at different times either "Cortijo y su Combo" or "Cortijo y su Bonche."

9. From *Esto Es Lo Mío* (Tico Records, 1978).

10. *Tres* is a Cuban six-string guitar typically associated with the music of *son*.

11. Calle Calma or Calma Street is the street where Ismael Rivera grew up.

12. https://tureng.com/en/spanish-english/sorongo.

13. As confirmed by the online edition of the dictionary of the Royal Spanish Academy of Language, www.rae.es.

14. It must be noted here that the term Congo in Spanish denotes, in the same manner as Kongo, a language, an ethnicity, and a political kingdom on the west coast of Africa.

15. From the release "Sorongo" on Tico Records, 1968.

16. Featuring Seun Kuti and Sammy Tanco from the Coss 2011 DVD release ¡*SONÓ, SONÓ . . . TITE CURET!*

17. From *Roberto Roena y su Apollo Sound X—El Progreso*, International Records, a Fania subsidiary, 1978.
18. The 2011 version of the song is available at YouTube.com.
19. The word *albañil* literally indicates construction worker; however, since in this case it is used as a last name I decided to use laborer since the term implies, much like *albañil*, a low-wage-earning, likely uneducated working-class person.
20. From the 1980 VAYA records release *Sentimiento tú*.
21. Estudia, trabaja y se gente primero. See chapter 4 for a full analysis of this song.
22. From *Apollo Sound 4*, released by International Records, a Fania subsidiary, 1972.
23. See chapter 4 for a full analysis of Blades's song.
24. For a full transcription of this piece, see the *Latin Real Book* by Dunlap and Mauleón-Santana (1997, 419).
25. La India and La Lupe are notable exceptions to this.
26. From *Giant Force/Fuerza Gigante*, released by Fania Records, 1980.
27. "Pacata" is an often-used Spanish onomatopoeia denoting something falling in front of you. The expression denotes something that is impossible to miss.
28. From *Metiendo Mano*, Fania Records, 1977.
29. *Soneos* is a synonym of *pregones*.
30. From the album *Cheo* released by VAYA (a subsidiary of Fania), 1972.

CHAPTER FOUR. RUBÉN BLADES'S MOVE INTO SALSA

1. Rubén Blades has a law degree from the University of Panama and an LLM in international law from Harvard University.
2. Ascanio Arosemena Chávez (Panamá, 22 December 1944–9 January 1964) was a student leader killed during the incidents that occurred on January 9th.
3. As performed by Bush y Su Nuevo Sonido. *Album unknown.*
4. 1970 by Alegre Records.
5. For specific details on the Colón/Lavoe collaboration see chapter 2.
6. This is a particularly important song, not only for its lyrical content, as it depicts the work conditions of Indigenous Latin Americans in 1745, but also in its sonic markers. I analyze the composition in depth in chapter 3 under the rubric of C. Curet Alonso.
7. *Siembra* refers to the command form of sowing seeds, as well as the period in which one would sow the seeds.
8. For a lengthier study of the significance of Salsa in Venezuela, see Berríos-Miranda, 2006.
9. The use of race here refers not to one in particular but rather to the Latin American people. The epithet is widely used by the Chicano community as in "viva la raza" (lit. long live the race, but understood as "long live the people"). In terms of Salsa, the term is later also used by Blades, although it refers to Latinos as it functions as a signifier of the formation of a cohesive group united by identity and ethnicity.
10. While the whole album was a massive commercial hit, the biggest hit of the album was the track entitled "Pedro Navaja." Despite the fact that this track is somewhat useful in understanding the *meta-barrio* concept as it presents the urbanized aspects and sounds of the city by introducing sirens in the opening, police radio narrations in its closing, and the archetypical characters of the playboy/gangster alongside the prostitute and the drunk man in the corner, I analyze two other tracks from the album as demonstrating steps taken in moving towards the idea of Latino consciousness and the role of *Latinidad* in the community.

11. As performed in the album *Siembra* by Rubén Blades and Willie Colón (Fania 1978).
12. This analysis stems from the fact that these types of concepts are also prevalent in other pieces by Rubén Blades, such as "Pedro Navaja," where the location is sonically determined as urban by the sounds of ambulances and traffic; or in "El padre Antonio y el monaguillo Andrés," where the South American location later presented lyrically is initially sonically evoked by the use of a 6/8 meter as utilized not in the classic Cuban referents of Salsa but as used in South American music (i.e., from Argentina, Peru, Chile).
13. This chorus is very unusual in its length and the way that it is presented. I develop this idea further as I analyze the musical aspects of the song.
14. See chapter 2 n.18 for a detailed description of this device.
15. I utilize the term *cuarto de coro* as opposed to the more grammatically correct *cuarto coro* in order not to cause confusion between *cuarto* denoting quarter and *cuarto* as in fourth.

CHAPTER FIVE. RUBÉN BLADES'S MOVE OUT OF SALSA

1. The first Salsa opera is actually *Hommy*, by Larry Harlow. The material of this is, however, an adaptation into a *Nuyorican* reality of the rock opera *Tommy* (1969) by The Who.
2. Dedicación: Dedico éste trabajo a 13 Oeste, a mi calle Segunda Carrasquilla y a la 25 arriba en el Chorrillo donde conocí a muchos de los protagonistas de ésta historia; y en especial deseo reconocer la ayuda espiritual de Paula Campbell, quien a pesar de nuestras diferencias me alentó y apoyó durante el período de creación y composición de "Maestra Vida."
3. Interestingly, *One Hundred Years of Solitude* is based around the fictitious town of Macondo, which can be considered analogous to the concept of the Latino meta-homeland.
4. Referring to the 1982 Falklands conflict between the United Kingdom and Argentina.
5. Sobre los imperios, Latino América.
6. This reference is to a common Spanish saying: "Camarón que se duerme, se lo lleva la corriente" [if the shrimp falls asleep, it is swept by the current]—i.e., sink or swim.
7. As a side note to "Ligia Elena," this set of characters inspired a very popular soap opera (telenovela) in Venezuela that aired in 1982-1983. The TV series was written by Cesar Rondón, journalist and author of *The Salsa Book* (1980/2008), narrator of "Maestra Vida," and close friend of Rubén Blades. While the soap opera also dealt with issues of class, the trumpet player in the series was not Black.
8. The word *niche* does not have a direct translation in English, yet in Spanish refers to a person of African descent, as well as denoting a person that comes from a poor background.
9. The name of the band is a play on words, as it can be understood in two different ways: *Six* from the tenement referring to the sextet formation of the band, or in a Puerto Rican fashion, understanding the word *seis* not as the number six but as the name of one of the countryside/*jíbaro* musical styles of the island, i.e., "music of the tenement."
10. Though the use of a vocal *guaguancó* is remarkably creative, the idea was not actually the creation of Blades or his band. Not only has vocalizing percussion been used for a very long time among percussionists, but the idea was originally recorded by Machito and his Afro-Cubans in the 1950s for the song "Bucabu."
11. Personally, as a conscious and revolutionary Latin American, I have followed suit and promoted the use of the accent in "América" when referring to the continent.
12. "Cuando lo malo te turbe y te nuble el corazón, piensa en América Latina y repite mi pregón." "Da la cara a tu tierra y así el cambio llegara."

13. Pero señoras y señores, En medio del plástico también se ven las caras de esperanza, se ven las caras orgullosas que trabajan por una Latino América unida y por un mañana de esperanza y de libertad.

14. "Usa la conciencia Latino, no la dejes que se te duerma, no la dejes que muera." "Hermano Latino, con fe y siempre adelante." "Conciencia familia."

15. This link references the fact that the United States calls itself "America," and the idea of a united América.

CONCLUSION

1. Latin American Liberation philosopher Enrique Dussel (n.d.) indicates the formation of Marxism in Latin America as a movement that has El Pueblo at its core: "In Latin America, Marxism from a political standpoint will move from a clearly Eurocentric position until, slowly throughout the 20th century, it will start to discover the concrete people, historic, oppressed and excluded, the latter becoming its principal political point of reference."

2. The large settling of Dominicans in Manhattan has happened specifically in Washington Heights and Inwood. Currently there is a large population of Dominicans in the Bronx.

3. As performed in the 2009 release *Mi Tumbao Social* by La Excelencia. Sung by Edwin Perez.

4. At the time of this writing (2019) the country of Chile is undergoing a very significant social revolution that has as one of its main concepts the drafting of a new constitution. Anita Tijoux has been very involved with the movement and even wrote a song called "Cacerolazo" (a popular term used to refer to protests that feature the beating of pots and pans—this is a very common practice in Latin America) to voice her support for the movement. The song can be heard directly at: https://www.youtube.com/watch?v=tVaTuVNN7Zs.

5. In the 2012 release *La Bala.* Composed by Anita Tijoux.

6. In the 2008 release 3rd World. Sung by Immortal Technique; composed by Immortal Technique.

7. https://www.npr.org/2008/09/03/94243997/tego-calderon-reggaeton-on-black-pride.

8. In the 2008 release *The Underdog/El Subestimado.* Sung by Tego Calderón; composed by Tego Calderón. *Ashé* (aché/asé) is a term commonly used in Cuba as part of the Yoruba-derived Regla de Ocha (Santería) religious practice. It literally means the power to make things happen. The religion has spread to many other locales, and is also practiced in Puerto Rico. Here Calderón uses it as a symbol of Africanness.

9. In the 2011 release *Entren Los Que Quieran.* Sung by Rene Perez (Residente); featuring Totó la Momposina, Susana Baca, and Maria Rita; composed by Rene Perez, Eduardo Cabra.

Bibliography

Acosta, Leonardo. 1997. "¿Terminó la polémica sobre la Salsa?" *Música Cubana*: 26-29.

———. 2004a. "Perspectives on 'Salsa.'" *Centro Journal* 16: 6-13.

———. 2004b. "The Year 1898 in the Music of the Caribbean: Cuba and Puerto Rico in the Machinations of the US Music Industry." *Centro Journal* 16, no. 1: 6-13.

Adorno, T. 1990. "On Popular Music." In *On Record: Rock, Pop, and the Written Word*, edited by S. Frith and A. Goodwin. London: Routledge.

Agawu, Victor Kofi. 1995. *African Rhythm: A Northern Ewe Perspective.* Cambridge University Press Archive.

Alegría, Ricardo E. 1956. "The Fiesta of Santiago Apostol (St. James the Apostle) in Loíza, Puerto Rico." *Journal of American Folklore* 69, no. 272: 123-134.

Althusser, Louis. 2006. "Ideology and Ideological State Apparatuses (notes towards an investigation)." *Anthropology of the State: A Reader* 9, no. 1: 86-98.

Amigo, Cristian. 2003. "Latino Music, Identity, and Ethnicity: Two Case Studies." PhD diss., University of California, Los Angeles.

Anderson, Benedict. 2006. *Imagined Communities: Reflections on the Origin and Spread of Nationalism.* Verso.

Aparicio, Frances R. 1998. *Listening to Salsa: Gender, Latin Popular Music, and Puerto Rican Cultures.* Wesleyan.

———. 2003. "Jennifer as Selena: Rethinking *Latinidad* in Media and Popular Culture." *Latino Studies* 1, no. 1: 90-105.

———. 2004. "US Latino Expressive Cultures." *Columbia History of Latinos in the United States since 1960*: 355-390.

Aparicio, Frances R., and Wilson A. Valentín-Escobar. 2004. "Memorializing La Lupe and Lavoe: Singing Vulgarity, Transnationalism, and Gender." *Centro Journal* 002: 78–101.

Arroyo, Jossianna. 2010. "'Roots' or the Virtualities of Racial Imaginaries in Puerto Rico and the Diaspora." *Latino Studies* 8, no. 2: 195–219.

Arteaga, José. 1990. *La Salsa*. 2nd rev. ed. Bogotá: Intermedio Editores.

Ashcroft, Bill, Gareth Griffiths, and Helen Tiffin. 2001. *Key Concepts in Post-colonial Studies*. Routledge.

Azank, Natasha. 2012. "'The Guerilla Tongue': The Politics of Resistance in Puerto Rican Poetry." PhD diss., University of Massachusetts Amherst.

Báez, Juan Carlos. 1989. *El vínculo es la Salsa*. Caracas.

Baron, Robert. 1977. "Syncretism and Ideology: Latin New York Salsa Musicians." *Western Folklore* 36, no. 3: 209–225.

Barton, Halbert. 2004. "A Challenge for Puerto Rican Music: How to Build a Soberao for Bomba." *Centro Journal* 16, no. 1. City University of New York. Centro de Estudios Puertorriqueños New York, Latinoamericanistas.

Benitez, John. 2013. Interview by the author. New York City, August 20, 2013.

Berríos-Miranda, Marisol. 1999. *The Significance of Salsa Music to National and Pan-Latino Identity*. University of California, Berkeley.

———. 2004. "Salsa Music as Expressive Liberation." *Centro Journal* 002: 158–173.

Berríos-Miranda, Marisol, and Shannon Dudley. 2008. "El Gran Combo, Cortijo, and the Musical Geography of Cangrejos/Santurce, Puerto Rico." *Caribbean Studies* 36, no. 2: 121–151.

Bhabha, Homi K. 1990. "The Third Space: Interview with Homi Bhabha." *Identity: Community, Culture, Difference*: 207–221.

———. 1994. *The Location of Culture*. Routledge.

Blades, Rubén. 1983. Interview with Uberto Sagramoso. *El Porteño* (September). Buenos Aires, Argentina.

———. 1986. Interview with Peter Hamill. *ASCAP in Action*. Spring.

———. 2008. Interview with Sara Del Valle Hernández. *El nuevo día*, June 8.

Blum, Joseph. 1978. "Problems of Salsa Research." *Ethnomusicology* 22, no. 1: 137–149.

Boggs, Vernon. 1992. *Salsiology: Afro-Cuban Music and the Evolution of Salsa in New York City*. Vol. 1992. Empire Pub Service.

Brennan, Timothy. 2008. *Secular Devotion: Afro-Latin Music and Imperial Jazz*. Verso Books.

Burgos, Adrian, Jr. 2001. "'The Latins from Manhattan': Confronting Race and Building Community in Jim Crow Baseball, 1906–1950." In *Mambo Montage: The Latinization of New York*, edited by Arlene Davila and Agustin Lao-Montes, 73–95.

Cabanillas, Francisco. 2004. "Entre la poesía y la música: Victor Hernández Cruz y el mapa musical Nuyorican." *Centro Journal* 002: 14–33.

Calderón, José. 1992. "'Hispanic' and 'Latino': The Viability of Categories for Panethnic Unity." *Latin American Perspectives* 19, no. 4: 37–44.

Caminero-Santangelo, Marta. 2007. *On Latinidad*. University Press of Florida.

Campbell, Patricia Shehan. 1996. *Music in Cultural Context: Eight Views on World Music Education*. Rowman & Littlefield Education.

Campbell, Susan Marie. 2005. "*Nuyorican* Resistance: Fame and Anonymity from Civil Rights Collapse to the Global Era." PhD diss., University of Minnesota.

Cano, Rubén López. 2009. "Apuntes para una prehistoria del mambo." *Latin American Music Review* 30, no. 2: 213–242.

Canovan, Margaret. 2005. *The People*. Polity.

Carp, David M. 2004. "Salsa Symbiosis: Barry Rogers, Eddie Palmieri's Chief Collaborator in the Making of La Perfecta." *Centro Journal* 002: 42–61.

Castañeda, Jorge G. 2012. *Utopia Unarmed: The Latin American Left after the Cold War*. Random House Digital, Inc.

Catapano, Peter. 1999. "A Blending of Latin Sounds." Salsa: Made in New York. *New York Times*. https://archive.nytimes.com/www.nytimes.com/library/music/102400salsa-essay.html.

Chen, Kuan-Hsing, and David Morley, eds. 1996. *Stuart Hall: Critical Dialogues in Cultural Studies*. Routledge.

Child, John. 2013. "Review of Canciones del Solar de Los Aburridos." Fania.com. https://www.fania.com/content/canciones-del-solar-de-los-aburridos.

Colón, Willie. 2008. Interview with Sara Del Valle Hernández. *El nuevo día*, June 8. San Juan, Puerto Rico.

Cortes, Felix, Angel Falcon, and Juan Flores. 1976. "The Cultural Expression of Puerto Ricans in New York: A Theoretical Perspective and Critical Review." *Latin American Perspectives* 3, no. 3: 117-152.

Cruz, Bárbara. 1997. *Rubén Blades: Salsa Singer and Social Activist*. Enslow Publishers.

Cruz, José E. 2003. "Unfulfilled Promise: Puerto Rican Politics and Poverty." *Centro Journal* 15, no. 1: 153-175.

Cruz-Malavé, Arnaldo. 2002. "Colonial Figures in Motion: Globalization and Translocality in Contemporary Puerto Rican Literature in the United States." *Centro Journal* 14, no. 2: 5-25.

Davies, Richard Arthur. 1999. "Cuban Trumpet Playing: The Solo Performance Style of Alfredo 'Chocolate' Armenteros." PhD diss., New York University, School of Education.

Dávila, Arlene. 2002. "Talking Back: Spanish Media and US *Latinidad*." *Latino/a Popular Culture*: 25-37.

Davis, Mike. 2001. *Magical Urbanism: Latinos Reinvent the US City*. Verso Books.

DeGraf, Galen Philip. 2009. "Situating Salsa through Tito Puente's Life and Music." *Honors Theses*: 337. http://wesscholar.wesleyan.edu/cgi/viewcontent.cgi?article=1336&context=etd_hon_theses.

DeSipio, Louis, and Adrián Pantoja. 2007. "Puerto Rican Exceptionalism? A Comparative Analysis of Puerto Rican, Mexican, Salvadoran, and Dominican Transnational Civic and Political Ties." In *Latino Politics: Identity, Mobilization, and Representation*, edited by Rodolfo Espino, David L. Leal, and Kenneth J. Meier, 104-120. Charlottesville, VA: University of Virginia Press.

Del Valle Hernández, Sara. 2008. Interview with Rubén Blades. *El nuevo día*, June 8.

De Maeseneer, Rita. 2002. "Sobre dominicanos y puertorriqueños: ¿movimiento perpetuo?" *Centro Journal* 14, no. 1: 53-73.

Domínguez, Daniel, and Muñoz, Roxana. 2008. "30 años de 'Siembra' y 'Pedro Navaja.'" Originally published October 5, 2008, on mosaico.com.

Duany, Jorge. 1984. "Popular Music in Puerto Rico: Toward an Anthropology of 'Salsa.'" *Latin American Music Review/Revista de Música Latinoamericana* 5, no. 2: 186-216.

———. 2002. *The Puerto Rican Nation on the Move: Identities on the Island and in the United States*. University of North Carolina Press.

———. 2005. "The Rough Edges of Puerto Rican Identities: Race, Gender, and Transnationalism." *Latin American Research Review* 40, no. 3: 177-190.

———. 2008. "Diasporic Dreams: Documenting Caribbean Migrations." *Caribbean Studies* 36, no. 1: 184-195.

———. 2010. "Anthropology in a Postcolonial Colony: Helen I. Safa's Contribution to Puerto Rican Ethnography." *Caribbean Studies* 38, no. 2: 33-57.

Dussel, Enrique. 2008. *Twenty Theses on Politics*. Duke University Press.

———. n.d. "El "giro descolonizador" desde *El Pueblo* y hacia la segunda emancipación." Departamento de Filosofía, UAM-I.

Easthope, Antony. 1998. "Bhabha, Hybridity and Identity." *Textual Practice* 12, no. 2: 341-348.

Enck-Wanzer, Darrel. 2006. "Trashing the System: Social Movement, Intersectional Rhetoric, and Collective Agency in the Young Lords Organization's Garbage Offensive." *Quarterly Journal of Speech* 92, no. 2: 174–201.

Enck-Wanzer, Darrel, Iris Morales, and Denise Oliver-Velez, eds. 2010. *The Young Lords: A Reader*. NYU Press.

Eriksen, Neil. 1980. "Popular Culture and Revolutionary Theory: Understanding Punk Rock." *Theoretical Review* 18: 13–35.

Espinosa, Gastón. 2007. "'Today We Act, Tomorrow We Vote': Latino Religions, Politics, and Activism in Contemporary US Civil Society." *Annals of the American Academy of Political and Social Science* 612, no. 1: 152–171.

Espinoza Agurto, Andrés. 2013. Interview with Andy Gonzalez. New York City, August 1.

Esteves, Sandra María. 2004. "'Poems,' 'Ode to Celia,' 'Puerto Rican Discovery # II Samba Rumba Cha-Cha Be-Bop Hip Hop,' 'Dance with Me.'" *Centro Journal* 002: 102–107.

Fairley, Jan. 1984. "La nueva canción latinoamericana." *Bulletin of Latin American Research* 3, no. 2: 107–115.

——. 1985. "Annotated Bibliography of Latin-American Popular Music with Particular Reference to Chile and to Nueva Canción." *Popular Music* 5, no. 1: 305–356.

Fernandez, Johanna. 2004. "Radicals in the Late 1960s: A History of the Young Lords Party in New York City, 1969–1974." PhD diss., Columbia University.

Findlay, Eileen J. 2009. "Portable Roots: Latin New Yorker Community Building and the Meanings of Women's Return Migration in San Juan, Puerto Rico, 1960–2000." *Caribbean Studies* 37, no. 2: 3–43.

Fiol-Matta, Licia. 2002. "Pop *Latinidad*: Puerto Ricans in the Latin Explosion, 1999." *Centro Journal* 14, no. 1: 27–51.

Fitzpatrick, Joseph P. 1966. "Intermarriage of Puerto Ricans in New York City." *American Journal of Sociology* 71, no. 4: 395–406.

——. 1971. *Puerto Rican Americans: The Meaning of Migration to the Mainland*. Ethnic Groups in American Life Series. Prentice-Hall.

Fitzpatrick, Joseph P., and Douglas T. Gurak. 1979. "Hispanic Intermarriage in New York City: 1975." Monograph No. 2. Bronx, NY: Hispanic Research Center, Fordham University.

Flores, Aurora. 2004. "¡Ecua Jei! Ismael Rivera, El Sonero Mayor (A Personal Reflection)." *: Journal of the Center for Puerto Rican Studies* 16, no. 2: 63–77.

——. n.d. "Review of Alma de Poeta." Fania.com. http://www.fania.com/products/tite-curet-alon-so-alma-de-poeta.

——. n.d. "Review of *Maestra Vida Volume 1*." Fania.com. http://www.fania.com/content/maes-tra-vida-vol-1.

Flores, Carlos. 2004. "Five Decades of the Puerto Rican Music Scene in Chicago: A Personal Recollection." *Centro Journal* 16, no. 1: 140–153.

——. 2001. "Remembering 'Las Caras Lindas.'" *Dialogo Magazine*.

Flores, Juan. 1993. *Divided Borders: Essays on Puerto Rican Identity*. Arte Público Press.

Flores, Juan, and Jorge Matos Valldejuli. 2004. "Tremendo rumbón: una entrevista con Genaro "Heny" Álvarez." *Centro Journal* 001: 120–131.

Flores, Juan, and Wilson A. Valentín-Escobar. 2004. "Puerto Rican Music and Dance: RicanStructing Roots/Routes, Part II." *Centro Journal* 002: 4–5.

Freidenberg, Judith. 1998. "The Social Construction and Reconstruction of the Other: Fieldwork in El Barrio." *Anthropological Quarterly* 71, no. 4: 169–185.

Freire, Paulo. 1970. "Pedagogy of the Oppressed." Translated by Myra Bergman Ramos. New York: Continuum.

Frith, Simon. 1996. "Music and Identity." *Questions of Cultural Identity* (1996): 108-127.

Fuentes-Rivera, Ada G. 2002. "Barrio, ciudad y 'performance': cruce de fronteras en el proyecto mural de James De La Vega." *Centro Journal* 14, no. 2: 65-97.

García, David F. 2004. "'Contesting That Damned Mambo': Arsenio Rodriguez, Authenticity, and the People of El Barrio and the Bronx in the 1950s." *Centro Journal* 16, no. 1.

———. 2006. *Arsenio Rodríguez and the Transnational Flows of Latin Popular Music.* Philadelphia: Temple University Press.

Gallo, Laura P. Alonso. 2002. "Latino Culture in the US: Using, Reviewing, and Reconstructing *Latinidad* in Contemporary Latino/a Fiction." *KulturPoetik*, no. 2: 236-248.

Gerard, Charley. 1989. *Salsa! The Rhythm of Latin Music.* Crown Point, IN: White Cliffs.

Gartner, Kurt Raymond. 2001. "Analysis of the Stylistic Development of Selected Tito Puente Timbale Solos in the Mambo Style." PhD diss., University of Northern Colorado.

Glasser, Ruth. 1997. *My Music Is My Flag: Puerto Rican Musicians and Their New York Communities, 1917-1940.* Vol. 3. University of California Press.

Golash-Boza, Tanya. 2006. "Dropping the Hyphen? Becoming Latino(a)-American through Racialized Assimilation." *Social Forces* 85, no. 1: 27-55.

Gonzalez, Juan. 2012. "From Crown Heights Brutality to $500M City Time Fraud; Juan Gonzalez Recalls 25 Years of His Greatest Scandalous Scoops." *New York Daily News*, December 23, 2012.

Gonzalez, Nelly S. 1980. *Doctoral Dissertations on Latin America and the Caribbean: An Analysis and Bibliography of Dissertations Accepted at American and Canadian Universities, 1966-1970.* No. 10. Urbana, IL: Latin American Studies Association.

Guerra, Damaris Elizabeth. 2005. "Del 58 al siglo XXI: Memoria histórica, espacios y proyecciones de la poesía panameña." PhD diss., Michigan State University.

Guillén, Nicolás, Amadeo Roldán, Alejandro García Caturla, Eliseo Grenet, and Emilio Grenet. 1980. *Motivos de son.* Editorial Letras Cubanas.

Gurak, Douglas T., and Joseph P. Fitzpatrick. 1982. "Intermarriage among Hispanic Ethnic Groups in New York City." *American Journal of Sociology* 87, no. 4: 921-934.

Guzmán, Betsy, and Eileen Diaz McConnell. 2002. "The Hispanic Population: 1990-2000 Growth and Change." *Population Research and Policy Review* 21, no. 1-2: 109-128.

Guzman, Pablo. 2006. "Ray Barretto, 1929-2006: *Mi amigo*, Latin Music's Most Intellectual Cat, Made Sure We Listened." Obituary. *Village Voice*, 27 February 2006. http://216.92.211.74/radio/archives/misc/ray_barretto_vvoice_2_27_06.php.

Hall, Stuart. 1991. "What Is This 'Black' in Black Popular Culture?" *Social Justice* 20, no. 1/2 (51-52): 104-114.

———. 1995. "New Cultures for Old." In *A Place in the World? Places, Cultures and Globalization*, edited by D. Massey and P. M. Jess, 175-213. Oxford University Press.

———. 1996. "Who Needs Identity?" *Questions of Cultural Identity* 16, no. 2: 1-17.

———. 2002. "Political Belonging in a World of Multiple Identities." In *Conceiving Cosmopolitanism: Theory, Context, and Practice*, edited by Steven Vertovec and Robin Cohen, 25-31. Oxford University Press.

———. 2003. "Cultural Identity and Diaspora." In *Theorizing Diaspora: A Reader*, edited by Jana Evans Braziel and Anita Mannur, 222-237. Blackwell Publishing.

Hargreaves, David J., Dorothy Miell, and Raymond A. R. MacDonald. 2002. "What Are Musical Identities, and Why Are They Important?" *Musical Identities*, 1-20. Oxford University Press.

Hemenway, David, Kate Wolf, and Janet Lang. 1986. "An Arson Epidemic." *Journal of Behavioral Economics* 15, no. 3: 17-28.

Hilton, Ronald, ed. 1969. *The Movement toward Latin American Unity.* New York: F.A. Praeger, 1969.

Hooker, Juliet. 2005. "Indigenous Inclusion/Black Exclusion: Race, Ethnicity and Multicultural Citizenship in Latin America." *Journal of Latin American Studies* 37, no. 2: 285-310.

Huntington, Samuel P. 2004. "The Hispanic Challenge." *Foreign Policy* 141, no. 2: 30-45.

Hutchinson, Sydney. 2004. "Mambo on 2: The Birth of a New Form of Dance in New York City." *Centro Journal* 16, no. 2: 109-137.

Irazábal, Clara, and Ramzi Farhat. 2008. "Latino Communities in the United States: Place-Making in the Pre-World War II, Post-World War, and Contemporary City." *Journal of Planning Literature* 22, no. 3: 207-228.

Irizarry, Ralph. 2013. Interview by the author. New York City, August 22.

Jimenez, Yuniel. 2013. Interview by the author. New York City, July 24.

Juliá, Edgardo Rodríguez. 2004. *Cortijo's Wake*. Duke University Press.

Kaufmann, Karen M. 2003. "Cracks in the Rainbow: Group Commonality as a Basis for Latino and African-American Political Coalitions." *Political Research Quarterly* 56, no. 2: 199-210.

Kempton, Arthur. 2005. *Boogaloo: The Quintessence of American Popular Music*. University of Michigan Press.

Kent, Mary. 2005. *Salsa Talks! A Musical Heritage Uncovered*. Digital Domain.

Kögler, Hans-Herbert. 2006. "Music and Identity: Adorno and the Promise of Popular Culture." http://www.philosophyofculture.org.

Kotarba, Joseph A., Jennifer L. Fackler, and Kathryn M. Nowotny. 2009. "An Ethnography of Emerging Latino Music Scenes." *Symbolic Interaction* 32, no. 4: 310-333.

Laclau, Ernesto. 2005. *On Populist Reason*. Verso.

Lankford, Andrew Brian. 1999. "The Integration of the Trombone into the Conjunto Ensembles of Salsa Music." PhD diss., University of North Carolina at Greensboro.

Lapidus, Benjamin. 2004. "'Yo tengo sentido, tengo rima': Cano Estremera and the Art of the Soneo." *Centro Journal* 002: 174-182.

Leymarie, Isabelle. 2003. *Cuban Fire: The Story of Salsa and Latin Jazz*. London: Continuum.

Lie, John. 1995. "From International Migration to Transnational Diaspora." *Contemporary Sociology* 24, no. 4: 303-306.

Loza, Steven. 1996. "Steven Loza on Latino Music." In *Music in Cultural Context: Eight Views on World Music Education*, edited by P. S. Campbell, 58-65. Rowman & Littlefield

———. 1999. *Tito Puente and the Making of Latin Music*. Urbana: University of Illinois Press.

Luciano, Felipe. 2000. Interview in *Salsa: Latin Pop Music in the Cities*. DVD (Shanachie 1203). PBS, released 1988, reissued 2000.

———. 2013. Interview by the author. New York City, June 5.

Lukács, György. 1971. *History and Class Consciousness: Studies in Marxist Dialectics*. MIT Press.

Lucas, Maria Elizabeth. 1989. "Directory of Latin American and Caribbean Music Theses and Dissertations (1984-1988)." *Latin American Music Review/Revista de Música Latinoamericana* 10, no. 1: 148-176.

Manuel, Peter. 1988. *Popular Musics of the Non-Western World*, 46-50. New York: Oxford University Press.

———, ed. 1991. *Essays on Cuban Music: North American and Cuban Perspectives*. Lanham, MD: University Press of America.

———. 1994. "Puerto Rican Music and Cultural Identity: Creative Appropriation of Cuban Sources from Danza to Salsa." *Ethnomusicology* 38, no. 2: 249-280.

———. 2006. *Caribbean Currents: Caribbean Music from Rumba to Reggae*. 2nd ed. Philadelphia: Temple University Press.

Marquez, Benjamin. 2007. "Latino Identity Politics Research: Problems and Opportunities." In *Latino Politics: Identity, Mobilization, and Representation*, edited by R. Espino, D. Leal, and K. Meier, 17–26. Charlottesville: University of Virginia Press.

Marre, Jeremy, and Hannah Charlton. 1985. *Beats of the Heart: Popular Music of the World.* New York: Pantheon.

Martí, José. 1942. *Versos sencillos, y otros poemas.* Ediciones "Mirador."

Martinez, Pedro. 2013. Interview by the author. New York City, August 19.

Marton, B. 2001. "Rubén Blades (1948–) Singer, Actor, and Political Activist. Panamanian." In *Making It in America: A Sourcebook on Eminent Ethnic Americans*, edited by Elliott Robert Barkan. ABC-CLIO.

Massó, Jose. 2013. Interview by the author. Boston, June 24.

Mastosantos, Jose. 1991. "Between the Trumpet and the Bongo: A Puerto Rican Hybrid." *Massachusetts Review*, no. 3: 428–437.

Mauleón, Rebeca. 1993. *Salsa: Guidebook for Piano and Ensemble.* Petaluma, CA: Sher Music Co.

Mavra, Miroslav, and Lori McNeil. 2007. "Identity Formation and Music: A Case Study of Croatian Experience." *Human Architecture: Journal of the Sociology of Self-Knowledge* 5, no. 2.

Meléndez, Edgardo. 2003. "Puerto Rican Politics in the United States: Examination of Major Perspectives and Theories." *Centro Journal* 15, no. 1 (Spring). New York: City University of New York, Centro de Estudios Puertorriqueños.

Mendoza, Cynthia. 2008. "In El Norte Con Calle 13 and Tego Calderón: Tracing an Articulation of Latino Identity in Reguetón." PhD diss., University of Florida.

Miller, Marilyn. 2004. "Plena and the Negotiation of 'National' Identity in Puerto Rico." *Centro Journal* 16, no. 1: 36–59.

Miranda, Marisol. 2003. "Con Sabor a Puerto Rico." In *Musical Migrations: Transnationalism and Cultural Hybridity in Latin/o America*, ed. Frances Aparicio and Cándida Jáquez. New York: Palgrave Macmillan.

Mitchell, Katharyne. 1997. "Different Diasporas and the Hype of Hybridity." *Environment and Planning D* 15: 533–554.

Montalvo, Eddie. 2013. Interview by the author. New York City, July 24.

Moore, Kevin. 2009. "Beyond Salsa Piano." Self-published.

———. 2010. *Beyond Salsa Percussion.* Self-published.

———. 2012a. "Beyond Salsa for Beginners." Self-published.

———. 2012b. "Beyond Salsa for Ensemble." Self-published.

———. 2013. "Beyond Salsa Bass." Self-published.

Moore, Robin. 1995. "The Commercial Rumba: Afrocuban Arts as International Popular Culture." *Latin American Music Review/Revista de Música Latinoamericana* 16, no. 2: 165–198.

Morales, Ed. 2003. *The Latin Beat.* Da Capo Press.

Moreiras, Alberto. 1999. "Hybridity and Double Consciousness." *Cultural Studies* 13, no. 3: 373–407.

Moreno, Jairo. 2001. "Tropical Discourses: Community, History, and Sentiment in Rubén Blades's Latin Music(s)." *Journal of Popular Music Studies* 13, no. 2: 133–163.

———. 2004. "Bauza-Gillespie-Latin/Jazz: Difference, Modernity, and the Black Caribbean." *South Atlantic Quarterly* 103, no. 1: 81–99.

Moreno Vega, Marta. 1995. "The Yoruba Orisha Tradition Comes to New York City." *African American Review* 29, no. 2: 201–206.

Mugge, Robert, dir. 1985. *The Return of Rubén Blades.* DVD. London: Channel Four Films.

Mujcinovic, Fatima. 2001. "Critical Positioning In-Between Two Cultures." *Centro Journal* 13, no. 1: 45–59.

Negron, Marisol. 2006. *Hecho in Nuyorican: An Analysis of the Creation, Circulation, and Consumption of Salsa in 1970s New York.* Stanford University.

Negrón-Muntaner, Frances. 2000. "Feeling Pretty: West Side Story and Puerto Rican Identity Discourses." *Social Text* 18, no. 2: 83-106.

Ochse, Markus. 2004. "Discutiendo la autenticidad en la música Salsa." *Indiana* 21: 25-33.

Padilla, Felix M. 1985. *Latino Ethnic Consciousness: The Case of Mexican Americans and Puerto Ricans in Chicago.* Notre Dame, IN: University of Notre Dame Press.

———. 1989. "Salsa Music as a Cultural Expression of Latino Consciousness and Unity." *Hispanic Journal of Behavioral Sciences* 11, no. 1: 28-45.

———. 1990. "Salsa: Puerto Rican and Latino Music." *Journal of Popular Culture* 24, no. 1: 87-108.

Padura Fuentes, Leonardo. 1999. "Johnny Pacheco: del nuevo tumbao al tumbao añejo. Crónica mayor de la Salsa." *Guaraguao* 3, no. 9: 207-216.

———. 2002. "Salsa y conciencia." *Guaraguao* 6, no. 15: 119-123.

———. 2003. "Faces of Salsa: A Spoken History of the Music." Translated by Stephen J. Clark. Washington, DC: Smithsonian Books.

Party, Young Lords. 1970. *Palante* 2, no. 2 (8 May).

Pearce, Diana. 1978. "The Feminization of Poverty: Women, Work and Welfare." *Urban and Social Change Review* 11.

Peñalosa, David, and Peter Greenwood. 2009. *The Clave Matrix: Afro-Cuban Rhythm: Its Principles and African Origins.* Bembe Books.

Perez, Brittmarie Janson. 1987. "Political Facets of Salsa." *Popular Music* 6, no. 2: 149-159.

Perez, Gina M., Frank Andre Guridy, and Adrian Burgos. 2010. *Beyond El Barrio: Everyday Life in Latina/o America.* NYU Press.

Pinckney, Warren R. 1989. "Puerto Rican Jazz and the Incorporation of Folk Music: An Analysis of New Musical Directions." *Latin American Music Review/Revista de Música Latinoamericana* 10, no. 2: 236-266.

Pratt, Mary Louise. 1992. *Imperial Eyes: Travel Writing and Transculturation.* New York: Routledge.

Priestley, George. 2007. "Ethnicity, Class, and Race in the United States: Prospects for African-American/Latino Alliances." *Latin American Perspectives* 34, no. 1: 53-63.

Quintana, Ismael. 2001/2004. Interview with Eric González. Herencia Latina. September 28, 2001 and October 13, 2004. http://www.herencialatina.com.

Quintero-Herencia, Juan Carlos. 2005. *La máquina de la Salsa: Tránsitos del sabor.* Ediciones Vértigo.

Rajs, Timoti. 2007. "Reflections on Music and Identity in Ethnomusicology." *Muzikologija* 7: 17-38.

Rama, Carlos M. 1980. *La independencia de las antillas y Ramón Emeterio Betances.* Instituto de Cultura Puertorriqueña.

Ramirez, Yasmín. 2002. "Passing on *Latinidad*: An Analysis of Critical Response to El Museo del Barrio's Pan-Latino Mission Statements." Paper given at Interpretation and Representation of Latino Cultures: Research and Museums Conference, Washington, DC, 2002.

Randel, Don Michael. 1991. "Crossing Over with Rubén Blades." *Journal of the American Musicological Society* 44, no. 2: 301-323.

Renta, Priscilla. 2004. "Salsa Dance: Latino/a History in Motion." *Centro Journal* 002: 138-157.

Rinaldo, Rachel. 2002. "Space of Resistance: The Puerto Rican Cultural Center and Humboldt Park." *Cultural Critique* 50, no. 1: 135-174.

Rivera, Angel G. Quintero. 1998. *Salsa, sabor y control: sociología de la música "tropical."* Siglo XXI Ediciones.

———. 2002. "Salsa, identidad y globalización. Redefiniciones caribeñas a las geografías y el tiempo." *Transcultural Music Review/Revista Transcultural de Música*, no. 6.

———. 2004. "¡Salsa! y democracia." *Iconos. Revista de Ciencias Sociales* 018: 20-23.

———. 2007. "Migration, Ethnicity, and Interactions between the United States and Hispanic Caribbean Popular Culture." *Latin American Perspectives* 34, no. 1: 83-93.

———. 2009. *Cuerpo y cultura: las músicas mulatas y la subversión del baile.* Estudios de la Cultura de América Latina, no. 24. Iberoamericana Editorial.

———. n.d. "El debate sociedad-comunidad en la sonoridad." http://biblioteca.clacso.edu.ar/ar/libros/mato2/quintero.pdf.

Rivera, Angel G. Quintero, and Luis Manuel Alvarez. 1990. "La libre combinación de las formas musicales en la Salsa." *David y Goliath, Revista del Consejo Latinoamericano de Ciencias Sociales* 19, no. 57: 45-51.

Rivera, Angel G. Quintero, and Roberto Marquez. 2003. "Migration and Worldview in Salsa Music." *Latin American Music Review* 24, no. 2: 210-232.

Roberts, John Storm. 1972. *Black Music of Two Worlds.* New York: Praeger.

———. 1979. *The Latin Tinge: The Impact of Latin American Music on the United States.* New York: Oxford University Press.

Roman-Velazquez, R. 1999. "The Embodiment of Salsa: Musicians, Instruments and the Performance of a Latin Style and Identity." *Popular Music-Cambridge* 18, no. 1: 115-132.

Romero, Enrique. 2002. *Salsa: el orgullo del barrio.* Celeste Ediciones.

Rondón, César Miguel. 2008. *The Book of Salsa: A Chronicle of Urban Music from the Caribbean to New York City.* Translated by Frances R. Aparicio with Jackie White. University of North Carolina Press.

Roxborough, Ian. 1984. "Unity and Diversity in Latin American History." *Journal of Latin American Studies* 16, no. 1: 1-26.

Ruiz, Lissette S. 2009. *De aqui y de alla: La reconstruccion nacional de la nacion puertorriqueña.* ProQuest.

Rumbaut, Rubén, and Kenji Ima. 1988. "The Adaptation of Southeast Asian Refugee Youth: A Comparative Study." Final report. Washington, DC: US Office of Refugee Resettlement.

Rutherford, Jonathan. 1998. *Identity: Community, Culture, Difference.* Lawrence and Wishart Ltd.

Sala, Jhair. 2013. Interview by the author. New York City, July 23.

Salazar, Max. 1991. "What Is This Thing Called Salsa?" *Latin Beat Magazine* (November).

———. 2000. "Gabriel Oller: Aguinaldos de Salsa." *Latin Beat Magazine* (March).

———. 2002. *Mambo Kingdom: Latin Music in New York.* Schirmer Books.

Salazar, Norma, 2007. *Tite Curet Alonso: lírica y canción.* EMS.

Saldívar, José David. 1986. "Towards a Chicano Poetics: The Making of the Chicano Subject, 1969-1982." *Confluencia* 1, no. 2 (1986): 10-17.

———. 1990. "The Limits of Cultural Studies." *American Literary History* 2, no. 2: 251-266.

Sanabria, Izzy. 1979. "Salsa: The Bittersweet Experience." *Latin New York Magazine* 11, no. 8 (August): 29-32.

———. n.d. "What Is Salsa? Where and How Did It Start?" *Latin New York Magazine.*

Santana, Sergio. 1992. ¿Que es la Salsa? Buscando la melodía. Medellín: Ediciones Salsa y Cultura.

Santiago-Valles, Kelvin A., and Gladys M. Jiménez-Muñóz. 2004. "Social Polarization and Colonized Labor." In *The Columbia History of Latinos in the United States since 1960,* edited by David Gutiérrez. New York: Columbia University Press.

Santos Febres, Mayra. 1997. "Salsa as Translocation." In *Everynight Life: Culture and Dance in Latin/o America,* edited by C. Delgado and J. Muñoz, 175-188. Duke University Press.

Sher, Chuck, ed. 1997. *The Latin Real Book: The Best Contemporary and Classic Salsa, Brazilian Music, Latin Jazz.* Vol. 1. Sher Music Co.

Shohat, Ella. 1992. "Notes on the 'Post-Colonial.'" *Social Text* 31/32: 99–113.

Siebert, Robert Eric. 2010. "Salsa and Everyday Life: Music and Community." PhD diss., State University of New York.

Simpson, Katherine. 2002. "Media Images of the Urban Landscape: The South Bronx in Film." *Centro Journal* 14, no. 2: 99–113.

Sinfield, Alan. 1996. "Diaspora and Hybridity: Queer Identities and the Ethnicity Model." *Textual Practice* 10, no. 2: 271–293.

Singer, R., and E. Martínez. 2004. "A South Bronx Latin Music Tale." *Centro Journal* 16.

Singer, Roberta L. 1982. *My Music Is Who I Am and What I Do: Latin Popular Music and Identity in New York City.* Indiana University.

Slobin, Mark. 1994. "Music in Diaspora: The View from Euro-America." *Diaspora: A Journal of Transnational Studies* 3, no. 3: 243–251.

Sollors, Werner. 1986. *Beyond Ethnicity: Consent and Descent in American Culture.* Oxford University Press on Demand.

Steward, Sue. 2000. "Cubans, Nuyoricans and the Global Sound." In *World Music*, vol. 2, *Latin and North America, Caribbean, India, Asia and Pacific*, edited by Simon Broughton and Mark Ellingham, with James McConnachie and Orla Duane, 488–506. London: Rough Guides.

Sublette, Ned. 2007. *Cuba and Its Music: From the First Drums to the Mambo.* Chicago Review Press.

Tammelleo, Steve. 2011. "Continuity and Change in Hispanic Identity." *Ethnicities* 11, no. 4: 536–554.

Taylor, Paul V. 1993. *The Texts of Paulo Freire.* Buckingham, UK: Open University Press.

Thomas, William Isaac, and Florian Znaniecki. 1958. *The Polish Peasant in Europe and America.* Vol. 1. New York: Dover.

Thoms, Renato. 2013. Interview by the author. New York City, August 20.

Torres, Cecilia A. R. 2008. "The Construction of Identity and Musical Identities: A Literature Review." *Visions of Research in Music Education* 11: 1–11.

Torres-Padilla, José L. 2002. "When 'I' Became Ethnic: Ethnogenesis and Three Early Puerto Rican Diaspora Writers." *Centro Journal* 14, no. 2: 181–197.

Trujillo, Ariacne. 2013. Interview by the author. New York City, August 19.

Unterberger, Richie. 1999. *Music USA: The Rough Guide.* Rough Guides.

Vázquez, Lourdes. 2004. "Si de cantar se trata." *Centro Journal* 16, no. 1: 132–139.

Vázquez, Papo (Angel). 2013. Interview by the author. New York City, June 13.

Vázquez-Cofresi, José. 2013. Interview by the author. New York City, July 22.

Vega, Ana Lydia, and Mark McCaffrey. 1985. "Lyrics for Puerto Rican Salsa and Three Soneos by Request." *New England Review and Bread Loaf Quarterly* 7, no. 4: 550–554.

Vega, Carmen Haydée Rivera. 2010. "'Bugalú y otros guisos' (review)." *Caribbean Studies* 38, no. 1: 190–195.

Wagner, Lauren. 2012. "Feeling Diasporic." Tilburg University.

Washburne, Christopher. 2008. *Sounding Salsa: Performing Latin Music in New York City.* Philadelphia: Temple University Press.

Waxer, Lise. 1994. "Of Mambo Kings and Songs of Love: Dance Music in Havana and New York from the 1930s to the 1950s." *Latin American Music Review/Revista de Música Latinoamericana* 15, no. 2: 139–176.

———. 2002a. *The City of Musical Memory: Salsa, Record Grooves, and Popular Culture in Cali, Colombia.* Middletown, CT: Wesleyan University Press.

———, ed. 2002b. *Situating Salsa: Global Markets and Local Meanings in Latin Popular Music.* New York: Routledge. 2002.

Wilson, Kathryn E. 2003. "Building El Barrio: Latinos Transform Postwar Philadelphia." *Pennsylvania Legacies* 3, no. 2: 17–21.

Wong, Ketty. 1999. "Directory of Latin American and Caribbean Music Theses and Dissertations (1992–1998)." *Latin American Music Review/Revista de Música Latinoamericana* 20, no. 2: 253–309.

Yakan, Muḥammad Zuhdī. 1999. *Almanac of African Peoples and Nations.* Transaction Books.

Young, Robert. 1995. "Hybridity and Diaspora." In *Colonial Desire: Hybridity in Theory, Culture and Race,* 1–28. Routledge.

Zea, Leopoldo. 1986. "La *Latinidad* y su sentido en América Latina." Symposium. México: UNAM.

Zimmerman, Marc. 2003. "Erasure, Imposition and Crossover of Puerto Ricans and Chicanos in US Film and Music Culture." *Latino Studies* 1, no. 1: 115–122.

Zuckermann, Ghil'Ad. 2004. "Cultural Hybridity: Multisourced Neologization in 'Reinvented' Languages and in Languages with 'Phono-Logographic' Script." *Languages in Contrast* 4, no. 2.

DISCOGRAPHY

Afro-Cubans, Machito and His. *Freezelandia* (1947–1949). © Tumbao 2004.

——. *Ritmo Caliente.* © Proper Records 2004.

All Stars, Fania. *Live at Yankee Stadium Volume 1.* © 1975 by Fania Records. SLP-476.

Barretto, Ray. *Together.* © 1969 by Fania Records. SLP-378.

——. *Power.* © 1970 by Fania Records. SLP-391.

——. *The Message.* © 1971 by Fania Records. SLP-403.

——. *Giant Force Fuerza Gigante.* © 1980 by Fania Records. Fania 579.

Bataan, Joe. *Subway Joe.* © 1968 by Fania Records. SLP-345.

——. *Riot!* © 1968 by Fania Records. SLP-354.

——. *Salsoul.* © 1973 by Mericana Records. XMS-124.

Blades, Rubén. *De Panama a Nueva York.* © 1970 by Alegre Records. SLPA-8850.

——. *Maestra Vida Volume 1.* © 1980 by Fania Records. Fania 576.

——. *Maestra Vida Volume 2.* © 1980 by Fania Records. Fania 577.

——. *Buscando América.* © 1984 by Elektra/Asylum Records. 7559-60352-1.

——. *Caminando.* © 1991 by Sony Music International. CD-80593.

Bush y Su Nuevo Sonido. *Lo mejor de Bush y su Nuevo Sonido.* n.d.

Calle 13. *Entren Los Que Quieran.* © 2010 Sony Music Latin. CD #773433.

Caney, Cuarteto. *Cuarteto Caney (1939–1940) Featuring Machito.* © 1991 Tumbao tcd-005.

Casino de La Playa, Orquesta. *Beyond Patina Jazz Masters: Orquesta Casino de la Playa.* © Beyond Patina 2012.

Colón, Willie. *El Malo.* © 1967 by Fania Records. SLP-337.

——. *The Hustler.* © 1968 by Fania Records. SLP-347.

——. *Guisando/Doing a Job.* © 1969 by Fania Records. SLP-370.

——. *Cosa Nuestra.* © 1970 by Fania Records. SLP-384.

——. *The Big Break/La Gran Fuga.* © 1971 by Fania Records. SLP-394.

Colón, Willie, and Rubén Blades. *Willie Colon Presents Rubén Blades: Metiendo Mano.* © 1977 by Fania Records. SLP-500.

——. *Siembra.* © 1978 by Fania Records. Fania 537.

——. *Canciones del Solar de Los Aburridos.* © 1981 by Fania Records. Fania 597.

Cortijo, Rafael, y Su Combo. *Baile con Cortijo.* © 1960 by Seeco Records SCLP-9130.

Cortijo, Rafael, y Su Bonche. *Sorongo.* © 1968 by Tico Records. LP-1170.

Cuba, Joe Sextet. *Estamos Haciendo Algo Bien! (We Must Be Doing Something Right!)* © 1966 by Tico Records. LP-1133.

——. *Wanted Dead or Alive (Bang! Bang! Push, Push, Push).* © 1966 by Tico Records. SLP-1146.

Feliciano, Cheo. *Cheo.* © 1972 by Vaya Records. VS-5.

——. *Sentimiento tú.* © 1980 by VAYA Records. VS-95.

Palmieri, Eddie. *Azucar Pa' Ti (Sugar for You).* © 1965 Tico Records. SLP-1122.

——. *Justicia.* © 1969 by Tico Records. LP-1188.

——. *Vamonos Pa'l Monte.* © 1971 by Tico Records. LP-1225.

——. *With Harlem River Drive: Recorded Live at Sing Sing.* © 1972 by Tico Records. LP-1303.

——. *Eddie Palmieri: Recorded Live at Sing Sing, Vol. 2.* © 1974 by Tico Records. LP-1321.

Puente, Tito. *Top Percussion.* © 1958 by RCA Victor. LSP-1617.

——. *Tambó.* © 1960 by RCA Victor. LPM-2257.

——. *The Best of Tito Puente.* © 1965 by RCA Victor. LSP-2974.

——. *The Complete 78's Volume 1, 1949–55.* © 2010 Fania Records #7102.

Rivera, Ismael. *Esto Es Lo Mío.* © 1978 by Tico Records. JMTS-1428.

Rodríguez, Arsenio. *Cumbanchando con Arsenio (Fiesta en Harlem).* © 1960 SMC Pro-Arte. SMC-1074-1.

——. *El Alma de Cuba: Grabaciones completas RCA Victor Volumen 3, 1940–1956.* © Tumbao Cuban Classics. B0011X0LMW.

Rodriguez, Tito, and His Orchestra. *Three Loves Have I.* © 1958 RCA Victor. LPM-1389.

Rodriguez, Tito. *Nostalgia con Tito Rodríguez (Recordings from 1949–1958).* © 1972 by Tico Records-Fania Legend.

——. *Mambo Mona (1949–1950).* © Tumbao 2005. TCD-014.

Roena, Roberto, et al. *Roberto Roena y Su Apollo Sound 4.* © 1972 International Records. SLP 00423.

——. *Roberto Roena y Su Apollo Sound X—El Progreso.* © 1978 International Records. JMINT 934.

Salsa con Conciencia, Orquesta (formerly La Excelencia). *Mi Tumbao Social.* © 2009 Handle With Care. HWC4720.

VIDEOGRAPHY

Cocolos y Rockeros. VHS. Directed by Ana Maria Garcia. San Juan, Puerto Rico, Pandora Filmes, 1992.

Las Caras Lindas de Tite Curet Alonso. DVD. Directed by Sonia Fritz Macias. San Juan, Puerto Rico, 2004.

Latin Music USA: The Salsa Revolution. Video. Directed by Adriana Bosch. PBS, New York, 2009.

Our Latin Thing (Nuestra Cosa). VHS. Directed by Leon Gast. New York, A&R Studios, Fania Records, 1972.

The Return of Rubén Blades. DVD. Directed by Robert Mugge. London, UK Channel Four Film, Mug-Shot Productions, 1985.

Rubén Blades Seis del Solar Todos Vuelven Live. DVD. Directed by Wilfredo Martinez Soza. Recorded by Guillermo Gomez and Oscar Marin. New York, Ariel Rivas Music, 2011.

Salsa: Latin Pop Music in the Cities. DVD. Directed by Jeremy Marre and Hannah Charleton. PBS, 1979; reissued 1988, 2000.

¡SONÓ, SONÓ . . . TITE CURET! DVD. Directed by Gabriel Coss. San Juan, Puerto Rico: Rojo Chiringa Producciones, 2011.

Index